Card Play Technique

Card Play Technique

or The Art of being Lucky

Nico Gardener
Victor Mollo

B. T. Batsford Ltd • London

First published 1955

First published by B.T. Batsford Ltd 1995

Reprinted 2000, 2001

© Nico Gardener Victor Mollo 1955, 1971

0 7134 7916 7

A CIP catalogue record for this book is available
from the British Library.

Printed by The Bath Press, Bath.

Published by B.T. Batsford Ltd, 8 Blenheim Court,
Brewery Road, London N7 9NY.

A member of the Chrysalis Group plc

A BATSFORD BRIDGE BOOK

CONTENTS

6

INTRODUCTION

Fortune only smiles on the brave. She positively beams on the skilful, versed in the technique of wooing her. For to be lucky is an art which can be mastered like any other.

You, dear reader, can hold much better cards than you do at present—not by dealing yourself more Aces and Kings, but by getting a higher return from your existing ration. Persuade the cards to work harder for you than they do for your opponents. Therein lies the formula of success.

The purpose of this book is to point the way, to enlist on your side, whether you be declarer or defender, fifty-two sturdy and loyal allies.

Does a mischievous gremlin haunt you at the table, bewitching every finesse, spoiling the distribution of every suit? If so, you can exchange him for a friendly leprechaun. He will sit behind you, averting bad breaks, warning you against impending ruffs and inspiring the luckiest leads. Better still, if you propitiate him, he will pierce the linen curtain and reveal to you the holdings of your opponents.

The art of card-reading, "seeing" the hands of the other players, is one of the secrets of being lucky. That is why we expound it in some detail, and engage to assist you, the ever-friendly leprechaun.

Complex coups, which happen once a decade or so, receive little prominence in these pages. Our concern is essentially with the plays that win rubbers and bring in the match points, not with the spectacular hands which sometimes astound, but rarely instruct.

We have endeavoured to describe all the moves in the thrust and parry of the eternal struggle between declarer and defence. But in every chapter, and in the exercises which follow, the spotlight is on everyday situations and on how to handle them. Leaving double-dummy problems in the shade, keeping the focus on the real, vibrant hands that recur again and again, we seek to make theory the hand-maiden of practice.

Cards have their magic. We pass on the incantations and ask you to weave the spells.

DUMMY PLAY

CHAPTER I

On Not Playing High Cards

By tradition, every Bridge book opens with a chapter on the simple finesse. Every reader, of course, knows all about it, and seeing the familiar diagram with the A Q over the King, wishes that he had stuck to horror comics.

Why, then, do authors, raring to get their teeth into Smother Plays and Trump Coups, expend their pent-up energies on the seemingly obvious? Is it lack of appreciation for the erudition of the average reader? Perish the thought—and the authors.

Naturally, every reader knows how to take a finesse. He knows, too, that it is an even-money chance, and that if it fails, it is just another case of bad luck. But does he know, also, how to convert a fifty-fifty bet into an odds-on proposition? Does he know, in fact, how to load the cards in his favour?

The essence of every finesse is HOPE—the hope that a missing card is where you want it to be, under a card above it. That, too, is the basis of some of the most complex plays in Bridge. And in both situations, the simple and the complex, technique consists in backing the right hope, at the right time, against the right defender.

Since one finesse is too simple, let us start with two. What is the way to deal with x x x opposite A J 9 in dummy? The play may not be very difficult, but the reasons behind it are not always apparent.

The finesse against the ten must be taken *first*. If the nine falls to the King or Queen, a second finesse develops against the other court card. But the order of precedence cannot be reversed, because the second finesse does not exist until the first—against the ten—has succeeded.

In executing the double manœuvre, declarer assumes *split honours*—the Queen in one hand, the King in the other. To do that, when there is no indication, is a fundamental of good play. It is a case of playing with the odds—in other words, of being "lucky".

Simpler still, on the face of it, is this very humdrum position:

J 9 2 opposite Q 4 3

To make one trick, declarer finesses against the ten, and half the time he succeeds. What is worse, the other half of the time he fails, and that is not quite good enough.

Of course, the ideal is to do nothing at all—until opponents open the suit. Then one trick is certain. But if we are driven to take the initiative, let us at least snatch some sort of advantage. It costs nothing to lead the deuce towards the Queen. The next man may have a doubleton honour. Or the ten singleton. Or even—he may make a mistake. It all improves the chances, and if nothing materialises, there will still be time to finesse against the ten.

Just as a good player avoids committing his own high cards, so he should give his opponents every opportunity to commit theirs.

Playing Towards Honours

This brings us to an important principle, which sometimes escapes identification until it is too late. To illustrate it in its simplest form assume that you hold

K Q J 2 opposite 3 4 5

With plenty of entries everywhere, what do you do to avoid losing more than one trick?

You play low *towards* the honours, twice and three times, if need be. What you do will make no difference if the suit breaks 3–3. You can't go wrong. And you will not escape the loss of two tricks if A 10 x x are over the honours. For then you can't do right.

But correct play makes all the difference if the suit is divided 4–2 and the Ace is *under* the honours. Then laying down the King is bound to cost a trick.

The rule is never to lead a high card when a small one will do. Don't *spend* an honour by laying it down. Lead an x towards it—and towards honour sequences.

Confronted by a diagram, there is little temptation to err, for the position is clear. But at the card table the inexperienced player must stop to think. The expert need not, for it is an instinct with him to economise his own high cards and to by-pass those of his opponents.

Good players, however, have been known to mishandle

K Q x x opposite J x x

Yet it is precisely the same idea as in the more obvious example above.

Declarer ignores a 3–3 break, for then nothing matters, and hopes to avoid the loss of two tricks in the event of the more * probable 4–2 split. He leads an x towards the K Q x x. If the Ace does not come up, and the King wins, the process is repeated. Maybe the player sitting under the two honours holds the doubleton Ace. Let him use it on a lowly x.

Playing towards the Knave will not work the same way, for should it hold the trick, declarer may still lose the King to a doubleton Ace. The objective should be to come through that Ace *twice*. Hence the play towards the two honours.

At no time is the need to husband high cards more urgent than with

K 4 3 2 opposite Q 7 6 5

The only hope of landing three tricks is to find a doubleton Ace, locate the culprit and play through him. If you guess right and the King (or Queen) wins, play low from both hands to the next trick—and hope that you bring down the Ace. It must be bought for two xs, for that is all you can afford.

The distribution you need is

K 3 2 2

```
      N
 W        E
      S
```

A 9   J 10 8

Q 7 6 5

Or vice versa for the East–West hands.

---

* As you will see when you come to Chapter IX, with six cards of a suit outstanding, there is a 48 per cent chance that they will be divided 4–2. A 3–3 break occurs only 36 per cent of the time.

Hope and guesswork are present again in this picture:

J 5 3

```
    ┌───────┐
    │   N   │
    │ W   E │
    │   S   │
    └───────┘
```

A Q 4 2

You collect three tricks with your eyes shut if the suit breaks 3–3. And if you open your eyes, you may be able to do the same against a 4–2 split. Should the bidding or the play to previous tricks suggest that West owns the King, lead low towards the Knave. If you think that the King is more likely to be with East, play small towards the A Q, finesse, and hope to bring the King down on the Ace.

Apply the same principle to the common finesse

A 10 6 5 opposite Q J 3 2

If dummy has plenty of entries, play the deuce, just in case there is a singleton King under the Ace. It is the sort of bad luck that a good player learns to avoid. With no further entry to dummy, you can't afford the premium on the insurance. The Queen must be led, for if you hold the trick, you want to play from dummy once more.

9 6 5 opposite A Q 10 3

Assuming adequate entries, lead a small one, not the nine. Should the defender under the honours hold the bare K J, all four tricks can be made. But not if you play the nine. For if one defender holds the K J alone, the other must have the 8 7 4 2. And if the nine is absorbed—needlessly—in the first three tricks, the eight will be top dog on the fourth.

A Finesse Takes Shape

Some situations do not lend themselves to a finesse until the other side paves the way. The more missing links there are in a suit, the better it is to have it opened by the defenders.

12

The reason is that, being last to play, declarer's side can prac-
tise the greater economy in high cards.

With A 10 x opposite K 9 x you can finesse nothing. But
if the enemy makes the first move, a finesse position develops
at once, and unless both the missing honours are in the wrong
hand—with the opener's partner—you are bound to win all
three tricks.

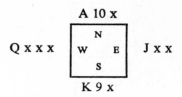

If West leads, the King takes the first trick, killing the Knave
and the finesse against the Queen is taken on the next round.
If the lead comes from East, South plays low, and the second
round finesse is taken against the Knave.

Here, again there is no finesse—not quite:

If dummy's seven grew into the eight, South could make a
trick by finessing against West's Knave. As the cards are,
it won't help even if the Knave is in the right place. Declarer
can do nothing but hope—that the enemy will fire the first
shot. Then a finesse position appears immediately and the
prospects of winning a trick are no worse than fifty-fifty. If
West leads, declarer plays low from dummy and hopes that
the Knave is not with East. Next time, he plays the ten and
runs it, unless West covers. If East makes the first move,
South plays low from his hand, and again a finesse position
takes shape against the Knave.

This is peculiar to suit contracts, because the mechanism hinges on the CONTROL power vested in trumps. A ruff does the work normally assigned to an Ace. Here it is.

♠ A Q J 10
♡ Q 9 x x
◇ x x x
♣ A x

♠ x
♡ A K J 10 x
◇ K x x
♣ x x x x

West leads a trump against Four Hearts. As soon as East follows, you can be certain of ten tricks. Five trumps, the Ace of Clubs, one Club ruff in dummy (maybe two), and three Spades, make up the total. The only danger is that *before* you can set up the Spades, a Diamond may be played *through* your King. Don't let that happen. After drawing trumps, lay down the Ace of Spades, then lead the Queen. If the King does not go up, discard a Diamond. Now you will have only one more Diamond loser, because the lead will be with West. Alternatively, if opponents don't play the Diamonds for you— you can discard the other two on the Spades.

The singleton Spade gives you control of the situation. It is almost as if you had it in your power to decide which of your opponents should hold the Spade King. For, of course, if the K x x of Diamonds were in dummy, you would take a natural, not a ruffing finesse. It would be West, not East, you would try to keep out.

With a void, *only* a ruffing finesse is possible. Change the hand slightly and see what happens.

♠ A Q J 10
♡ Q 9 x x
◇ K x x
♣ A x

♠ —
♡ A K J 10 x
◇ x x x x
♣ x x x x

Much as you would like to keep West out of the lead, it can't be done, and you are reduced to the traditional hope that the missing honour is where you want it.   This time, with East.

A feature of the ruffing finesse is that declarer reverses the normal procedure.   Instead of " hoping " that a missing honour is *under* the one above it, he hopes that it is *over* it. And instead of covering, he ruffs.

When the Queen is the missing link, this position arises:

A K J 10

x x

Declarer plays off the Ace and King, exhausting his own holding in that suit.   Then he leads the Knave and runs it, unless East covers.

In this case, declarer can play either opponent for the Queen.   His decision between the natural and the ruffing finesse will depend largely on which defender he is anxious to keep out of the lead.

Résumé

(1) When two honours are missing, and there is no indication of where they are, declarer should play for *split honours*—assuming that each defender has one.

(2) Wherever possible, avoid leading out high cards. Play *towards* honours and also towards honour sequences (Q J 10 2 or K Q J 9).

(3) A corollary to the above is that you should seek to lose your xs, not your honours or intermediates, to the top cards of the opponents.

(4) The more chinks in your suit, the more urgent it is to husband your honours and intermediates, and whenever possible, to wait till the suit is opened by opponents.

(5) Sometimes a finesse position does not exist, but takes shape as soon as a suit has been opened by defenders.

(6) The characteristic of a ruffing finesse is that the missing honour is assumed to be *over*, not *under*, the card above it. The play depends on having a shortage in one hand opposite an honour-combination in the other.

(7) A singleton (or doubleton, if the Queen is missing) enables declarer to choose between a natural and a ruffing finesse. With a void he is compelled to rely on the latter.

Foreword to Exercises

Weaving their pattern through this book, Dummy-Play and Defence counter one another in alternating chapters. Each one is followed by Exercises to which the answers will be found on pp. 353–381. Their purpose is not to tease or puzzle the reader, but to provide him with material for practice. As the book unfolds, the plays and defences grow more advanced, and the Exercises with them. But easy or difficult, every example is designed to illustrate a method, to bring out a specific point in the mechanics of card play. No problems are intended, no riddles and no mystification. For success in Bridge lies not in solving problems, but in finding none. In the manifold situations to which the distribution of the pack lends itself, no element of mystery is present—only a challenge to technique. Every card combination carries within itself the key to its solution. Approached with the right password, it will yield it readily enough. The object of the Exercises is to let the reader pick up the key for himself. It may grate a trifle, at first, but as he learns the secrets of the lock, he will find that it fits every time.

Exercises

Assuming adequate entries, how do you play?

(1) A x x opposite Q J x x in dummy to make three tricks.

(2) Same as above, but no side entry to your hand.

(3) Q x x opposite K 10 x to make two tricks.

(4) A 4 3 2 opposite Q 10 9 8 to make three tricks.

(5) A 4 3 2 opposite Q 10 6 5 to make three tricks.

(6) Q 9 8 opposite 10 7 4 to make one trick.

(7) Sitting West, you are in Five Clubs.   A Spade is led.

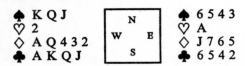

```
♠ K x x                         ♠ A x x
♡ —             N               ♡ K Q J 10
◇ K J 9 x    W     E            ◇ x x
♣ A K Q 10 x x      S           ♣ J 9 x x
```

What is your plan of play?

(8) You are in Six Diamonds.   A Heart is opened.   What card do you play to the second trick?

```
♠ K Q J                         ♠ 6 5 4 3
♡ 2              N              ♡ A
◇ A Q 10 4 3  W     E           ◇ J 6 5 2
♣ A K Q J          S            ♣ 6 5 4 2
```

(9) Same contract and same lead as in (8).   What card do you play to the second trick?

```
♠ K Q J                         ♠ 6 5 4 3
♡ 2              N              ♡ A
◇ A Q 4 3 2   W     E           ◇ J 7 6 5
♣ A K Q J          S            ♣ 6 5 4 2
```

DEFENCE

CHAPTER II

Trick Promotion

Live and let live is not a maxim applicable to Bridge. Declarers do live, as we all know, but it is the mission of the defence to make their lives as unhappy as possible. South, the man who plays the hand in most of the diagrams, must never be allowed to play too well. And it is not only a case of preventing him from making bricks without straw. Whenever possible, the straw itself should be taken from under his nose.

The first chapter opens merrily with an autopsy of the finesse. To complete the picture, let us carry out the dissection from the point of view of the defence.

Promotion

You sit over dummy's Q x x with K 10 9. Declarer plays the Queen, and, of course, you cover. But why? The answer is that you have everything to gain and nothing to lose. Clearly, declarer has the Ace and Knave. Otherwise, he would not be leading the Queen. Mind you, he should not do it anyway. But that is another matter. Declarers sometimes make that play, and that is all that concerns us for the present. Covering the Queen ensures a trick eventually. The Ace takes the King. The Knave drops the nine. Then, on the third round, the ten comes into its own. That was the point in covering the Queen—to PROMOTE the ten.

And what if you hold K 3 2—no ten or nine this time? You still cover, because partner may have them. If you knew for certain that he did not, it would not matter.

Defence against the finesse rests on the principle of PROMOTION. Take a look at that first trick. The four cards are made up of the Ace, King, Queen and some small x—

partner's contribution. Declarer had to use the Ace and Queen to capture the King. That is two high cards for one—an excellent rate of exchange for the defence. The profit lies in the PROMOTION of that ten, and the dividend is the same, whether it is in your hand or in partner's. Of course, declarer may have the whole sequence, but then nothing is lost. PROMOTION means a black eye to nothing—for declarer.

That is the essence of the stratagem, and hence the ancient adage: Cover an honour with an honour. But parrot cries are made for parrots, not for players holding high honours. Apply the adage to this situation:

When Not to Cover

Declarer is in Six Hearts and dummy's trumps are Q x x x x x. You sit over them with K x. What card do you play on the lead of the Queen? A small one? Certainly. But why?

The reason is that partner is most unlikely to hold the Knave, and even if he did, it would be a singleton. Work it out. Declarer must have at least four Hearts—since to be declarer he must have bid Hearts in the first place. This leaves partner with one or none. So you can *promote* nothing in his hand.

Probably declarer can see eleven trumps—five in his own hand and six in dummy. He does not know whether to finesse against the King or to play for the drop. As it costs him nothing, he plays the Queen and hopes that if you have K x, you will oblige by covering. By playing low you give him a guess, a fifty-fifty chance to go wrong. To put up the King saves declarer the guess. Don't save him anything.

Partner leads the eight of Hearts. The contract is Four Spades—or Three Diamonds or anything else for that matter. You sit over dummy's Q J 10 9 with K 6 4 2. Do you cover? Of course the idea does not even occur to you. Why? Because you cannot promote anything, anywhere. Unless partner is being revoltingly clever, his eight spot is the top of nothing. So declarer holds A x or A x x. If you cover, he can make four Heart tricks. If you don't, he cannot make more than three. But your primary reason for not covering is that there is not anything you can hope to promote.

Now try this situation. South bids a Spade. North raises to Three, and the final contract is Four Spades. Dummy goes down with A 4 3 2 of trumps. Declarer wins the opening lead and plays the Knave of Spades. This is the position.

(*Dummy*)
A 4 3 2

(*You*)
Q 7 6

```
    N
 W     E
    S
```

Well? What do you do to that Knave? Do you follow the slogan—cover an honour with an honour? Or do you turn your mind to PROMOTION?

It need hardly be said that you play the six or seven at a fraction over dictation speed. Partner cannot have the ten, so there is nothing to PROMOTE. If, by some chance, partner did have the ten, there would still be nothing to PROMOTE. So you do not cover.

The point is that South must have four or five Spades. Therefore, partner has, at best, a doubleton. Even if it happens to be the ten and nine there is nothing to PROMOTE. They will both drop on the Ace and King. Another consideration is that declarer has the ten himself. Otherwise he would not play the Knave.

Perhaps you feel tempted to ask: Well, why does declarer play the Knave? What is he up to? Broadly speaking, there are two possibilities. Life may present itself to declarer in this shape.

A 4 3 2

```
    N
 W     E
    S
```

K J 10 9 (8)

He would very much like to know which of his two dis-agreeable opponents harbours the Queen. Knowing nothing, he leads the Knave in the hope that something will happen.

West—that is you, by the way—may cover and put him out of his misery. Or there may be a fidgeting and fumbling, which will amount to the same thing. If nothing happens, he will doubtless go up with the Ace, intending to finesse—or play for the drop—on the next round.

So don't cover, don't fidget, don't fumble. Let declarer guess.

The other possibility is that the trumps are divided like this:

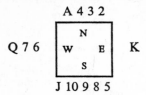

A 4 3 2

Q 7 6   K

J 10 9 8 5

Declarer expects to lose one trick, but must be prepared to concede two, if K Q x are over the Ace. Meanwhile, he leads the Knave, intending to play low if West follows with a small one. Should you be so ill-advised as to cover the Knave with the Queen, your side will not make a trick at all.

So let this rule be your guide: Cover to PROMOTE, but *don't* cover—or think about it—when it is self-evident that there is nothing to promote.

Now what happens here?

You hold K 7 6 over dummy's Q J 2. To cover or not to cover? The answer is: Cover the *second* time, but not the first. Going up with the King on the Queen can't promote partner's Knave. He has not got it. But he might have the ten and this will be established if the *second* trick—after the Queen has gone—accounts for the Ace and Knave.

Covering the first time is not only pointless. It can actually cost a trick. The position may be this:

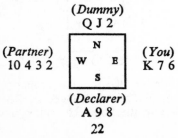

(*Dummy*)
Q J 2

(*Partner*)   (*You*)
10 4 3 2   K 7 6

(*Declarer*)
A 9 8

22

If you cover the first time, declarer wins with his Ace and finesses against partner's ten, making *three* tricks in the suit.

It is sound practice not to cover the *first* of two touching honours without some good reason, such as

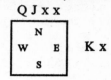

Q J x x

K x

Now you must hope that partner holds something like 10 9 x or 10 8 x. If he does not, it is just too bad. But if he does—and you don't cover—declarer can play a small one on the second round, drop your King and still retain the Knave in dummy to slaughter partner's ten. The whole picture will be:

Q J x x

10 9 x

K x

A x x x

But, of course, if declarer had opened the bidding with Four Spades and had found the Q J x x in dummy, there would be no sense in covering. Now partner is pretty well marked with a void.

The defender's main trouble is that he does not know how the suits are distributed. He can only speculate. So he must draw inferences from the bidding and decide—each time—whether by covering an honour he can promote any card in his own or in partner's hand. Think. Guess. Calculate. But *don't* cover through sheer force of habit.

And now take a case like this:

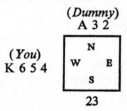

(*Dummy*)
A 3 2

(*You*)
K 6 5 4

The bidding has been One No-Trump—Three No-Trumps. No help at all. The Queen appears from the closed hand. What's your reaction?

You have no indication of how solid may be declarer's sequence. But you must not cover, because your King is safe in any case. He can't be caught. Suppose declarer started with Q J 10 9 (or Q J 8 7 for that matter); then, by covering, you allow him to make *four* tricks in the suit. Playing low keeps him to three—and sets up a trick for yourself.

Making Declarer Guess

This is an appropriate moment for a little fifth-column activity.

In the last chapter our overture showed declarer how to set about making two tricks out of: x x x opposite A J 9. But like the Vicar of Bray, we have changed sides.

Sometimes, you sit West with

```
                    (Dummy)
                     A J 9
                  ┌─────────┐
       (You)      │    N    │
       K Q x      │  W   E  │
                  │    S    │
                  └─────────┘
```

Declarer plays a small card. If he needs *two* tricks in the suit, he will normally finesse the nine. So *don't* split your honours. Play low and give partner a chance to make his ten. Of course, it may be more important for you to make a trick quickly, than to prevent declarer making two. Perhaps it is a question of the setting trick. Or maybe you need an entry and have no time to spare. Then split your honours. But always bear in mind that declarer may intend to play the nine. He does not *know* the position. Let him GUESS.

The beauty of guessing is that it must go wrong sometimes.

Imagine that you are defending against Six No-Trumps. You lead a Heart and dummy goes down with

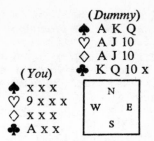

(Dummy)
♠ A K Q
♡ A J 10
♢ A J 10
♣ K Q 10 x

(You)
♠ x x x
♡ 9 x x x
♢ x x x
♣ A x x

Dummy's ten holds the trick, and declarer proceeds to play four rounds of Diamonds. On the last Diamond a small Club is played from the table, while partner discards a Spade. So far, so bad. Now declarer leads a Club and you play low. The King wins, and declarer returns to his hand by overtaking a Heart, to lead another Club.

What do you play this time? Quite right. You play low again, hoping that declarer will mis-guess. You can see that to play the Ace would be tantamount to surrender. A second Club trick would be declarer's twelfth, and that would be that. So it is easy to do the right thing. But now imagine that you are sitting East. Same contract. Same dummy.

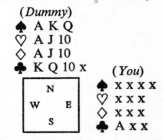

(Dummy)
♠ A K Q
♡ A J 10
♢ A J 10
♣ K Q 10 x

(You)
♠ x x x x
♡ x x x
♢ x x x
♣ A x x

Again South plays off four Diamonds and leads a Club, going up with the King from dummy. And you play . . .?

It is really the same situation as before. You cannot beat the contract—*unless* declarer mis-guesses. By winning the trick with your Ace you virtually compel him to guess right He is almost bound to land that second, vital, Club trick by finessing against the Knave on the next round. But if you play low, he won't know what to do.

25

To take Kings with Aces is the most natural thing in the world. But it is not always the most profitable. When that King is the one trick declarer needs for his contract, you seize it with gusto. But when it is apparent that your Ace must make sooner or later, it is sometimes best to put off the happy moment. Keep declarer in suspense. By making him guess, you give him a chance to *mis-guess*.

Having come to the end, let us go back to the beginning. The first stage in Defence is the opening lead. Often it is the most ticklish part, and more will be heard of it later. But there is one aspect, which belongs essentially to the realm of the finesse. *DON'T* take a finesse for declarer before the dummy goes down.

You may see this picture in the course of the play:

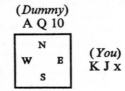

(*Dummy*)
A Q 10

(*You*)
K J x

You don't normally play the suit, but allow declarer to do his own finessing. You expect two tricks, because the distribution of the suit is lucky for you. Finessing is based on the hope that missing honours are well placed, and here they are not.

The same situation as above may arise, unknown to you, when you make the opening lead. If you lead from a King, you may be playing into the A Q.

IN CHOOSING AN OPENING LEAD, BEWARE OF PRESENTING DECLARER WITH THE FRUITS OF A FINESSE WHICH FATE INTENDED HIM TO LOSE.

Résumé

(1) The defence against finessing is based on the principle of PROMOTION.

(2) You should cover an honour with an honour to promote a lesser honour (or a nine and even an eight) in your own hand or in partner's. But—

(3) Do *not* cover honours when there is nothing to promote.

(4) When declarer leads the top of two touching honours, cover the *second* time—unless you have a doubleton honour yourself.

(5) With a doubleton honour—especially K10—cover the first time. But—

(6) When you know that partner can only have a void, singleton or worthless doubleton, *do not cover*. The bidding and dummy's holding must be your guides.

(7) If your honour cannot be caught, do not cover. This situation arises when your honour is guarded by more small cards than the higher honour in the hand over you (e.g., K x x x under A x x).

(8) Do not split your honours if you suspect that declarer is attempting a " deep " finesse (e.g., K Q 2 under A J 9). Declarer does not know your holding and you must not help him.

(9) In selecting your opening lead, bear in mind the risk of playing into a tenace. Avoid leading from unsupported honours (K x x) or from your tenace positions (A Q x or K J x).

27

Exercises

(1)

(*Dummy*)
Q J 9 8

```
    N
 W     E    (You)
    S       K 10
```

The Queen is led.   Do you cover?

(2)

(*Dummy*)
Q J 9 8

```
    N
 W     E    (You)
    S       K 10 x
```

Same lead.   Do you cover?

(3)

(*Dummy*)
Q J 4 2

```
    N
 W     E    (You)
    S       K 5
```

Same lead.   Do you cover?

(4)

(*Dummy*)
A 6 5 3

```
(You)    N
Q 9 2  W     E
         S
```

South leads the Knave.   Do you cover?

(5)

                               (*Dummy*)
                                A J 6

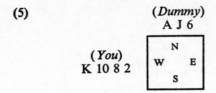

(*You*)
K 10 8 2

Queen led.   Do you cover?

(6)

                  (*Dummy*)
                  J 10 2

(*You*)
Q 9 4

The Knave is led.   Do you cover?

(7)

                  (*Dummy*)
                  J 10 8

(*You*)
Q 9

Same lead.   Do you cover?

(8)

                  (*Dummy*)
                A K 10 9 3

(*You*)
Q J 5 2

South, Declarer, leads the four.   What card do you play?

(9)

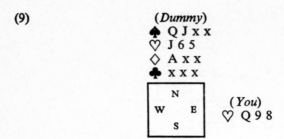

(Dummy)
♠ Q J x x
♡ J 6 5
◇ A x x
♣ x x x

N
W   E
S

(You)
♡ Q 9 8

The bidding was: South, One Heart; North, One Spade; South, Four Hearts.

Partner opens the King of Diamonds. Declarer wins in dummy with the Ace and plays the Knave of Hearts. Do you cover?

(10) What opening lead do you make against Four Spades (bidding was One Spade—Four Spades)?

Your hand is ♠ Q 3   ♡ 7 5 2   ◇ K 9 7 3   ♣ A Q J 6

DUMMY PLAY

CHAPTER III

To Ruff or Not to Ruff?

You may have heard about those poor fellows who sleep at night on the Embankment, exposed to the cold winter winds. Their plight is ascribed to the fact that they did not lead trumps at the first opportunity. Since much of the present chapter is devoted to not leading trumps, let us look into this Embankment legend more closely.

Why should declarer lead trumps at all? The usual reason is that he has more of them than the opponents. That is why he made them trumps in the first place. Doubtless, he wants to ruff his losers with dummy's small trumps. But certainly he does not want opponents to ruff his winners with *their* small trumps. So he draws trumps until the other side has no more. The idea is excellent, when there are enough trumps in the *two* hands to put it into practice. When there are not, drawing trumps *and* ruffing losers in dummy becomes more difficult. The one must be done before the other. Take this example:

♠ A K Q x x	N	♠ x
♡ x	W E	♡ K Q x
♦ Q J x x x	S	♦ 10 9 x
♣ A K		♣ J x x x x

Play the hand, first in Spades, then in Diamonds, and note the difference in technique. A Club is led to both contracts, and there are no bad breaks.

(1) THE CONTRACT IS THREE SPADES:

As always, count your winners and losers at the outset. You expect four trump tricks, allowing for one loser; three Diamonds, and two Clubs. So far so good.

31

There is only one danger. If you fail to draw three rounds of trumps first, one of the opponents may ruff a Diamond, and it may be the WRONG OPPONENT.

With ordinary luck the outstanding trumps will be divided 4–3. Obviously, the defender with four trumps will have to make one, so you don't much care whether he ruffs a Diamond or not. His trump is a winner anyway. But his partner's three trumps are all losers. They can be painlessly extracted by your Ace, King and Queen. If *he* ruffs, you are ditched, because he will make a trick with a *losing* trump. That is why, before developing the Diamonds, you draw three rounds of trumps, leaving one—a winner—outstanding. This will be the position :

```
    ♠ x x            ┌──────────┐            ♠ —
    ♡ x              │    N     │            ♡ K Q
    ◇ Q J x x x      │ W     E  │            ◇ 10 9 x
    ♣ A              │    S     │            ♣ J x x x
                     └──────────┘
```

and everything in the garden will be lovely. Opponents can collect four tricks, but no more.

All very simple. Lead trumps and keep away from the Embankment on cold nights. And now, to make quite sure, play the hand all over again, but this time in Diamonds.

(2) CONTRACT FOUR DIAMONDS :

Counting the losers, you can see : two trumps, one Heart and a Spade, two if you are unlucky enough to find a 5–2 Spade break. Even without the slings and arrows of outrageous fortune, you are still confronted by four losers, and that is one more than you can afford. Of course, you get rid of it by ruffing a small Spade in dummy. But it must be done *immediately*. If at trick two—after winning the opening Club lead—you so much as touch a trump, all may be lost. With good defence, you will be hoist with your own petard. Opponents will *play back* trumps. Three rounds will denude dummy and that losing Spade will remain forever unruffed.

This time, it is *not* leading trumps that will keep you from the Embankment.

Observe that though you make the same number of tricks in your own hand, there is one more winner in Diamonds than in Spades. So long as the defence does not open up with three sizzling rounds of trumps, dummy contributes by producing a ruff. Those little xs take tricks, just like Aces. Hence the importance in bidding of finding a " fit "—a contract in which dummy's small cards will play a useful part.

And now that we have drawn, and not drawn trumps, we can draw the moral. The underlying principle is this :

DRAW trumps when you fear that opponents may ruff winners in your side-suits.

DON'T DRAW trumps—prematurely—when you want to ruff losers in dummy.

Here is another illustration of the ruffing technique :

```
♠ K Q J 10 9        ♠ x x x
♡ K Q x             ♡ x x
♢ A x               ♢ x x x x
♣ x x x             ♣ A K x x
```

The deuce of Clubs is opened against Three Spades. What do you play at trick two? Many declarers will be tempted to lead a trump, " just one round ". And that is just one round too soon. The defence will return a *second* trump. Then, when they come in with the Ace of Hearts, the third, fatal trump will glide across the table, and dummy's last trump will vanish without justifying its existence.

To make sure of his contract, declarer must play a Heart at trick two. Then—if the Ace is on the wrong side—nine tricks are still made by ruffing a Heart in dummy.

It is all a question of timing. By not playing a Heart immediately, declarer misses his turn. Technically speaking, he " loses a tempo ".

The following hand is only a slight variation on the same theme :

```
♠ A K Q J 10        ♠ x x x
♡ K Q J             ♡ x x
♢ K x x             ♢ A x x
♣ A K               ♣ x x x x x
```

A Club is opened against Six Spades. If you are not careful, you can lose two tricks—a Heart and a Diamond. But as long as nothing unlucky happens, and you don't miss a tempo, you are safe. Drive out the Ace of Hearts. Then discard a Diamond from dummy on the third Heart. Finally, ruff a Diamond in dummy. But beware of playing trumps twice, before clearing the Hearts.

A feature of this type of hand is that, at first, no ruffing position exists. Dummy and declarer start with the same length in Diamonds. A Diamond shortage is *created* by means of a discard on a set-up Heart.

Cross-ruff

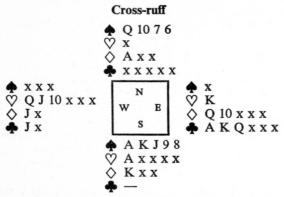

The Queen of Hearts is opened against a Spade contract by South. Four is easy, but try to make as many tricks as you can. On a complete cross-ruff—every trump being made separately—the hand will yield twelve tricks. The total is made up of nine trumps, the Ace of Hearts and two Diamonds.

Before going any farther, make your plan. In which order do you play the cards? Are you ready? Then answer this question. At which stage did you cash the Ace and King of Diamonds? That is the main point of the hand. If you left them till the end, you lost your chance to make twelve tricks. Imagine for the sake of argument—but only for the sake of argument—that you take the first Heart, ruff a Heart and come back to your hand three times with Club ruffs to trump the remaining three Hearts in dummy.

34

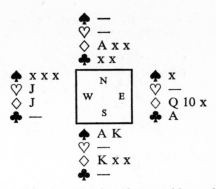

Had you been in a slam the situation would now be hopeless. West has one trump more than you have. He will ruff the second Diamond and play a Heart.

What went wrong? The answer is that you omitted to cash the two top Diamonds *before* embarking on the cross ruff. The salient feature of this play is that declarer and dummy make their trumps separately. Therefore, at the end, declarer is short of trumps and cannot draw them. Trump control passes to the defenders, who had every opportunity to discard from their short suits, and can now ruff Aces and Kings in declarer's side-suits. So take this precept to heart:

BEFORE beginning a cross-ruff, CASH your winners in the side-suits. See how it works out in practice by playing that Spade contract all over again. This time, play off the top Diamonds first.

Note that a slam could not be made against a Spade lead. It would have the same fatal effect as "just one round of trumps" by declarer, reducing the total ruffs from nine to eight.

Dummy Reversal

It is akin to a law of nature that trumps are drawn from the closed hand and losers are ruffed in dummy. Sometimes nature refuses to co-operate. Then declarer must resort to the unnatural. A "dummy reversal" consists in ruffing losers in *declarer's own hand* and drawing trumps—eventually —from *dummy*.

You are in Seven Hearts. A Spade is opened and all you have to do is to make thirteen tricks.

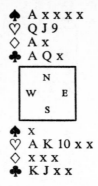

♠ A x x x x
♡ Q J 9
♢ A x
♣ A Q x

♠ x
♡ A K 10 x x
♢ x x x
♣ K J x x

On top you see eleven winners: One in Spades, five in Hearts, the Ace of Diamonds and four Clubs. Not enough.

Now perform a gentle exercise in acrobatics. Change places, mentally, with dummy and imagine that your hand is down on the table.

How would it be if that powerful trump suit—A K 10 x x—were used, not for its natural purpose of drawing trumps, but for the unnatural one of ruffing Spades? Of course, we can't do both—draw trumps and ruff—with the same Hearts. So we can only count three Heart tricks proper—North's Q J 9. But now we can see four ruffs which did not exist before!

Let us count again: The Ace of Spades and four Spade ruffs in declarer's hand, make five. Dummy's three Hearts; the Ace of Diamonds, and four Clubs; a grand total of thirteen.

The play takes this course: The Spade Ace wins the first trick and a small Spade is ruffed. A small Club to the Queen and a second Spade ruff. A Club to the Ace and a third Spade ruff. Now back to dummy with the Ace of Diamonds and the last Spade is trumped (if it is not already a master).

Dummy now has:

♠ —
♡ Q J 9
♢ x
♣ x

All is plain sailing, so long as you *unblocked* the trumps.
Your last five cards should be:

♠ —
♡ x (!)
◇ x x
♣ K J

and you cross to dummy with a *small* Heart, draw the trumps—
discarding two Diamonds from your own hand—and take the
last two Clubs.

But observe the *unblocking play*. Dummy's last two Spades
must be trumped with the Ace and King of Hearts! Otherwise you will not have a small Heart left to overtake in dummy.
And you must enter dummy to DRAW TRUMPS.

The question of entries is always important, and never more
so than in dummy reversals. It is all very well for declarer to
ruff losers in his own hand. First he must be able to get at
them, and that means an entry to dummy for every loser he
intends to trump. To succeed, the dummy reversal technique
requires:

    (1) Enough entries in dummy to reach *all* the losers
that are to be ruffed in the closed hand.

    (2) Yet *another* entry in dummy to draw opponents'
trumps.

    (3) Trumps of quality in dummy—even if there are only
three of them—to perform the drawing process.

A grand slam by dummy reversal does not happen every day.
But the principles which it involves, arise again and again.
Try this:

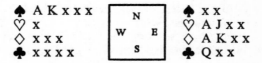

♠ A K x x x   ♠ x x
♡ x   N   ♡ A J x x
◇ x x x   W   E   ◇ A K x x
♣ x x x x   S   ♣ Q x x

The deuce of Hearts is opened against Two Spades. What is
your best chance of gathering eight tricks?

The trumps will yield four tricks if the suit breaks 3–3, and
three tricks if—as is more likely—it breaks 4–2. Add

dummy's Ace, and A K, and you have a total of 6–7 tricks. One short, at least.

Now apply the dummy reversal technique. Use the three red entries to dummy to ruff losers in your own hand. If the Hearts break—as the lead indicates—you are home in a canter.

This time, there is no question of drawing trumps from dummy. So it is only a *partial* reversal. But the basic idea is the same: ruffing losers in declarer's hand may produce more tricks than setting up the trump suit as such.

On Not Ruffing

After so much about ruffing, it is only fitting that we should conclude with a few words on when NOT to ruff.

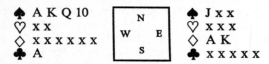

The Ace, King and Queen of Hearts are led against Four Spades—a contract which it is reasonable to be in, but most unreasonable to get into. Trumps may break 4–2. They probably will. So you cannot afford to be *forced*—to be deprived of a precious trump—by that third Heart. Let it go, discarding one of those promising little Diamonds. Now all should be well. Take the next trick, whatever it is, and play off the A K of Diamonds. Back to your hand with a Spade and ruff a Diamond with the Knave. Draw trumps and put your hand down. Nothing can break the contract, so long as trumps and Diamonds are reasonably divided (not 5–1 and 4–1 respectively).

But if you ruff the Queen of Hearts, a simple 4–2 trump break will upset the whole apple-cart.

It is true that *Five* Spades can be made if the trumps break 3–3; but you are not in Five. So play SAFE and try to make Four.

The question arises: when should declarer refuse to be forced?

The answer is: when he *can* afford to lose that particular trick, but fears losing control of the trump suit.

Résumé

(1) Draw trumps at once, when you fear that opponents may ruff winners in your side-suits.

(2) Don't draw trumps *prematurely*, when you intend to ruff a loser—or losers—in dummy.

(3) It is not always necessary to draw *all* the trumps. You may have to leave opponents with the *best* trump—one that will make a trick in any case. It is their *losing* trumps that you must extract—those which cannot take tricks in their own right, but may ruff your winners—given the opportunity.

(4) When dummy and declarer have equal length in the same side-suit, no *immediate* ruffs in that suit are possible. But the holdings may be *made unequal* by discarding a loser in one hand on a winner in the other.

(5) *Before* embarking on a cross ruff, CASH your winners in the side-suits. Otherwise opponents may ruff them in the end game.

(6) In a dummy reversal, declarer ruffs dummy's losers in his *own hand*, and then draws trumps *from dummy*. This play hinges on adequate entries and good trumps in dummy.

(7) The purpose of both the cross ruff and the dummy reversal is to make *separately* the trumps in the two hands. The difference is that in the cross-ruff the trumps in *both* hands are used for ruffing; in the dummy reversal only *declarer's* hand ruffs, while dummy's holding is used to draw opponents' trumps.

(8) The dummy reversal technique may be employed *partially*. Declarer uses dummy's quick entries to ruff losers in his own hand, but does *not* draw trumps from dummy. This method is adopted when declarer can make *more trump tricks* by ruffing than by setting up an uncertain trump suit.

(9) Refuse to be *forced*—to ruff opponents' winners—when you can afford to lose a particular trick or tricks, but *cannot* afford to shorten your trumps. This will enable you to retain TRUMP CONTROL.

39

Exercises

(1) North leads the ten of Diamonds against Three Spades by West.

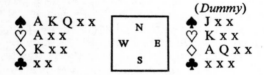

♠ A x x x   ♠ x x x x
♡ K Q x x   ♡ x
◇ A Q x   ◇ K x x x
♣ x x   ♣ A x x x

(*a*) Where do you take the trick?
(*b*) What card do you play at trick two?

(2) The Knave of Clubs is led against Four Spades by West. South overtakes with the King, and follows with the Ace and Queen of Clubs.

(*Dummy*)

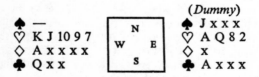

♠ A K Q x x   ♠ J x x
♡ A x x   ♡ K x x
◇ K x x   ◇ A Q x x
♣ x x   ♣ x x x

What card do you play on the Queen of Clubs (trick three)?

(3) A trump is opened against Four Hearts by West.

(*Dummy*)

♠ —   ♠ J x x x
♡ K J 10 9 7   ♡ A Q 8 2
◇ A x x x x   ◇ x
♣ Q x x   ♣ A x x x

What should be the first three tricks?

40

(4) The deuce of Clubs is opened against Five Diamonds by West.

(*Dummy*)

West	Dummy
♠ x x	♠ A x x
♡ A x x	♡ x x
◇ K Q J x x	◇ 10 x x
♣ K J x	♣ A Q x x x

What do you play at trick two?

(5) The Queen of Hearts is led against Four Spades by West.

(*Dummy*)

West	Dummy
♠ A K Q 8	♠ J 10 9
♡ K	♡ A x x x x x
◇ x x x x	◇ A x x
♣ x x x x	♣ A

(*a*) Which ten tricks will you make, assuming that neither defender has a void in any suit?

(*b*) Which ten tricks would you expect to make on a trump lead?

(6) The Knave of trumps is opened against Two Diamonds by West.

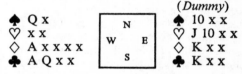

(*Dummy*)

West	Dummy
♠ Q x	♠ 10 x x
♡ x x	♡ J 10 x x
◇ A x x x x	◇ K x x
♣ A Q x x	♣ K x x

What cards do you play to: (*a*) the first two tricks; (*b*) the next three tricks?

(7) You are West in Two Hearts. North leads the deuce of Spades.

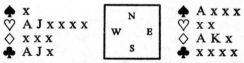

West	East
♠ x	♠ A x x x
♡ A J x x x x	♡ x x
◇ x x x	◇ A K x
♣ A J x	♣ x x x x

(*a*) What card do you lead from dummy at the second trick?

(*b*) Which eight tricks do you expect to make?

41

DEFENCE

CHAPTER IV

The Trump Lead—and After

The first move in defence—and sometimes the most difficult —is the opening lead. We are all familiar with the spectacle of the defender who fingers a Knave, strokes an Ace, then hovers round a deuce, only to close his hand again in doubt and dejection. Even Master players experience at times a sense of uncertainty. There is no infallible answer to the problem. What is a good lead in one situation becomes execrable in another, and every case has to be judged on its merits.

Trump Leads

An all-important clue is the bidding. To foil declarer one must first know his intentions. Listen carefully: Opener, " One Spade "; Responder, " Three Spades "; Opener, " Four Spades ". What does the exchange of messages convey? Presumably dummy will turn up with four trumps or thereabouts. And presumably there will be on the table some doubleton or singleton—maybe even a void. After all, one of the attractions of seeking game in a suit—as opposed to the cheaper No-Trump contract—lies in dummy's ruffing value.

Listening attentively is almost as good as peeping at dummy. The next stage is to apply the information. Your thoughts should follow this course : " Evidently declarer hopes to ruff something in dummy. That way he may dispose of two, three or conceivably four, losers. But perhaps I can put a spoke in his wheels by *opening* a trump, and if I can get in quickly, I will apply a second spoke, and maybe, a third. The more trumps I lead, the fewer will remain in dummy to ruff losers."

The kernel of the argument is this : What is good for

declarer is bad for the defence. If the bidding indicates that he hopes to make tricks by ruffing in dummy, then it must be a good idea for me to remove dummy's trumps.

Let us put on our earphones once more:

One Spade	.	.	Two Diamonds
Two Hearts	.	.	No Bid

Perhaps we hold some juicy Spade combination like A Q 10 or K J 9 x or A J 9 x. This looks like an auspicious moment to open a trump. By passing, declarer's partner has shown preference for Hearts. He may have two Spades and three Hearts or one Spade and two or three Hearts. We don't know the exact position, but we do know that dummy will be *shorter in Spades* than in Hearts. So we attack trumps to prevent declarer ruffing too many of his Spade losers—and our winners—in dummy.

Here is another situation which invites an attack on dummy's trumps.

One Heart	.	.	Three Hearts
Three No-Trumps	.	.	Four Hearts

The opening bidder knows from the first response that he will find good Heart support, but suggests game in No-Trumps. Yet his partner prefers the *more expensive* contract in Hearts. His only reason can be DISTRIBUTION. Clearly, his double raise was based more on shape than on high cards. In short, his ruffing value is particularly good. And that is a particularly good reason for attacking it.

One or two examples will illustrate the damaging effects of a trump opening. You may recall this hand:

In the last chapter declarer had no difficulty in making Four Diamonds—on a Club opening. The point of the hand was that trumps must not be touched by declarer until *after* he had ruffed a Spade in dummy. But what if the defence does

43

the touching at trick one, *before* declarer has any say in the matter? Three rounds of trumps can be taken by the defence *immediately*, without letting in declarer. Dummy's ruffing value is eliminated, that losing Spade remains unruffed, and the contract is beaten.

Now take a look over declarer's shoulder as he plays this one in Four Hearts.

♠ A x	N	♠ J x x x
♡ K 10 x x	W E	♡ Q J x x
◇ J x x x	S	◇ Q
♣ A Q x		♣ K J 10 x

Top tricks come to eight—three trumps, four Clubs and the Ace of Spades. To get home, declarer will need *two* Diamond ruffs in dummy, and if a trump is not opened, he will almost certainly get them. Work it out. Declarer wins the first trick and concedes a Diamond. Defenders may now switch to a trump, but it is too late. Only two rounds can be drawn before allowing declarer to regain the lead. And that still leaves two trumps in dummy to ruff Diamonds. That second Diamond ruff is the tenth, decisive trick, and only a *trump opening* can remove it. If it is wasted, a tempo is lost and it may be too late to make up for it afterwards.

There are exceptions to every rule, but this broad principle is worth following.

OPEN A TRUMP, when the bidding indicates that declarer will lean heavily on dummy's RUFFING VALUE to fulfil his contract.

Leading from an Honour

Even after deciding that the situation—and particularly the bidding—calls for a trump opening, there may still be cause for fingering and fidgeting. Which trump? With x x or x x x there is not much scope for profound reflection. But what happens with A x x or K x x or Q x x?

At first sight, A x x seems to call for the Ace with a small one to follow. That will account for two of dummy's potential ruffs at one fell swoop. The only trouble is that, in that case, there may be no second swoop, and therefore, no chance to play a *third* trump—the one that usually does the damage It is all a question of entries and communications. Let us look into it more closely.

At trick two declarer probably gains the lead. If he can retain it until he has finished ruffing in dummy, there is nothing much that you can do about it. But he may have to let your side in, and it may be, not you, but partner. Now partner may have started with two trumps only. If you take them both with your lead of A x, how is he to put you in to play the third round? Even if you have an entry, partner may fail to find it. Of course, the same difficulty arises— still more directly—if the second trick is won, not by declarer, but by partner.

The lead of a small one from A x x allows partner, if he wins an early trick, to put you in with his second trump. Admittedly, he may not have even two trumps, but as against that, he can have a singleton King, and what could be more galling than to bring it down on your Ace at the first trick?

Try out these leads on the two examples in the preceding pages.

The Four Diamond contract is broken on the lead of a small trump from A x x (or K x x). It succeeds against the Ace. The same situation arises on the Four-Heart hand. If the lead is Ace and another trump from A x x, declarer wins the second trick and plays the Queen of Diamonds. It is a tragedy for the defence if the wrong man holds both the Ace and King of the suit. His two trumps have been taken out by an unkind partner and the culprit himself has no entry, and therefore, no way of taking that third round of trumps.

Again a small one from A x x cooks declarer's goose. Winning the second trick, the right-hand opponent still has a trump to lead and the defence takes three rounds before the ruffing can start.

If your trump holding is A x x (or K x x), partner may well have a doubleton. Don't sever connections between the two hands by robbing him thoughtlessly of both his little xs. He may sorely need them. The motto should be: PRESERVE THE LINE OF COMMUNICATIONS.

The Attack Continues

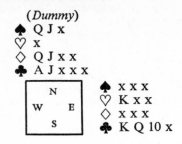

(*Dummy*)
♠ Q J x
♡ x
◇ Q J x x
♣ A J x x x

♠ x x x
♡ K x x
◇ x x x
♣ K Q 10 x

Against Four Spades by South, partner opens the Ace of trumps, followed by another. Declarer wins in dummy and leads a Heart. Most defenders in East's position will play low unhesitatingly. One or two will hesitate, but still play low. Only the expert will go up with the King as a matter of course. The reason is that East needs an *ENTRY* and needs it desperately. Declarer's play shows that he intends to ruff a Heart in dummy, and only East can stop him, because only he has another trump. Therefore, East must go up with that Heart King, hoping to hold the trick and to torpedo dummy's ruffing potential with his third, precious trump.

Of course, if declarer has the Ace of Hearts, East's King will be a casualty and dummy will still ruff. What of it? If declarer has the Heart Ace, it will probably not matter much what East does. But if West holds that Ace, East's play will make all the difference.

It comes to this: in certain circumstances, going up with the King of Hearts will gain a trick. In no circumstances is it likely to *lose* a trick.

We have established that the bidding may call for an immediate onslaught on dummy's ruffing value. The opening phase in the offensive is a trump lead. The second phase is a trump continuation, and this demands that the RIGHT defender—the one who still has a trump—should be on play when his side next gets in.

Tactically, the two defenders must nurse each other's entries—sometimes purely hypothetical entries—to put the right man in at the right time. Conversely, they must see to it, that through inadvertence, the wrong man does not find himself on play at the wrong time.

Unfortunately for defenders, who happen to be on lead against suit contracts, destiny does not always provide them with comfortable trump holdings like A x x or K x x—or for that matter—x x x. Sometimes they may be dealt Q x x. Then it is usually best to think of something else. The risk of losing a trick is too great. With J x x lead a small one. Even that will cost a trick at times.

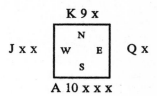

Given a little judicious guessing, South will now lose no trick at all. Still, when a trump attack is indicated, x from J x x will gain more on the swings than it will lose on the round-abouts.

From J 10 x lead a *small* one. Partners sometimes hold singleton honours. Maybe the position is:

J 10 x opposite Q (or K)

and it is distinctly undignified to make no trick at all out of three honours. What if South plays small from dummy?

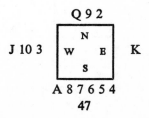

Both the Knave and the King fall to the Ace. Declarer then finesses against the ten.

A great statesman once said: " Above all, not too much zeal." He had in mind his country's diplomatic service, but the injunction is also applicable to trump leads. Don't overdo it.

Egregiously bad is the opening of a *singleton* trump.

If one defender has a singleton, the chances are that his partner holds three or four—maybe Q x x or Q 10 x x or K J x. Declarer suspects nothing. Left to himself he may well lose one or two trump tricks. A singleton lead may present him with a photograph of the defence—a plan of the traps and minefields of distribution. With this up his sleeve, declarer may not lose a trick at all—not even to K J x x.

Forcing Declarer

A particularly good moment not to lead trumps is when you have four of them. The situation generally calls for a FORCING game—forcing declarer to ruff in his hand. In its simplest form, the idea can be expressed like this : If declarer has four trumps and I can FORCE him to ruff once, I shall be left with more trumps than he. In fact, I shall have trump control. If declarer has five trumps, I may still gain control by FORCING him twice.

This is the sort of thing that happens.

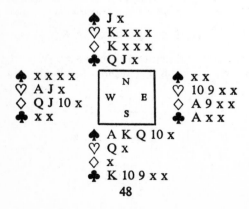

On the face of it, declarer should have no trouble in Four Spades. A trump lead presents him with the contract, all signed, sealed and delivered. But a Diamond offensive makes his life very awkward. The second Diamond reduces his trumps to four. And there is bound to be a third Diamond before the Clubs can be cashed. From now on, West will have one trump more than declarer.

Here is an extreme case to illustrate the FORCING principle.

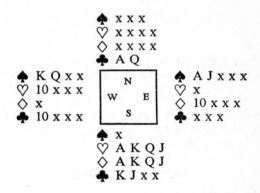

South can make a small slam in three suits if Spades are not attacked at once. But the second Spade FORCES him and trump control passes to the defence.

At this point, it is appropriate to revert to the defender with a singleton trump. Most of the time he should act just as if he had three more. An enlightened soliloquy would take this form and explain the paradox.

"The bidding suggests that opponents have about eight trumps between them. As I have one only, partner may have four. Therefore, I must endeavour to FORCE declarer. If he shortens himself twice—maybe even once will be enough—he will have fewer trumps left than my partner. And won't that be good!"

When declarer sets out to ruff—or cross ruff—one of his constant fears is that he may be over-ruffed. Then he loses, not only a trick, but also the initiative.

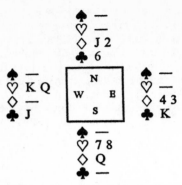

Diamonds are trumps in this three-card ending. Declarer needs to make all the tricks and succeeds, if the Hearts are divided. But to do so, he must ruff the first Heart with the *deuce*. He must chance it, for there is no other way. Alas, East *over-ruffs*, and plays the last trump, bringing down the Knave and Queen together. Where he hoped to make three tricks, declarer makes only one.

On Not Over-ruffing

But what happens here:

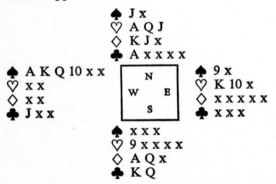

Four Hearts for South looks eminently reasonable. West opens the King of Spades, notes East's nine and continues with the Ace *and* Queen. Declarer ruffs with the Knave in dummy.

50

What next?

Have you worked it out? If East over-ruffs, the contract can't be lost. If he doesn't, it can't be made. Why? Because of that thing PROMOTION on which we put so much emphasis in Chapter II. The ten has been promoted. With the Knave out of the way, East's trump holding becomes, to all intents and purposes, K J x. But if the King is used to over-ruff, the 10 x goes back to being itself. Dummy's A Q will draw them and that will be that. Promotion has failed to be consummated.

K 10 x over A Q J is a flagrant case. Try this one:

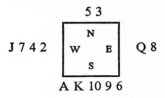

East plays something, which declarer ruffs with the ten. Most defenders in West's position over-ruff like lightning. It is an instinctive reflex, and sometimes an expensive one. Of course, West does not *know* that his partner possesses the Q 8. But he has nothing to *gain* by over-ruffing. His Knave will make a trick, anyway. So he may as well wait a minute or two, just in case partner has the right cards to PROMOTE the seven. Yes, even sevens make tricks, especially after the tens, nines and eights have fallen on the baize battlefield.

Is there any rule to follow, any principle that determines when to over-ruff and when to hope for the promotion of some modest middle card? There is no cast-iron formula. But follow this general idea and you won't be far out:

It is seldom wise to over-ruff with an honour—especially when it is flanked by middle cards (tens and nines). With a natural trick in trumps—one that can't be taken from you—think twice before over-ruffing—and then, for the most part, don't.

Conversely, over-ruff declarer's small trumps gleefully with your own. If you have been dealt the six and the three, you will be doing well to make a trick with one of them. Holding

K 5 over the Ace, make the five—should the happy occasion arise—and hope to make the King as well.

The best time of all to over-ruff is when you want an entry—to play another trump, to give partner a ruff, or in some other good cause.

Résumé

(1) When the bidding indicates that declarer will find ruffing value in dummy, the most effective opening lead is often a trump.

(2) From A x x (or K x x) the correct lead is a small one. Partner is more likely to have two trumps than three, and it is good tactics to leave him a trump to play back, if he happens to win the first trick for the defence.

(3) From J 10 x, lead a small one.

(4) Opening a singleton trump is nearly always bad. The effect may well be to destroy a trick—or tricks—in partner's hand.

(5) With four trumps, a trump lead is generally to be avoided—particularly when the bidding indicates that declarer has no more than four or five trumps himself. The best strategy for the defence is to *FORCE* declarer—to make him shorten his trumps.

(6) A defender should not over-ruff declarer or dummy automatically. The main consideration is the likelihood or otherwise of developing another trump trick.

(7) With a natural trump trick—one that must make in any any case—don't over-ruff unless: (*a*) you want the lead; (*b*) you hope to get a *second* ruff.

Exercises

(1)

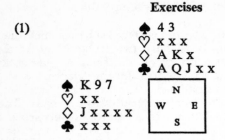

♠ 4 3
♡ x x x
♢ A K x
♣ A Q J x x

♠ K 9 7
♡ x x
♢ J x x x x
♣ x x x

South is in Four Spades. East has bid Hearts and West leads the top of his doubleton. East plays the King, Ace and Queen of Hearts. Declarer ruffs the third round with the Knave of Spades. What should West do?

(2) Same bidding and play as in (1).

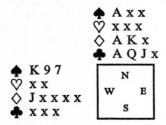

♠ A x x
♡ x x x
♢ A K x
♣ A Q J x

♠ K 9 7
♡ x x
♢ J x x x x
♣ x x x

What should West do at trick three?

(3)

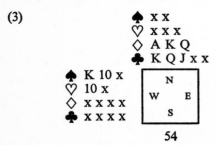

♠ x x
♡ x x x
♢ A K Q
♣ K Q J x x

♠ K 10 x
♡ 10 x
♢ x x x x
♣ x x x x

South is in Two Spades. East has bid Hearts and West leads the ten to his partner's King. East plays the Ace of Clubs and continues with the Ace and Queen of Hearts. Declarer ruffs with the Knave. What should West do?

(4)

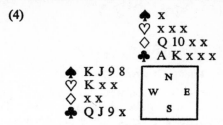

♠ x
♡ x x x
◇ Q 10 x x
♣ A K x x x

♠ K J 9 8
♡ K x x
◇ x x
♣ Q J 9 x

West opens a small trump against Four Hearts. Declarer wins with the Knave in his hand and plays the Queen of Spades. Should West cover?

(5) Bidding was:

South (dealer)	West	North	East
One Spade	Two Clubs	Two Spades	Three Clubs
Four Spades	No Bid	No Bid	No Bid

Sitting West, what do you lead from:

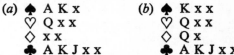

(a) ♠ A K x
♡ Q x x
◇ x x
♣ A K J x x

(b) ♠ K x x
♡ Q x x
◇ Q x
♣ A K J x x

(6) South, dealer, opened Four Hearts and all passed. What do you lead from:

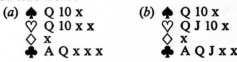

(a) ♠ Q 10 x
♡ Q 10 x x
◇ x
♣ A Q x x x

(b) ♠ Q 10 x
♡ Q J 10 x
◇ x
♣ A Q J x x

DUMMY PLAY

CHAPTER V

Trump Control

Our purpose this time is to demonstrate the fallacy of that specious saying: " You can't make a silk purse out of a sow's ear." Of course you can. In Chapter III we learned to transform losers into winners by ruffing with little xs. The trump magic that turns nondescript cards into tricks is only one of the charms of suit contracts. Another is CONTROL —the right to say " stop " or " go ", and to divert the card traffic across the table.

Here is a flagrant case:

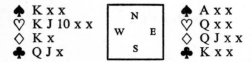

♠ A K Q 10 x   ♠ J x
♡ K x   ♡ A Q J 10 x
◇ x x   ◇ x x
♣ K x x x   ♣ A Q J x

East–West can make eleven tricks in Spades, Hearts or Clubs. In No-Trumps, somebody will be able to reel off at least five Diamonds. There is no need to ruff anything, but there is every need for trumps of some kind. A suit contract will give declarer CONTROL—the right to say " stop " to those sickening Diamonds.

Now try this:

♠ K x x   ♠ A x x
♡ K J 10 x x   ♡ Q x x
◇ K x   ◇ Q J x x
♣ Q J x   ♣ K x x

Opponents open the Queen of Spades. How do you propose to make Four Hearts? Think it over slowly on the basis of a common and garden distribution.

Ready? What card did you play at trick two? Was it a Diamond? No? Then you have cooked your goose. Anything else—including a trump—will be seized avidly by opponents. Another Spade will flash back. Whatever you do next, the defence will collect three Aces *and* a Spade. Result: one down.

The King of Diamonds at trick two is a *sine qua non* or what philosophers would probably call a "categorical imperative". The reason is that a Diamond trick must be set up for a Spade discard *quickly*—before the Ace and King of Spades are knocked out. Note that it is no good playing a small Diamond. It must be the King. Otherwise the suit is blocked.

At this point another question must be asked: Where did you take that first Spade? Not in dummy? Good. Because if you did, the contract is doomed. Opponents hold off the first Diamond, take the second and drive out the King of Spades. Now dummy cannot be reached in *time* for the discard. TIME is the operative word.

Imagine, for a horrible moment, that you must play the hand in Three No-Trumps. Ten tricks are there—two in Spades, four in Hearts and two tricks in each of the minors.

Unfortunately, in No-Trumps, TIME is on the side of the defenders. They can set up five tricks before you set up nine. Again, there is no "ruffing value" about. But the suit contract is worth at least two tricks more than No-Trumps—more if one of the defenders has five Spades.

It comes to this: You can make ten tricks. They can make five. Whoever CONTROLS the ebb and flow of battle, decides the issue. In No-Trumps, the defence is in command. Three Aces give three entries—three opportunities to attack the weak spot in Spades. But in Hearts declarer can say "stop" to the Spades. He takes CONTROL, and that is what makes a suit contract so often superior to No-Trumps.

One more illustration—with a sting in the tail.

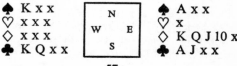

♠ K x x
♡ x x x
◇ x x x
♣ K Q x x

N
W E
S

♠ A x x
♡ x
◇ K Q J 10 x
♣ A J x x

57

No-Trumps is out of the question, since opponents can peel off anything up to nine Hearts, at sixty miles an hour. In Diamonds, the Hearts are stopped at trick two and ten tricks can be made without trouble. The three inescapable losers are: the Ace of trumps, one Heart and one Spade.

Now try Clubs as trumps. This time—unless trumps break 4–1—you make not ten tricks, but *eleven*. That little Spade is no longer a loser. It is neatly parked on the Diamonds.

To compare the two contracts, count the winners in each case: Spades, two; Hearts, 0; and Diamonds, four; the total is the same for both minors. But Clubs yield an *extra* trick as trumps.

After discarding a small Spade on East's Diamonds, West can ruff a Spade in his own hand, raising the Club winners to five—when they are trumps.

The 4–4 Trump Fit

This brings out the advantage of a trump suit divided 4–4 between declarer and dummy. A long side-suit is used for discards and the fourth trump—in either hand—produces an additional trick by ruffing.

Modern bidding places so much emphasis on this particular trump fit—four in each hand—that the mechanics of playing the combination are worth another thought. Picture the hands in terms of shape alone:

	(Dummy)		
♠	♡	◇	♣
5	4	2	2

	(Declarer)		
♠	♡	◇	♣
3	4	3	3

Count the tricks in the majors, assuming all to be winners. With Spades as trumps there are *nine*: five Spades and four Hearts. But in a Heart contract there may well be ten. Declarer may be able to discard two Clubs or two Diamonds

58

on dummy's Spades and to ruff in his hand, bringing the total Heart winners to *five* instead of *four*.

Now fill in the picture:

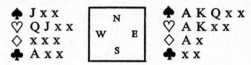

♠ J x x ♡ Q J x x ◇ x x x ♣ A x x

♠ A K Q x x ♡ A K x x ◇ A x ♣ x x

In Spades, eleven tricks is the limit of the hand. There is no means of disposing of two losers—one in each minor. But in Hearts the addition comes to twelve. Two Diamonds (or two Clubs) are deposited on the Spades and a ruff yields the odd trick.

Of course, this situation will not arise every time. Opponents may be able to take their tricks first, and then there will be nothing sufficiently worthless to discard and to ruff. But on balance, there is a distinct advantage in making trumps the suit divided 4–4, and in using the 5–3 suit for discards, with a view to an extra ruff.

Even on the sketchiest hands the 4–4 pattern proves surprisingly resilient. With careful handling, an extra trick seldom fails to materialise, so long as the trumps break 3–2—the normal expectation.

Two Hearts is the contract.

♠ K Q x
♡ 10 x x x
◇ x x
♣ K x x x

♠ A J x
♡ A Q x x
◇ K x x x
♣ x x

West opens the Queen of Diamonds. East wins with the Ace and returns a trump. Play low—in common parlance, duck. West, let us say, takes the trick with the Knave and plays a Club. Up with the King, like a man. East wins with the Ace and plays another trump. Now what?

Before coming to a decision, take stock of the position. The defence is bound to make another Club, and you have lost three tricks already. If the King of Hearts is wrong—over the A Q—the score against you will be five. So you must ruff both your losing Diamonds in dummy. Therefore, you cannot afford to duck the trump lead again. West may grab the trick with the King and return a *third* trump. That will leave one trump only in dummy to deal with two Diamonds. Play the Ace of Hearts and this will be the position:

♠ K Q x
♡ 10 x
◇ x
♣ x x x

N
W　E
S

♠ A J x
♡ Q x
◇ K x x
♣ x

The rest should be easy, because you are now in CONTROL. Play off the King of Diamonds and ruff a Diamond. Back to your own hand with a Spade and ruff the last Diamond. One of the defenders may ruff something, sometime. You could not care less. The King is the only trump out, and it must make anyway.

The feature of the hand is the handling of the trumps. If you go up with the Heart Ace at trick two and begin ruffing the Diamonds, the last one may be over-ruffed by East—and you may still lose two tricks to West. That will be three trump winners for the opponents—in addition to two Clubs and the Ace of Diamonds.

The purpose in ducking on the first round of trumps, and winning the second, is to absorb four of the enemy's five trumps. Then, and only then, can you set about ruffing Diamonds.

Correct timing—playing the Ace of Hearts at the right time —enables declarer to retain CONTROL throughout.

A side-light on the strength of the 4–4 trump division is that declarer need not fear a FORCING game by opponents. If East continues with Clubs, after winning trick three, South still lays down the Ace of trumps. He then crosses into dummy with a Spade and ruffs the last Club with the Queen of Hearts in his hand—a touch of the dummy reversal technique.

With the 4–4 trump pattern, *either* hand can make the extra trick by ruffing.

How do you play this in Four Spades? A Club is opened:

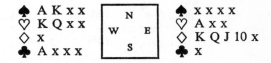

<pre>
♠ A K x x   ♠ x x x x
♡ K Q x x   ♡ A x x
♢ x   ♢ K Q J 10 x
♣ A x x x   ♣ x
</pre>

One of the best ways of not playing the hand is to begin by laying down the Ace and King of trumps. Most of the time, nothing will go wrong and no one will notice anything out of the ordinary. But once in four times, or thereabouts, the trumps will break 4–1. Before ten tricks are made, the defence will come in with the Ace of Diamonds. If the wrong man has it, declarer will suffer the indignity of having his trumps drawn by the opponents. And then will come a succession of Clubs, which he will be powerless to stop.

Ruffing Clubs is also inadvisable—if only because someone may over-ruff the third Club, put partner in with the Diamond Ace and over-ruff again.

The correct procedure is to play a Diamond immediately— at trick two. As soon as that Ace is out of the way, all is plain sailing. Declarer is in full control. He plays off the Ace and King of Spades, and continues with Diamonds for ever. A 4–1 trump break bothers him no longer, because he is one move *ahead* of the defence.

Play Safe

Many fair players will have a lapse here:

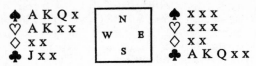

♠ A K Q x   ♠ x x x
♡ A K x x   ♡ x x x
♢ x x   ♢ x x
♣ J x x   ♣ A K Q x x

Four Spades is the contract. Opponents open the Ace and King of Diamonds and switch to a Heart.

There is nothing to ruff and nothing to establish. Trumps must be cleared quickly. But how?

Gallup Poll statistics would show the great majority of declarers leading out the three top Spades. Then rather more than half would curse their habitual bad luck. A 4–2 trump break—which is likely enough—blows the contract to bits. The defender with the fourth trump sits pretty until the third—or fourth—round of Clubs. At that point he ruffs, cutting off dummy in the prime of life. A Diamond robs declarer of his last, precious trump, and the probable result is: one down, maybe two.

The answer is: Play a trump at trick four—but a *small* one. With the next trick the defence must let you in. Now play off the Ace, King and Queen of Spades. This way you draw *four* rounds of trumps instead of three. And you retain CONTROL.

Of course, if the trumps happen to break 3–3, the correct play costs a trick. You make ten tricks instead of eleven. But it is well worth insuring the contract at the price of a trick, which you can afford to lose.

The Suicide Ruff

Ruffing is an expedient, not a principle. Ruff, not just to make tricks, but to make *extra* tricks—tricks you could not make otherwise. When dummy has a long suit, its trump holding may be worth more as a means of access to the length, than as ruffing value. A ruff, as such, is worth one trick. An entry may be worth three, four or five.

Here is an illustration of the suicide ruff from real life:

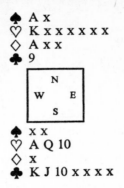

♠ A x
♡ K x x x x x x
♢ A x x
♣ 9

```
        N
    W       E
        S
```

♠ x x
♡ A Q 10
♢ x
♣ K J 10 x x x x

Against Five Hearts by North, East opened a Spade.

How would you plan the campaign?

This is how the gruesome story unfolded itself. Declarer won the first trick with the Spade Ace and ran the nine of Clubs. West gathered the trick with the Queen, cashed the King of Spades and led a Diamond. At this point, declarer decided to commit hara-kiri.

After winning the Diamond return with the Ace, he *ruffed a Diamond*. Back to his hand with a Club ruff, and another Diamond ruff on the table. Now he was firmly wedged in dummy. The only way out, after playing off the Ace of Hearts, was by way of yet another Club ruff. A surprised East over-ruffed with the Knave, and it was all over.

Begging for mercy afterwards, declarer pleaded: "I had two losing Diamonds."

So he had. But he could not afford to ruff them. And there was no need to resort to such masochism. Dummy's Clubs could have absorbed those Diamonds in comfort—if declarer had not cut off all access to them by slaughtering his precious trump entries.

With a long suit in dummy and the necessary entries to set it up, declarer should learn to make the TABLE GOOD. Dummy will take the tricks. The losers in his own hand won't matter. They will be absorbed automatically by dummy's winners.

In such cases the motto should be: TAKE CARE OF THE WINNERS AND THE LOSERS WILL TAKE CARE OF THEMSELVES.

The last hand was a freak. Here is an everyday affair to bring out the same point.

♠ A K Q J x		♠ 10 x x
♡ K x x		♡ J x
◇ x x		◇ A x x x x x
♣ A J x		♣ x x

North opens a Heart against Four Spades. South takes the trick with the Ace and returns a trump. How do we proceed?

Two ruffs in dummy would bring our total of winners to ten. But before we can set up a Club ruff, we shall have to let opponents in once more. Another trump by them is a certainty, and that will leave one trump in dummy to deal with two losers. No good.

So we go for the Diamonds. At trick three we play a Diamond and—*duck*. Whatever the return, we win, cash the Ace of Diamonds and ruff another with an honour. Then we draw trumps ending up in dummy with the ten.

There are two points to note: First, as in the last example, it would be suicidal to ruff a Heart in dummy. The entry to the Diamonds would disappear and we should pay with three (Diamond) tricks for the pleasure of making one (the Heart ruff).

Secondly, you cannot set up the Diamonds without ducking on the first round. The suit must be played three times, because one of the defenders is bound to have three Diamonds. And dummy is short of an entry. The ducking technique has the effect of creating one.

A Transgression

To conclude here is a hand with a . . . No, work out for yourself what it is.

♠ A K Q J 10 x		♠ x x
♡ x x		♡ A K Q x x x
◇ A Q x		◇ x x
♣ A Q		♣ x x x

A trump is opened against Six Spades. Well? How do you play it?

The slam is certain if you can make four tricks in Hearts. Therefore, after drawing trumps, *duck* a Heart. This is a SAFETY PLAY to guard against a 4–1 split. The price you pay is to give up all hope of that thirteenth trick, which you can make if the suit breaks 3–2.

A Digression

Let us admit it candidly. That last hand appears right out of its context. As a subject, the mechanics of PLAYING SAFE will later claim a whole chapter. Why, then, jump ahead? The answer is that Safety Plays call for no special technique and apply, in principle, to all hands, rather than to any particular type. Convenient though it be to group together a number of standardised situations, Safety Plays have a right to inclusion in every chapter, and it can never be too soon to turn the searchlight on their sterling virtues.

The term Safety Play implies nothing more than giving priority to the contract at the expense of probable tricks in excess of the required minimum. That, of course, is the correct approach to contracts of every size and colour. With the Master, it is an automatic reaction, a habit of which he is often unconscious. To condition the reflexes during the present, adolescent phase, we have gate-crashed, before our time, into Chapter XIII. It is only for a moment, though we shall do it again. And if that is a transgression, we can plead, at least, that we have not erred in innocence, but with malice aforethought.

Résumé

(1) In a suit contract, declarer can ruff, not only to make dummy's trumps separately, but also to exercise tactical control: to stop the play of a suit of which he has no more, and to attack another which he seeks to develop.

(2) With weak trump holdings, declarer may have to set up his side-suits or ruffing positions, before attempting to draw trumps; otherwise—

(3) If trumps break badly, opponents may gain CONTROL and cash their winners before declarer can cash his own.

(4) It is sometimes correct for declarer to play a small trump from both hands, even when his holding contains the Ace or A K. This enables him to remain in CONTROL if trumps break badly.

(5) With eight trumps between declarer and his dummy, a 4–4 division often possesses an added trick-taking capacity. A side suit can be set up through ruffs in one hand, while trump control is retained in the other.

(6) When trumps provide entries to a long suit, declarer should avoid ruffing losers in that hand. A trump is often more valuable as an entry to several tricks than as the means of winning one trick by ruffing.

Exercises

(1) ♠ x x   ♠ A K x x x
     ♡ K x   ♡ A x x
     ◇ A K Q J 10 x   ◇ x x
     ♣ A x x   ♣ x x x

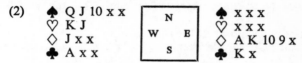

A trump is opened against Six Diamonds. After drawing trumps, which card will you play from your hand? What card will you play from dummy?

(2) ♠ Q J 10 x x   ♠ x x x
     ♡ K J   ♡ x x x
     ◇ J x x   ◇ A K 10 9 x
     ♣ A x x   ♣ K x

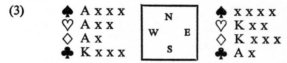

Against Three Spades, opponents lead the Ace, King and a small trump. No more trumps are out.

(a) How do you play the Diamonds?

(b) How do you play the Diamonds if the contract is Four Spades?

(3) ♠ A x x x   ♠ x x x x
     ♡ A x x   ♡ K x x
     ◇ A x   ◇ K x x x
     ♣ K x x x   ♣ A x

A Club is opened against Four Spades. What cards do you play from your hand, and from dummy, to trick two?

(4) ♠ A K Q J x   ♠ x x
     ♡ x x x x   ♡ A K x
     ◇ J x x   ◇ K Q 10 9 x x
     ♣ x   ♣ x x

The Ace, then the King of Clubs are led against Four Spades.

(a) What card should declarer play to the second trick?

(b) What should declarer lead when he wins his first trick?

(5)   ♠ A K Q J x   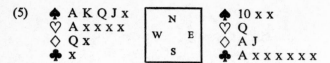   ♠ 10 x x
       ♡ A x x x x   ♡ Q
       ◇ Q x   ◇ A J
       ♣ x   ♣ A x x x x x x

A Heart is opened against Six Spades by West. South plays the King and West wins. What cards should declarer play to: (*a*) trick two; (*b*) trick three; (*c*) trick four; (*d*) trick five?

(6)   ♠ A K Q x x   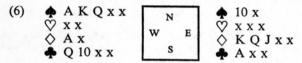   ♠ 10 x
       ♡ x x   ♡ x x x
       ◇ A x   ◇ K Q J x x
       ♣ Q 10 x x   ♣ A x x

The contract is Four Spades. Opponents lead the three top Hearts.

(*a*) Should declarer ruff the third Heart?

(*b*) What card should declarer play when he wins his first trick?

DEFENCE

CHAPTER VI

Attack on Suit Contracts

Time is more than money. It represents tricks. Often enough declarer can make his ten tricks and yet the defence can make four—or five. To flash first past the post, you must make yours *before* he makes his. That is the time to be aggressive.

To be or not to be dynamic. That is the question for the defence. In Chapter IV we learned spoiling tactics—the art of interfering with declarer. It was clear from the bidding that dummy would have a singleton or doubleton. So we opened a trump to reduce the ruffing value. But what if the bidding suggests, not ruffing value, but a good side suit in dummy? Or simply that the other side has most of the cards? Then attack may be the order of the day. Gather your tricks quickly, before declarer can gather his.

Of all leads the most dynamic is a singleton. Partner wins with the Ace and gives us a ruff. Or else, declarer takes the trick, but has to let partner in, while we still have a trump, and the result is the same.

The ideal, of course, is to lead the singleton of a suit bid by partner. That he has bid the suit holds out some hope that he may have the Ace. And the fact that he was good enough to bid at all, suggests that he will have an entry—the hope of a second ruff.

When partner has not said a word, the issue is not quite so clear. Leading a singleton will only help declarer—if partner never gets in to give us that ruff. Will he or will he not? That is the point to consider. So make a good guess. It is not as difficult as it sounds. Weigh the evidence.

Let us suppose that declarer is in Four Spades and that you hold a couple of Aces and a King. Now partner is unlikely to

69

hold much in the way of high cards. Unless the distribution is freakish, opponents won't bid game with so much out against them. And if partner is weak, he won't come in to give you a ruff. So let us think of an alternative to that singleton.

Conversely, you may have next to nothing in your hand. This time partner must have some high cards, if only because opponents made no effort to reach a slam. An ideal moment to open a singleton.

It adds up to this: the better your hand, the less chance there is of hurting declarer with a singleton lead. The worse your hand, the rosier will be your prospects of getting a ruff or two.

Doubleton Leads

And now what about doubletons? There was once a strong prejudice against having anything to do with them. But on many hands it is still the best lead.

The second thing to do is to think it out. The first is to tune in to the bidding.

We hear: One Spade;   Two Hearts;
            Two No-Trumps;   Four Hearts;

You are on lead and hold:

     ♠ K x x x   ♡ A x x   ◇ 10 x   ♣ x x x x

The situation is particularly unpromising, because that Spade King is probably in the wrong place. In short, it looks as if the hand will play well for declarer. Given time, he may be able to set up the Spade suit. Don't give him time. Attack with the ten of Diamonds—always the top from a doubleton. If you are very lucky, partner will have the A Q over the opener's King. But without going to extremes, you may well find partner with the Ace—or the King over the Ace. And you are playing *through* the strong hand—the hand that has advertised something in Diamonds by its Two No-Trumps rebid. So you are unlikely to do much damage.

70

You may ask: How will partner know whether I have led from a doubleton or a singleton? Even if he has the Ace of Diamonds and plays back the suit, I can't ruff. And how shall I put him in afterwards?

The answer is that partner can, and must, work it out. Sometimes he will go wrong, but more often than not he will get there. Let us switch to his chair and see why.

Now, from a new angle we see that ten of Diamonds glide across the table. Dummy goes down with:

♠ A J 10 x   ♡ K J   ◇ K Q 9 x   ♣ Q x x

We, ourselves, in our new seat, find:

♠ Q x x x   ♡ x x   ◇ A x x   ♣ K J x x

Well, is that ten a singleton or a doubleton lead? Seven Diamonds stare us in the face—four on the table and three in our hand. Partner's card is the eighth. So, if it is a singleton, declarer must have five, and the bidding makes that distinctly unlikely. He has shown at least six Hearts. If he had five Diamonds as well, he might have said something about it.

Have another guess:

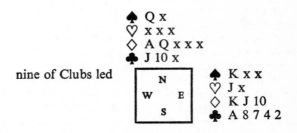

```
              ♠ Q x
              ♡ x x x
              ◇ A Q x x x
              ♣ J 10 x
nine of Clubs led   ┌──────────┐   ♠ K x x
                    │    N     │   ♡ J x
                    │ W     E  │   ◇ K J 10
                    │    S     │   ♣ A 8 7 4 2
                    └──────────┘
```

The bidding was:

East	South	West	North
One Club	One Spade	No Bid	Two Diamonds
No Bid	Two Hearts	No Bid	No Bid

Is that nine a singleton?

71

Declarer has shown at least nine cards in Spades and Hearts, for it is unlikely that he overbid One Spade on a four-card suit, missing the K Q. It is most improbable that he has K Q x x of Clubs as well. And if he has not, the lead cannot be a singleton. If partner started with three Clubs, holding up the Ace will cost nothing, and if he led from a doubleton, it may gain a trick.

Not every situation will lend itself to accurate analysis. But " 'tis better to have guessed and lost, than never to have guessed at all ".

Leading from doubletons should not become a hobby. But it can be a useful opening sometimes, and if we leave out of our calculations the very possibility that partner has struck that lead, then the defence will be robbed of a useful weapon.

After the diagnosis, the cure. If partner leads a singleton and you have the Ace, there is nothing much to think about. Take the trick and give him a ruff. But if the lead is from a doubleton, it won't do. Partner can't ruff yet, and it is up to you to make sure that you have the bowling, when he can ruff, on the third round. Of course, you may have no say in the matter. Declarer may be able to draw trumps, and that will be that. On the other hand, partner may have a quick entry—a trump trick, perhaps. He will try to put you in to give him that ruff and will search for an entry to your hand. The Ace of his doubleton suit ensures accessibility. Hold it up, if you decide that the lead is from a doubleton. That will leave open the lines of communication.

Let us turn back to that Two Heart contract. Having deduced that the nine of Clubs is no singleton, we play the seven or eight, a " come-on " card. More will be heard of this side of it later. Meanwhile, we can put on record that we want to attract partner's attention—to encourage him. Hence the seven or eight, and not the deuce. Maybe partner will be the next to come in with a trump. Then, if he started with a doubleton Club, he can still reach across the table, because we *did not* play that Ace and have left him a Club to return.

Now try it out on the first hand of the chapter. Here it is :

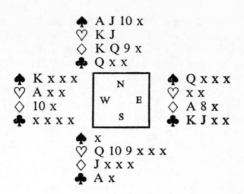

♠ A J 10 x
♡ K J
◇ K Q 9 x
♣ Q x x

♠ K x x x
♡ A x x
◇ 10 x
♣ x x x x

♠ Q x x x
♡ x x
◇ A 8 x
♣ K J x x

♠ x
♡ Q 10 9 x x x
◇ J x x x
♣ A x

If East wins the Diamond opening with his Ace, the contract is unbeatable. West comes in with the Ace of trumps, but can't give East the lead. Communications have been severed. Conversely, if East holds up the Ace, West can put him in with his other Diamond, and the ruff kills the contract.

One question remains to be answered before we leave East's comfortable seat. Must that ten of Diamonds be a singleton or a doubleton? Could it not be the top of three or four?

To which the answer is: hardly. West cannot have a sequence, because the nine is on the table. If he held four Diamonds—without the nine—he would have started with the smallest, not the ten. It is conceivable that he had three, but then no harm is done by holding up the Ace. We shall make it later, rather than sooner, and that is all. It can't run away.

Let us now return to West's seat and probe farther into the whys and wherefores of leading against suit contracts. Tune in:

South	*North*
One Heart	Two Diamonds
Three Diamonds	Three Hearts
Four Hearts	

Sitting West, your hand is:

♠ Q J 10   ♡ K x   ◇ x x x x x   ♣ A x x

What is your first reaction? A natural one would be

pleasurable expectancy. Declarer will probably go down, for it looks very much as if he is going to be unlucky.

What else? First and foremost there is an interesting Diamond position. The bidding suggests that North–South have at least seven Diamonds between them, perhaps eight. That means that partner has a void or singleton. Lead a Diamond confidently. Even if nothing happens on the first round, there is a good chance that you will come in with the King of trumps. Partner can hardly fail to ruff a second Diamond. With any luck, he may get another ruff, too, after giving you the lead with that Ace of Clubs.

With four of the suit, instead of five, a Diamond is still the attacking lead. But without length in Diamonds, the Spade Queen is the best opening.

So far, we have dealt with two aspects of defence: manœuvring for a ruff and contriving one for partner.

Trump Promotion

Another stratagem that occurs in the initial phase of operations is TRUMP PROMOTION. We met it in Chapter II. The principle is always the same, but the practice takes many different forms.

This time we will begin from the other side of the table:

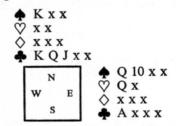

♠ K x x
♥ x x
♦ x x x
♣ K Q J x x

♠ Q 10 x x
♥ Q x
♦ x x x
♣ A x x x

After the uninspiring sequence—South, One Heart; North, Two Clubs; South, Two Hearts—partner leads out the three top Diamonds, and all follow. Then comes the thirteenth Diamond. Declarer discards a Spade from dummy. And you?

First ask yourself: Why did partner lead that Diamond, knowing that declarer had no more? By far the most likely reason is that he has a promising trump holding and wants you to FORCE an honour from declarer's hand. So trump—with the Queen. If it is over-ruffed with the Ace, your side is pretty certain to make a handsome profit. Study some of the possibilities. Lay out the cards, giving partner K 10 8 or A 10 8 or J 10 2, and work it out. With the first two combinations he will now make *three* tricks. With the J 10 2 he will make two. 10 8 3 2 will also yield two tricks, whereas an apparently useless trump holding like 9 4 3 2 will now produce one trick. Had you not gone up with that Queen, your side would have made one trick less each time. By driving out the Ace (or King) you PROMOTED—raised by one grade—every trump in partner's hand.

Now walk back to West's chair and give him a problem.

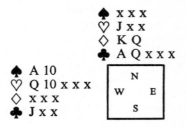

       ♠ x x x
       ♡ J x x
       ◇ K Q
       ♣ A Q x x x

♠ A 10
♡ Q 10 x x x
◇ x x x
♣ J x x

South is in Four Spades after some such bidding as:

South	*North*
One Spade	Two Clubs
Two Spades	Three Spades
Four Spades	

Sitting West, you open a small Heart. Partner proves his worth. He produces the Ace and King of Hearts, but, alas, a third one, too. This is ruffed by declarer, who enters dummy and leads a trump to his King.

Take stock. Always take stock in defence, but above all, at the beginning.

The Ace of trumps is your third trick. You need one more to defeat the contract. Where is it coming from?

75

Reading declarer's hand—envisaging what he must or may have—is the hallmark of the expert defender. To the inexperienced player it does not come easily. But everyone should try to get in the way of it. Few habits give better results.

Let us do it now. South opened the bidding and found a little extra to go the Fourth Spade over North's Three. To justify his calls he must have the Ace of Diamonds and almost certainly the King of Clubs as well. So it is no use looking for another trick in the side-suits. A second trump trick is the only hope; not a very bright one, but still a hope. Clearly, declarer started with the King and Queen of Spades. There is just a chance, though, that partner has the Knave. Admittedly if South's trumps are headed by the K Q, without the J 10 behind them, he probably has six of them. A little more " reading " should show that he would have passed three spades on just five to the K Q nothing, an Ace and a King.

Where are we? We have established that only trumps can provide the setting trick; that to do it partner must have the Knave, and that if he has, it is a doubleton. So, after taking the King with the Ace, we shall be left with the ten bare and partner—if our hopes come true—with the bare Knave. It won't be long before declarer plays his Queen and drops the two together unless—unless PROMOTION comes to the rescue. Can you beat that contract now? For the sake of convenience here is the hand again.

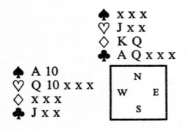

♠ x x x
♥ J x x
♦ K Q
♣ A Q x x x

♠ A 10
♥ Q 10 x x x
♦ x x x
♣ J x x

Four tricks have gone. Three Hearts, the last one ruffed by declarer; then a Spade, our Ace taking South's King.

Lead a Heart. Let East—who has no more—ruff with that

76

hypothetical Knave. Declarer can over-ruff, but that will make your ten good. With the disappearance of the Knave and Queen, the ten becomes master.

This particular type of promotion play is known as the UPPERCUT. Defenders contrive to use their trump honours *separately*. One of them goes up with an honour, forces declarer to over-ruff and thereby promotes an honour in partner's hand.

To exploit this situation, declarer must be *forced* to over-ruff. Otherwise, he will discard a loser and preserve his trump honours intact. In other words, before embarking on trump promotion, defenders must cash their winners—much as declarer does when he embarks on a cross-ruff (see Chapter III).

We will refashion that last hand a little to bring out the point. Make the contract *Three* Spades and give West the Ace of Diamonds.

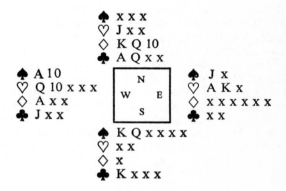

The first four tricks are the same. South ruffs the third Heart and loses the King of trumps to West's Ace. Now what about that uppercut? If West leads a Heart for East to ruff with the Knave, the blow is wasted. South just gets rid of his losing Diamond. That Diamond Ace must be cashed *before* the uppercut.

Defenders should always be on the look-out for the chance to promote each other's trumps. But promotion does not arise while declarer still has losers to discard.

Ruffing Winners, Not Losers

This sort of situation occurs every now and then:

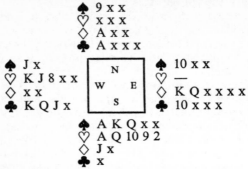

West opens the King of Clubs against Four Spades. Declarer wins with dummy's Ace and leads a Heart. That is his normal line of play. Since one of dummy's two entries is knocked out at the first trick, he takes the opportunity to finesse the Hearts. Doubtless, he hopes to use dummy's second entry for another finesse later, and to draw trumps in between.

But what about East? Work out what will happen: (*a*) if he ruffs, and (*b*) if he does not.

Take (*a*) first. Declarer will part cheerfully with the deuce of Hearts, ruff the Club return and draw trumps in two rounds. Now he will cash the Ace of Hearts and lay down the Queen. West will glare furiously at East, and East will wear a look of injured innocence. For this will be the unhappy picture.

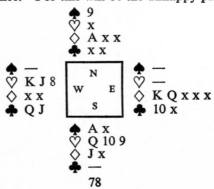

The defence is powerless. West can take his Heart King, but the Knave is trapped. And it all happened because East ruffed so injudiciously.

The time has come to try (b). East discards a Diamond or a Club and sits back. Declarer is helpless. If he draws trumps, he will lose three Hearts. And if he does not, East will over-ruff a Heart—*after* West has gathered two tricks with his King Knave.

What exactly would a post-mortem reveal? Why was that ruff so fatal? Because, the coroner would say, East used a precious trump to ruff the *deuce of Hearts*. That is all he achieved. Later, at the Old Bailey, East might plead that " he did not know his trump was loaded ". He thought that it was of little use, anyway. That proved a serious error, but how was he to know?

The judge would rule that even a seemingly useless trump should not be wasted on a miserable deuce that was a loser from the start. And that is the kernel of the matter.

In other words, ruff CONSTRUCTIVELY—to deprive declarer of a winner, to promote a trump in partner's hand, to take the lead when you want to be on play. But do not ruff just because you think that your trump is not much good anyway.

Here is another instance of the RUFF PURPOSELESS:

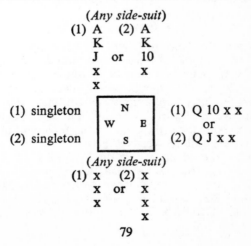

(*Any side-suit*)

(1) A	(2) A
K	K
J or	10
x	x
x	

(1) singleton   N   (1) Q 10 x x
   W   E   or
(2) singleton   S   (2) Q J x x

(*Any side-suit*)

(1) x	(2) x
x or	x
x	x
	x

79

Declarer plays dummy's Ace, enters his hand and leads towards dummy's K J x x or K 10 x.

If West ruffs, he is, in effect, trumping his partner's trick. Other things being equal, declarer will still make his King later. And such is the distribution, that he cannot hope to make anything else in that suit.

One final reflection on wanton ruffing: a trump is rarely useless. The fact that declarer does not know who has it or has no time to draw it, can in itself be an asset to the defence.

Make Him Guess

Some players are luckier than others. The reason is that they give their opponents the chance to be unlucky.

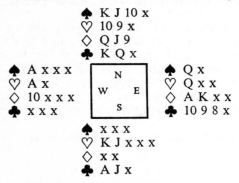

```
                  ♠ K J 10 x
                  ♡ 10 9 x
                  ◇ Q J 9
                  ♣ K Q x
  ♠ A x x x       ┌─────────┐     ♠ Q x
  ♡ A x           │    N    │     ♡ Q x x
  ◇ 10 x x x      │ W     E │     ◇ A K x x
  ♣ x x x         │    S    │     ♣ 10 9 8 x
                  └─────────┘
                  ♠ x x x
                  ♡ K J x x x
                  ◇ x x
                  ♣ A J x
```

West opens the deuce of Diamonds against a very ordinary Two Hearts. It looks as if declarer is bound to make it. The Queen of trumps is right and the Queen of Spades is wrong. So he will lose two Diamonds, two Spades and one trump.

The first few tricks are a matter of routine. East wins the Diamond, sees no future in the suit and shifts to the ten of Clubs. Declarer takes the trick on the table and finesses the ten of Hearts, losing to West's Ace.

Now what would an expert do in West's position? He can see that declarer has no losing Clubs, at most one more loser in Diamonds and no further worries in Hearts. Therefore, to beat the contract the Spades must somehow lead to three tricks. Can it be? Yes, if partner has a doubleton

Queen and declarer makes the *wrong guess*. Perhaps that is asking a lot of life, but good defence demands just that. When only a certain combination of cards can break the contract, back that combination.

You lead away from the Ace of Spades. Declarer does not know who has what. Some of the time he will go up with the King and make his contract. But the rest of the time he will play the Knave. East will win with the Queen—mildly surprised perhaps—and return another Spade. The third Spade is ruffed and the contract is beaten.

The feature of the hand is that declarer was given the chance to guess wrong—to be unlucky. And the moral is that in defence a little imagination goes a long way.

Punching Dummy

The last hand of the chapter will illustrate a new point and also several old ones.

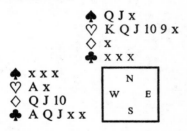

```
              ♠ Q J x
              ♡ K Q J 10 9 x
              ◇ x
              ♣ x x x
  ♠ x x x        ┌─────────┐
  ♡ A x          │    N    │
  ◇ Q J 10       │ W     E │
  ♣ A Q J x x    │    S    │
                 └─────────┘
```

The bidding was:

South	North
One Club	One Heart
One Spade	Two Hearts
Two Spades	Three Spades
Four Spades	

West nearly led a trump—to stop Club ruffs in dummy—but finally picked on the Queen of Diamonds. East produced the eight and declarer won the trick with the Ace. Next came a small trump, taken in dummy, and at trick three the King of Hearts. South discarded a Diamond and . . .

81

Over to West. He has had all the clues, and must now work out his own salvation.

This is the most advanced hand we have had up to now, so let West be an expert, and let us follow his thoughts. West will be saying to himself: " South may as well put his cards on the table, for I can read every one. He can't have more than five Clubs, because I can see the other eight. He has bid and rebid Spades, so he must have at least five. But he can hardly have six, or he would have bid them first, before the Clubs. In fact, he must have ten black cards—five in each suit. Nothing else will fit the bidding. Since he has shown out of Hearts on the first round, it is obvious that his Diamond holding is A x x. He might have the A K x, but partner's eight—an encouraging card—makes it unlikely."

By this time, without any cheating, West can see all the cards. We may as well join in.

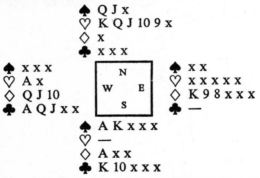

West pursues his soliloquy: " Not taking the Ace of Hearts won't help. South will only play another. And if I take it, what shall I do next? I could play my Ace of Clubs and give partner a ruff. But that only comes to three tricks, and if I do that, declarer will draw trumps, ending in dummy, and reel off the Hearts. How can I kill that dummy? The only hope is to *force* the table—to make declarer ruff. One trump has been played already. If dummy ruffs, it will leave one trump only on the table, and I shall have two. Here goes . . ."

We can now return to our own wavelength, just in time to hear that Knave of Diamonds hit the cloth.

If South does not ruff, he has had it. West remains on play to cash the Ace of Clubs and give his partner a ruff. But South does ruff. Not knowing about the Clubs, he fears that East will overtake the Knave of Diamonds and play a Club through. Besides, he still has a chance. If West is short of Hearts and has three trumps (as, in fact, he has) all may yet be well.

At trick five South leads a Heart from dummy, then another. West ruffs. But now he must lay down that Ace of Clubs and give East a ruff quickly. Otherwise declarer is home. He cannot be forced again in dummy, because he has no more Diamonds himself. And trumps can now be drawn. West and East have only one each. That was why South prayed so hard that the man who ruffed the Heart should have three trumps, not two. Of course, he could not foresee the nasty club break.

The main point of the hand is West's play at trick four. Technically, it is known as PUNCHING DUMMY—killing a trump entry to the table.

Whenever dummy has a long suit, that has been or can be established, and no entry outside trumps, the defence should consider this line of attack. FORCE dummy to ruff, because that trump may be worth more to declarer as an entry.

Note one or two other points about the hand :
West tuned in early and tried to work the hand out from the beginning. It is not always easy, but it is *always* the key to a really hot defence.

West knew that his partner had no Clubs, but he resisted the temptation to give him a ruff *prematurely*. Dummy had to be PUNCHED first.

Finally, West did not fumble when he ruffed that Heart. There was no more time to lose, because *all* declarer's cards were potential winners. Yes, even the Clubs would cease to be losers.

Dummy had been set up, subject to the trump break, and unless the defence took their tricks at that particular moment, they would not take them at all.

Declarer was unlucky on the hand, but not because of the bad Club break. His bad luck was West's good play. There is an ancient Chinese proverb which says : " If you defend well, you will meet many unlucky declarers."

Résumé

(1) Singleton leads are more likely to be effective on bad hands than on good ones. The fewer high cards you have yourself, the better your chance of finding partner with the entries he needs to give you ruffs.

(2) When the bidding indicates that partner must be short in a suit (perhaps both opponents have bid it on the way round), open that suit. It is the singleton lead *in reverse* and needs quick entries in your hand to give partner a ruff—or ruffs—while he still has trumps.

(3) If you suspect that partner is leading from a doubleton and you have the Ace of the suit, HOLD IT UP. Then, when partner takes a trick, he will be able to put you in to give him a ruff.

(4) By ruffing high—usually with an honour—a defender may promote his partner's trumps. To succeed, this play requires that declarer should be forced to OVER-RUFF. If he can discard a loser, the defence gains nothing on balance.

(5) Ruff winners, not losers. When you trump a master card (with a losing trump) you gain a trick. When declarer plays *towards* a master card, you do not necessarily gain anything by trumping. You may be taking a trick which partner would have made later.

(6) When it looks as if only " a miracle " can save the contract, play for the miracle. Base your defence on wishful thinking, envisaging singletons, doubletons and the exact honour combinations needed to beat declarer.

(7) When dummy turns up with a long suit, which can be easily set up, the first pre-occupation of the defence should be to knock out dummy's entries. If trumps provide the only entry, PUNCH dummy—force dummy to ruff.

Exercises

(1) You are West and hold:

♠ Q J 10 x   ♡ 10 x x x   ◇ x   ♣ A J x x

Bidding:

South	North
One Heart	Two Diamonds
Two Hearts	Four Hearts

What card do you lead against Four Hearts?

(2) You are West and hold:

♠ x x x x x   ♡ A x   ◇ x x x x   ♣ A x

Bidding:

North	South
One No-Trump	Three Spades
Three No-Trumps	Four Hearts
No Bid	

What card do you lead against Four Hearts?

(3)

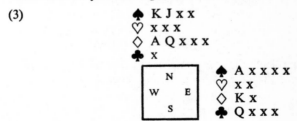

```
        ♠ K J x x
        ♡ x x x
        ◇ A Q x x x
        ♣ x
            N            ♠ A x x x x
        W       E        ♡ x x
            S            ◇ K x
                         ♣ Q x x x
```

Bidding:

South	North
One Heart	Two Diamonds
Two No-Trumps	Three Hearts
Four Hearts	

West opens the ten of Spades and dummy plays low. What card should East play?

(4) Same contract, same bidding and same lead as in (3) above. The dummy is also the same.

East
- ♠ A x x
- ♡ A x
- ◇ K 10 9 x x x
- ♣ x x

(*a*) Should East win the first trick?
(*b*) What line of defence should he adopt?
(*c*) Assuming the bidding to be correct, is declarer likely to make his contract?

(5)

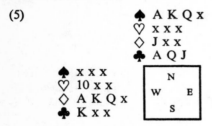

♠ A K Q x
♡ x x x
◇ J x x
♣ A Q J

♠ x x x
♡ 10 x x
◇ A K Q x
♣ K x x

Bidding:

North	*South*
One Spade	Two Hearts
Two No-Trumps	Four Hearts

West leads three top Diamonds to which all follow. What should he play at trick four?

(6)

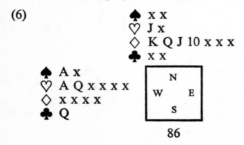

♠ x x
♡ J x
◇ K Q J 10 x x x
♣ x x

♠ A x
♡ A Q x x x x
◇ x x x x
♣ Q

Bidding:

North	South
Three Diamonds	*Four Spades*

West opens the Ace of Hearts on which declarer drops the King. What should West play at trick two?

(7)

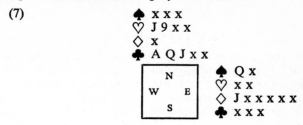

♠ x x x
♡ J 9 x x
◇ x
♣ A Q J x x

♠ Q x
♡ x x
◇ J x x x x x
♣ x x x

Bidding:

South	North
One Spade	*Two Clubs*
Three Spades	*Four Spades*

West leads the King of Hearts, followed by the Queen and the deuce. Declarer plays the nine from dummy. What card should East play?

DUMMY PLAY

CHAPTER VII

No-Trump Contracts

Most game contracts in No-Trumps fall into two categories: the hands on which declarer can see nine tricks, if only opponents would leave him alone; and the hands on which he is not sure of the contract, even if no one does anything particularly disagreeable. Some hands, of course, combine both characteristics. But let us begin with those that don't.

The Hold-up Play

Here is a perfectly respectable Three No-Trump contract.

```
        ♠ A x x
        ♡ x x
        ◇ A K J 10 8
        ♣ A x x

            ┌─────────┐
            │    N    │
            │ W     E │
            │    S    │
            └─────────┘

        ♠ K x x x
        ♡ A x x
        ◇ 9 x
        ♣ K x x x
```

West leads the King of Hearts and declarer—COUNTS. The most important step on any hand precedes the play of the first card.   COUNT the winners—the certainties, the probables and the possibles.   COUNT the losers—the inevitable and the not-so inevitable.

The hand in the above diagram offers seven solid tricks in Aces and Kings.   Two more winners can be developed in Diamonds, even if a trick is conceded to the Queen.   Losers are the only worry.   Opponents must not be allowed to grab more than three tricks in Hearts.   Four Hearts and the Queen of Diamonds will wreck the contract.   But unless West's King of Hearts is some sort of fancy lead, declarer can make an absolute certainty of the whole thing.   He passes the first Heart trick.   And the next one.   After winning the third Heart, declarer runs the nine of Diamonds.   Let East make the Queen if he has it.   What is more, let him return a Heart— if he has a Heart.   It won't matter, because it will mean that the suit was divided 4–4.   If that was the case, Three No-Trumps was cold from the start.   Only a 5–3 or 6–2 break was dangerous, and declarer guarded against that by holding up the Ace until the third round.   That way he made certain that if West had five Hearts, East could not play one back after getting in with the Queen of Diamonds.

The example is elementary, but its anatomy is worthwhile, because it illustrates a principle—the principle of the HOLD-UP play, which is to *sever communications* between opponents. Declarer makes certain of setting up his eighth and ninth winners without risk of losing the lead to West—the DAN-GEROUS OPPONENT.   East will not be dangerous after the third round of Hearts.

Now suppose that East has five—or six—Hearts.   Perhaps he called them at some stage and West led a Heart in response to his partner's bid.   Basically, the situation is the same as before.   Declarer must set up those two long Diamonds without letting in the dangerous opponent.   This time, how-ever, it is East, not West, who is DANGEROUS.   What can declarer do to keep out East?   Is it possible to keep him out at all, if he has that all-important Queen of Diamonds? The answer is : perhaps.

The natural way to play those Diamonds is to finesse—to run the nine.   There are six Diamonds out against declarer and they are probably divided 3–3 or 4–2. Nearly half the time (48 per cent) it will be 4–2, and just over a third of the time (36 per cent) 3–3. If East has three or four Diamonds to the Queen, he is bound to make a trick anyway. But if West has the Queen—even Q x x x—it can be caught by finessing. So, if declarer's aim in life were to make as many Diamonds as possible, he would have to run that nine. But, in point of fact, he would far prefer to lose a Diamond than to let in East, the DANGEROUS opponent. Therefore, the Ace and King of Diamonds are played off first. *Perhaps* East has a doubleton Queen. It is a chance to nothing. If the Queen does not drop, declarer is no worse off. He plays a third Diamond and hopes that the Queen is with West. Now— *provided* he held up that Heart Ace—he is home in a canter. West cannot have a Heart left, unless the suit is divided 4–4. And if it is, the contract is, in any event, unbeatable.

The first time—when West had the Hearts—declarer could make quite certain of his nine tricks. The second time he could not do more than give himself an extra chance. But both times he *must* hold up the Ace of Hearts till the third round—TO SEVER COMMUNICATIONS between his two opponents.

Often enough declarer is faced by a situation like this:

A J x x

K 10 x x

He can either lay down the King and play a small one towards the A J, hoping that West has the Queen, or he can start with the Ace and play up to the King, hoping that the Queen is with East. On such occasions finesse into the hand which is NOT DANGEROUS.

Try this variation:

♠ A x x
♥ x x
♦ A K Q x
♣ K 9 x x

♠ K x x x
♥ A x x
♦ x x
♣ A J x x

Against Three No-Trumps West opens the King of Hearts. How do you set about it? Count first, of course. Eight tricks can be seen at a glance. Clubs should provide the ninth and it is obviously the suit to develop.

The natural way to attack the Clubs is to finesse the Knave. But here the DANGEROUS opponent is West. Declarer does not mind losing a trick to East. He held up the Ace of Hearts, communications have been severed, and the twain shall never meet. But West must be kept out if humanly possible.

To give himself the best chance, declarer plays the Ace and leads towards the King, finessing the *nine*. East can make the ten, but so long as the clubs break 3–2—and the odds are 2–1 on—nine tricks are in the bag. Should West produce the ten, declarer goes up with dummy's King. Even if West shows out, there is no trouble. By finessing *away* from West—the DANGEROUS opponent—declarer ensures the contract, against every distribution except: Q 10 x (or Q 10 x x) of Clubs with West. And that would be a case of *force majeure*.

91

See if you can work this one out.

♠ x x
♡ K x x
◇ A x x
♣ A Q x x x

♠ A x x
♡ A x x x
◇ K x x
♣ x x x

Once more we are in Three No-Trumps, but just for a change, it is Spades, not Hearts, that fill us with alarm. East has bid the suit and West dutifully opens a Spade. Declarer *counts*. Six top tricks are readily available. For more he must look to the Clubs. That involves the risk of letting in East, the DANGEROUS opponent, but the risk must be taken. The Ace of Spades is held up till the third round and the Queen of Clubs is finessed with trepidation. It wins! Declarer is over the first hurdle. What next? This is the spot where a lot of good players have been known to take the wrong turning. What would you do?

There is an instinctive tendency to play the Ace, then a small one. If West wins the *third* trick with the King, all is well. He has no more Spades or else the suit breaks 4–4, which is just as good.

But West may have started with K x of Clubs only. Then, willy nilly, he will drop his King on the Ace and control of the suit will pass to East's Knave. The declarer, who thinks a move ahead and works it out, will make his contract. The others will be " unlucky ".

Having brought off the Club finesse, declarer returns to his hand with a Heart or Diamond and plays towards the Club Ace. If West's King goes up, he DUCKS—plays a small one from dummy, not the Ace. East, the DANGEROUS opponent, is powerless. He cannot overtake his partner's

King and he can have no possible entry outside Clubs. So long as the Clubs break 3–2 declarer is home.

If West plays low, then, of course, the Ace goes up from dummy. There is no risk of letting in East, since he can no longer have three Clubs.

Making the contract depends on two things: Firstly, holding up the Spade Ace, so as to make it safe to lose the lead to West, the HARMLESS opponent. And secondly, visualising the distribution of the five outstanding Clubs. To succeed, West *must* have the King. That is luck. The rest is good play.

We are still in the HOLD-UP business. Try to spot the new feature.

Hold-up with Two Stoppers

♠ K x x
♡ x x
◇ A K J 10 x
♣ A x x

♠ Q 10 9 x
♡ A K x
◇ 9 x
♣ K x x x

We are in Three No-Trumps again, and we revert to Hearts as the menace. This time, counting winners is slightly more complex. If the Queen of Diamonds is where we want her—under the A K J—there will be nothing to worry about. But if the Queen is with East, the ninth trick will have to be a Spade. That means that opponents will get in twice—with the Queen of Diamonds and with the Ace of Spades. That is why we must HOLD UP even with two stoppers. The position is the same as if we had one stopper only and might have to surrender the lead once.

West opens the Queen of Hearts and we let him hold the trick. Next time we win and . . .?

Everything may hinge on what we do at trick three. The obvious play is to run the nine of Diamonds. If West has the Queen, the contract is made. If not, it is bad luck—or is it?

If we *knew* for certain that East had no more Hearts, we could play that Diamond quite safely. But he can easily have a third Heart. If so, he will return the suit and knock out our Ace. At that point we shall have eight tricks only—the A K of Hearts, the A K of Clubs, and four Diamonds. To make the ninth we shall be compelled to let the defence in once more with the Ace of Spades. If West has it, he may reel off two more Hearts.

The correct play is a Spade at trick three. Either opponent may have the Ace. If East has it, he will no doubt take the trick and knock out our Ace of Hearts. But now we shall be in the same happy position as on the first hand of the chapter. The Diamond finesse can be taken into East's hand, and after *three* rounds of Hearts, he can do us no harm.

Declarer should follow this rule: When he has two stoppers, and is forced to allow the defence to gain the lead twice, he should try to lose to the DANGEROUS opponent the *first* time, *not* the second. In other words, he must knock out the DANGEROUS opponent's entry, while he can still stop the suit he fears. By the time the other opponent gets the lead, he may have no more of the feared suit to play.

A HOLD-UP, requiring more will-power, arises on hands like these:

♠ x x x
♡ K x
◇ A Q J x x
♣ J x x

```
        N
    W       E
        S
```

♠ K J x
♡ A Q x
◇ 10 9 x
♣ A K x x

The contract is Three No-Trumps as ever. West opens a small Spade and East produces the Queen. Let it go. Don't cover. It seems unnatural, but it is undoubtedly wise. Work it out on the same lines as the foregoing hands. If the Spades break 4–3, no one can do you an injury. The worst that can happen is that you will lose three Spades and a Diamond. All that worries you is a 5–2 division, because you cannot afford to lose *four* Spades and a Diamond.

Test it in practice :

(*a*) You take the Queen of Spades with the King and finesse the Diamond. East gets in with the King and flashes back a Spade—his *second* and *last* Spade. West sits over you with the A 10 and two small ones, and makes the lot. One down.

(*b*) You let East take the first trick with the Queen of Spades and he plays another. Whatever happens, you are now safe. If West wins with the Ace he can do no harm, because he will never get in again. If he ducks and East plays a third Spade, when he comes in with the King of Diamonds, the future will be just as secure. West can't have enough Spades to worry you. The DANGEROUS opponent was not so dangerous after all.

This is different :

♠ x x x
♡ A x x
◇ J x
♣ A K x x x

♠ K J x
♡ K x
◇ A Q 10 x x x
♣ x x

Same contract and same lead as last time, and again East plays the Queen of Spades. Here, however, the vital finesse will be taken into West's hand, so you win the first Spade, cross into dummy and run the Diamond Knave. If West has the King, good luck to him. He can do no damage.

When Not to Hold Up

How do you play this one in Three No-Trumps, after a Heart opening from West?

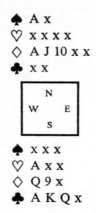

♠ A x
♡ x x x x
◇ A J 10 x x
♣ x x

N
W   E
S

♠ x x x
♡ A x x
◇ Q 9 x
♣ A K Q x

What card do you play to the first trick? There are two reasons for going up with the Ace quickly. The first, and best, is that given a chance, East may switch to Spades. Even if the black suit breaks 4–4, you cannot afford to lose one Heart, three Spades and a Diamond. The second reason is that the hold up is quite unnecessary, *because* you have seven Hearts between the two hands. The Diamond finesse will be taken into East's hand. If the finesse wins, all is well. If it does not, all is still well. Either East will have no Heart to return or else West will have started with four Hearts only.

Here are the answers to the question: to hold up or not to hold up; and if so, how often. To guard against a five-card suit, which may mean four losers:

(*a*) With five of the suit between you and dummy, hold up twice. Take the third one. That must sever communications between defenders, unless the suit breaks 4–4.

(*b*) With six, hold up once. Again you sever communications when the suit is divided 5–2.

(*c*) Holding seven, no hold up is necessary at all.

To conclude our piece on the hold-up play, let us return to the first hand and modify it slightly.

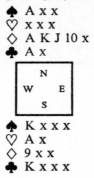

♠ A x x
♡ x x x
♦ A K J 10 x
♣ A x

♠ K x x x
♡ A x
♦ 9 x x
♣ K x x x

As before, the King of Hearts is opened against Three No-Trumps. With five Hearts we should like to hold up twice. Alas, the spirit is willing, but the doubleton is short. Still, even a single hold-up may help. If West started with six Hearts—as we hope and pray—East will have two only. By not playing our Ace till the second round we may exhaust his holding. Then, should he win a trick in Diamonds, he will have no Heart left to give the lead to the DANGEROUS opponent. You cannot make certain of the contract. But you can give yourself the best chance.

One final modification of this same hand to bring the subject to a close : West leads a Heart against Three No-Trumps.

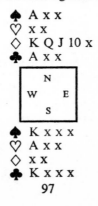

♠ A x x
♡ x x
♦ K Q J 10 x
♣ A x x

♠ K x x x
♡ A x x
♦ x x
♣ K x x x

97

Again declarer can do nothing to make *certain* of the contract. If West, the dangerous opponent, has the Ace of Diamonds, he will go down—unless the Hearts break 4–4. But the best chance still lies in holding up the Ace of Hearts till the third round. East *may* have that Ace of Diamonds and the Hearts *may* break 5–3. In the long run, those extra chances will make all the difference between being lucky and unlucky.

Ducking

Strictly speaking, holding up the enemy will not help you to make the contract. It will only help you not to lose it. And that is almost the same thing, but not quite.

To develop his own tricks, declarer first attacks length.

Here there is no doubt as to which suit declarer should develop first:

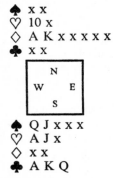

♠ x x
♡ 10 x
♢ A K x x x x x
♣ x x

♠ Q J x x x
♡ A J x
♢ x x
♣ A K Q

West opens a small Heart, and East's Queen falls to the Ace. The contract really depends on counting up to nine—before it is too late. By going into a huddle at trick one, declarer will discover that he needs a few tricks in Diamonds—just a few, not seven. Therefore he can afford to lose a trick in that suit, and he should do so forthwith. Much of the time the Diamonds will not break 2–2. But even if they did, considering the value of the game, there can be no solid future in laying about twenty to one against yourself for the sake of one more trick. The whole contract hinges on bringing in those Diamonds. And that means that *three* rounds must be played, *ending* in dummy. Declarer must duck on the *first* round. Opponents can cash three more tricks—the King of Hearts and two Spades, but that is all. If the Diamonds are no worse than 3–1 (90 per cent) declarer is home.

Just as the hold-up play depends on *severing* communications between opponents, so suit development depends on *preserving* communications between declarer and dummy.

The moral is: give up a trick, but hold on to an entry. With a long suit as the prize, an entry may easily be worth four tricks or more.

This situation is not quite so straightforward, but it involves the same principle.

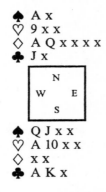

♠ A x
♡ 9 x x
◇ A Q x x x x
♣ J x

♠ Q J x x
♡ A 10 x x
◇ x x
♣ A K x

West opens a Spade against Three No-Trumps. Declarer plays low, but East wins with the King and returns another Spade, knocking out dummy's only entry to the Diamonds. What now? Only the Diamonds or a miracle can produce nine tricks. And the Diamonds are the better chance.

You can enter your hand and finesse. But even if the King is right, it won't help. Somebody will have three Diamonds, and the third one—the ten or nine maybe—will put an end to the suit. Once again, it is essential to play *three* rounds, in order to exhaust opponents. *Duck* the first time. Play low from both hands. Then, on the second round, finesse. If the Queen holds, and the suit breaks 3–2 (a 68 per cent chance) the contract is in the bag.

To give yourself a superior chance, play that first " ducking " Diamond, not from your hand, but from dummy. You are there already with the Ace of Spades, and it costs nothing. If East has K x only, he is almost certain to go up with the King.

The feature of this hand, and of the last, is that being short of entries, declarer ducks the first time so as to be able to play an extra round of the suit.

Work out the correct way to handle the Clubs on this deal :

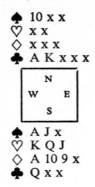

```
        ♠ 10 x x
        ♡ x x
        ◇ x x x
        ♣ A K x x x
              ┌─────────┐
              │    N    │
              │ W     E │
              │    S    │
              └─────────┘
        ♠ A J x
        ♡ K Q J
        ◇ A 10 9 x
        ♣ Q x x
```

West opens a Heart. East wins with the Ace and returns another Heart. Now everything is quite simple—provided that the contract is Three No-Trumps. If it is Two No-Trumps only, then—paradoxically enough—the hand requires more thought.

We should like to be in declarer's shoes, so let us tune in to his soliloquy.

" If the Clubs break 3–2, as they should do most of the time, nine tricks are cold. Yes, I wish we had bid game. Still, it is no use crying over spilt milk. We are in Two, which should be kindergarten stuff. Can anything go wrong? No one can possibly deprive me of my two Aces or of the K Q of Hearts, for that matter. So all I need is four Club tricks. What if I am unlucky? There could be four in one hand and a singleton in the other. That sort of thing happens more often than one would think, once every four times or thereabouts (28 per cent). So I had better be careful. If I play my Queen and then a small one towards dummy, I still won't

100

know. East may be the one to show out. I can only find out *after* playing from dummy, and if I put on the King, it will be too late to do anything about it. I shall have one Club left in my hand to West's two. Since I am not in Three No-Trumps, I can afford to lose a Club. That will make it a cinch. Queen first, then a small gift to opponents. Let them take the second Club. They can do nothing to upset me and I shall still have a Club left in my hand and the A K in dummy. This way I can draw *four* rounds and retain control. The last trick will be dummy's Ace and that fifth Club will be good —even if West has four."

In Two No-Trumps ducking a Club is a safety play. De-clarer can afford to lose a Club. He follows the technique of suit development to draw an extra round, just in case. Had the contract been Three No-Trumps, the safety play would not be available. Declarer would need five Clubs and must be con-tent to make his contract most of the time and to be un-lucky when the Clubs break 4–1. But in Two No-Trumps there is no need to be unlucky.

Talking of luck, we have held remarkably good cards in this chapter and it is only fair that the last deal should be played in a modest contract of One No-Trump.

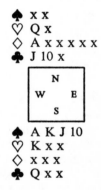

♠ x x
♡ Q x
◇ A x x x x x
♣ J 10 x

	N	
W		E
	S	

♠ A K J 10
♡ K x x
◇ x x x
♣ Q x x

West leads a Spade, East produces the eight-spot and our Knave wins. Let us scratch for our tricks together. Clearly West has the Queen of Spades, so that suit will not yield more than three winners. Hearts will contribute a trick. Clubs

101

are good for a trick, too, of course, but it would be inadmissible to set it up in our own time. Obviously we must look for sustenance to the Diamonds. Dummy has no entry, but with three of the suit ourselves, we need not worry about communications.

So, at trick two, we duck a Diamond. East makes the Knave and returns a Spade. At this point our contract is already safe. Since neither opponent showed out on the first Diamond, the suit must break 3–1 or 2–2. So we duck a second round of Diamonds—in case it is 3–1. Now our Diamond investment is worth four tricks—dummy's six, less the two " ducks ". We have already collected two Spades, and if another is played, that will be our seventh trick. An attack on Clubs or Hearts will lead to the same result. The worst that can happen is another Diamond. From the enemy point of view that play has the advantage of leaving us in dummy without visible means of access to the Ace of Spades. So let it be. We play off the Diamonds. Dummy's last five cards will be:

and our own

Now we play a Club or a Heart, and we don't care what happens. We are bound to make another trick.

The hand illustrates the way to handle a six-card suit to which no side entry is available. Duck *twice* to make sure that your one and only entry will enable you to reel off the rest of the tricks. Of course, if you needed five Diamond tricks, instead of four, you would duck once only. And you would hope that the suit was going to break 2–2.

Résumé

(1) When you fear that the defence may endanger a No-Trump contract by making too many tricks in a particular suit—presumably the suit opened by West—your first concern should be to SEVER COMMUNICATIONS between your two opponents.

(2) You endeavour to HOLD UP your control card in the suit until one of the opponents has no more.

(3) If eight cards of the suit are out against you, the danger is that it may be split 5–3 or 6–2. You are not concerned with an even 4–4 division.

(4) With five of the danger suit between your two hands, hold up until the THIRD round, because either: (a) the suit will break 4–4, or (b) one of the opponents will have no more after the third round.

(5) With six of the suit in the two hands, hold up once. Unless the suit breaks 4–3, the opponent with the shorter holding will run out after the SECOND round. But hold up *twice*, if you fear even a four-card suit.

(6) Seeing seven cards of the danger suit in his own hand and dummy, declarer needs no hold-up to protect himself against a five-card suit.

(7) Having held up his stopper long enough to make sure that—if a five-card suit is out against him—one of the opponents will have no more of it, declarer tries to prevent the *other* opponent from getting the lead.

(8) To keep out the DANGEROUS opponent, declarer may take unnatural finesses. Or he may play for a drop when, in other circumstances, it would be correct to finesse (9 x opposite A K J 10 x).

(9) With a double stopper—e.g., A K x opposite x x— declarer should still HOLD UP, if he may have to lose the lead *twice*.

(10) When the lead must be lost twice, declarer should seek to lose it to the DANGEROUS opponent the *first* time. Next time, if the other opponent gets in, he may have no more of the suit to play back. It follows that an Ace should be driven out *before* an honour,

103

which can be finessed *away* from the dangerous opponent. But if a finesse must be taken into the DANGEROUS hand, this should *precede* the attack on a suit in which opponents hold the Ace.

(11) Do not HOLD UP at all, when a switch by the defence to another suit appears to carry greater danger.

Exercises

(1)

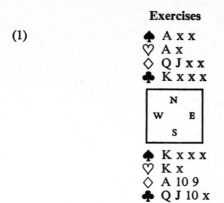

♠ A x x
♡ A x
◇ Q J x x
♣ K x x x

♠ K x x x
♡ K x
◇ A 10 9
♣ Q J 10 x

West, who had opened the bidding with Three Hearts, leads the Queen of Hearts against Three No-Trumps.

(a) Where do you take the trick?

(b) What card do you play to the second trick?

(2)

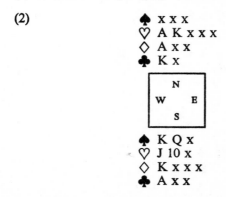

♠ x x x
♡ A K x x x
◇ A x x
♣ K x

♠ K Q x
♡ J 10 x
◇ K x x x
♣ A x x

West leads a small Spade against Three No-Trumps by South and East plays the Knave. What card should South play?

(3)

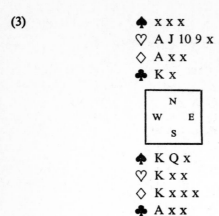

♠ x x x
♡ A J 10 9 x
◇ A x x
♣ K x

♠ K Q x
♡ K x x
◇ K x x x
♣ A x x

Same lead and contract as in (2).
(a) Sitting South, do you win the first trick?
(b) What do you do when you gain the lead?

(4) West leads a Spade against Three No-Trumps.

♠ Q J x
♡ K Q J 10 x
◇ x x x
♣ x x

♠ A x x
♡ x
◇ A x x x x
♣ A K Q x

What card do you play from dummy to the first trick?
106

(5) West leads a Heart against Three No-Trumps and East plays the Queen.

♠ K J x x
♡ —
♢ A J 10 x x
♣ Q 8 x x

♠ A x
♡ A K 4 3 2
♢ Q 9 x
♣ K 10 9

(*a*) Do you hold up or not?
(*b*) What card do you play after winning your first trick?

(6) The contract is Two No-Trumps.

♠ A x x
♡ x x
♢ A J 9 7 4 2
♣ x x

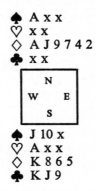

♠ J 10 x
♡ A x x
♢ K 8 6 5
♣ K J 9

West leads a Heart in response to his partner's bid. What card do you play from your hand when you gain the lead?

DEFENCE

CHAPTER VIII

Attack on No-Trump Contracts

According to the best authorities, the correct lead against a No-Trump contract is the King from K Q J 10 x x. Exponents of the classical school usually add that it is advisable on such occasions to hold a couple of Aces as likely entries. The dictum is sound. Its only drawback is that, like those exotic flowers that bloom every seventy-five years, you are never there to see it happen. Meanwhile, you must lead and you look, naturally, for something that will annoy declarer. The question arises: what do declarers fear most? And the answer is: xs. The smallest xs kill the toughest declarers.

Generally speaking, if a man elects to contract for Three No-Trumps, it is because his side holds a decided preponderance in high cards. The defence is most unlikely to muster enough Aces and Kings to break him. But declarers have their weak spots—suits which they can only stop once or twice. If those stoppers can be driven out, before declarer can set up enough winners for his contract, the xs come into their own. It becomes a race between the two sides: who can get going first? TIME is the vital element. That is why the advantage of the opening lead must be capitalised to the fullest extent.

When the bidding gives no clues, the best weapon in attack is usually LENGTH. Length is where the xs live. If you have six Spades, there are only seven out in the other three hands. Declarer—or his dummy—may have a doubleton. Someone, of course, will have three, but that someone may be partner. Whoever it is, the lead is unlikely to do much harm. Will it do any good? That is another point. Consider these two hands:

(a) ♠ x x x x x x (b) ♠ x x x x x x
♡ A x x ♡ x x x
◇ A x ◇ x x
♣ A x ♣ x x

The bidding has been : One No-Trump ; Three No-Trumps. What do you lead?

On (a) a Spade is positively a weapon of terror. Work it out. The opening lead drives out the Queen of Spades. You come in with your first Ace and drive out the King. Declarer lets you in with your second Ace and you set up the Spades for good and all. An Ace still remains in your hand, and if declarer needs even one trick in that suit, you have an entry for three little Spade xs that will wreck the contract.

A totally different picture is presented by (b). Without an entry to your name, the long, threadbare Spade suit is a hopeless proposition. Unless partner has three Spades, you can never come in at all. And even if he has three, it is essential that he should have a small one—something you can overtake. Otherwise the suit will be blocked. So don't bother with those Spades. Try a Heart, hoping that partner has length, and that it will do him some good.

Of course, most of the time you will have a hand somewhere between (a) and (b). That is, you will not be endowed with three almost certain entries. Neither will you hold a hopeless blizzard. You will lead from length, hoping to set up an x or so, hoping that partner will get in and play the suit back, and hoping that such high cards as you have, will enable you to get in and cash some midget to break the contract. That is the theory behind leading from LENGTH.

The next question is : what particular card should you lead?

With an honour sequence there is no problem, and the same is true of a near sequence. Lead the top from :

K Q J or K Q 10 x
Q J 10 or Q J 9 x
J 10 9 or J 10 8 x

From A K J x or A K J x x lead the King and look around.

The general idea is to switch to something else at the next trick, waiting for partner to come in and play *through* declarer's Queen—if he has it.

Holding A K x x x (x) or A Q x x x (x) lead the *fourth* highest. Why it should be the *fourth* will emerge later. The point is that it must be a little x. Why? Because it is a reasonable presumption that declarer can stop the suit once, to say the least. Partner may have—probably has—a doubleton only. Leave him one of the suit to play *back*. For all you know, he will get in before you do. It would be a thousand pities to have him play some other suit, just because he is without one of yours.

Third Hand

Now transpose yourself for a few minutes to the East position. Your last act as West was to lead the King of Hearts against Three No-Trumps. Soaring across the table, your spirit rests over East's shoulder to behold the A x of Hearts. To add point to the argument, East holds two other Aces. Squinting at dummy, you perceive x x x. What does it all amount to?

East *knows* that you led from K Q J or K Q 10. Otherwise you would have played a small Heart, not an honour. Unless he overtakes with his Ace, the suit will be blocked. His partner—whose uneasy spirit is now hovering over his shoulder —may have the rest of the Hearts. But he will never, never get in to make them. The fact that he, East, has two other Aces, makes it almost certain that the wretched West is without any kind of entry.

Those two Aces, of course, have been introduced to make it all more impressive and for no other reason. East must overtake in any case. First of all, West might switch to another suit. When all is said and done, he does not know that his partner holds the Ace of *his* suit. And even if he guesses it, there is no guarantee that declarer won't be able to reel off nine tricks before West comes in again. The deal may be something like:

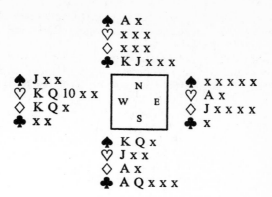

```
              ♠ A x
              ♡ x x x
              ◇ x x x
              ♣ K J x x x

♠ J x x                        ♠ x x x x x
♡ K Q 10 x x      N            ♡ A x
◇ K Q x        W     E         ◇ J x x x x
♣ x x             S            ♣ x

              ♠ K Q x
              ♡ J x x
              ◇ A x
              ♣ A Q x x x
```

Unless East overtakes the Heart and plays back another, the contract is unbeatable. Declarer has nine tricks on top—provided he does not lose five Hearts.

A similar situation arises if East's holding is J 2. He must play the Knave—if only to inform West that he has it. Otherwise West will switch to some other suit, thinking that declarer holds A J x.

The moral is this: if partner leads an honour, you must assume that it is the top of a sequence or a near sequence. So, holding a doubleton honour, get out of the way—UNBLOCK.

But as with all other plays, discretion is the better part of unblocking. Too much enthusiasm is fatal. West leads the King, and the table shows up with 10 x x x. You cannot afford to part with an honour.

Now let us get back to the West position. He has just picked up A J 10 8 x (x) and we are in time to see him lead the Knave. That is the correct play, because it offers the best chance of setting up the suit with the loss of one trick only. If declarer has K Q x, he will win the first trick. But partner will get in and play *through* him, trapping his second honour. If declarer finds Q x in dummy, he is no better off. If he takes the trick with the Queen, East can still play *through* his K x. If he wins with the King in his hand, the Queen will drop on the Ace next time.

The same idea inspires the opening of the Knave from K J 10 x x (x). There is a danger, of course, of leading into

111

declarer's tenace—A Q x.   But if the suit is to be played at all,
the Knave is the right card.   These combinations are known
as INTERIOR SEQUENCES.

The above leads are standardised.   East is expected to
recognise them and to co-operate.   Let us move round the
table again.   The contract continues to be Three No-Trumps.

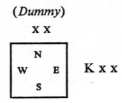

West leads the Knave.   The bidding having supplied no
clue, East does not know for certain what it is all about.
Perhaps West had J 10 9 x (x).   If so, nothing is lost by going
up with the King, and it will help West to know who had it.
But that Knave may have emerged from A J 10 x x.   Then the
King is imperative.   The position will be:

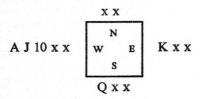

and five tricks can be cashed at top speed.

And what if East holds the Queen instead of the King?

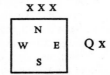

There is again no means of knowing definitely the background
to West's Knave.   If it is a J 10 9 sequence, nothing is lost by
going up with the Queen.   But if that Knave belongs to an

112

interior sequence, not playing the Queen can be catastrophic. The hand may well be something like:

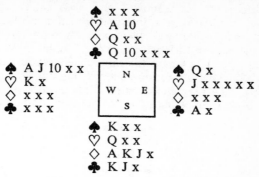

♠ x x x
♡ A 10
◇ Q x x
♣ Q 10 x x x

♠ A J 10 x x
♡ K x
◇ x x x
♣ x x x

♠ Q x
♡ J x x x x x
◇ x x x
♣ A x

♠ K x x
♡ Q x x
◇ A K J x
♣ K J x

Suppose that East, parsimonious by nature, feels reluctant to " waste " his Queen on partner's Knave. What happens? Imagine that an inspired declarer ducks, although he normally wouldn't. It is all over. If West continues with Spades, he will never get in again. If he switches, the situation will be still more humiliating. East will come in soon enough with that Ace of Clubs. But his Spade Queen will *block* the suit. Declarer won't cover, and West—foaming at the mouth—will be unable to overtake. Now declarer can't lose the contract.

By going up with the Queen at the first trick, East *forces* declarer to win it. If he does not, another Spade comes through and he is two down from the start. If he takes the trick, his discomfiture is delayed, but not by much. East seizes an early trick with his Ace of Clubs and produces that lethal Spade x.

Again it is a case of UNBLOCKING with a doubleton honour. And again there would be no excuse for doing the right thing at the wrong time. If dummy springs to life with 9 x x x, East must restrain himself.

Signalling

What does it all amount to? Is there any rule to guide East, sitting on declarer's right, as to what he should or should not do?

The first thing to remember is that opening leads are largely standardised. They *mean* something. West opens in the dark. He can't see dummy. But East can. And he is, therefore, in a position to interpret how the suit led is distributed round the table. His first endeavour should be to convey the pattern to West, as far as possible.

To flash pictures across the table defenders rely largely on SIGNALS. High cards are encouraging, and low cards discouraging. To play encouraging cards is known as " petering ". East peters when he wants the suit continued.

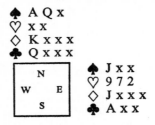

```
              ♠ A Q x
              ♡ x x
              ◇ K x x x
              ♣ Q x x x
          ┌─────────┐      ♠ J x x
          │    N    │      ♡ 9 7 2
          │ W     E │      ◇ J x x x
          │    S    │      ♣ A x x
          └─────────┘
```

Against One or more No-Trumps, West opens the Queen of Hearts. This is almost certainly the top of a sequence, though it could be from A Q 10 x x.

East should reflect on these lines : " Partner has made a safe lead. Even if it is a four-card suit and declarer has A K 8 x, it won't cost a trick. My nine may be quite important. I hope that when West gets in again, he will play another Heart. We may be able to set up a couple of tricks there, and anyway I don't want him to switch. A Diamond or a Club will probably help declarer. So I will give partner a ' come-on ' signal. I will *peter* with the seven."

Will West guess that the seven is a peter? More often than not, he will. An experienced player is always on the look-out for the small cards. If a deuce or three is " missing ", he will draw inferences. Either declarer is false carding—discarding a higher card than he need do—or else partner is signalling. Sometimes it is a matter of guesswork. But usually there are indications. When two small cards are missing, West is unlikely to guess wrong. The bidding generally limits the number of cards declarer can have in a

114

particular suit. If the deuce and three are both missing from the first trick the odds are that partner has one of them. On the other hand, the deuce is nearly always unmistakable. Partner is *not* encouraging. And if the deuce is in dummy—or West himself has it—the three conveys the same message.

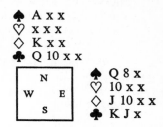

♠ A x x
♡ x x x
♢ K x x
♣ Q 10 x x

♠ Q 8 x
♡ 10 x x
♢ J 10 x x
♣ K J x

The bidding was:

South	*North*
One No-Trump (vulnerable)	Three No-Trumps

West opens the Knave of Spades, and declarer plays low from dummy.

If East is a good player, a picture will have formed itself already in his mind—a splash of black pips fading in the distance. East begins to " see " his partner's hand. That Knave can hardly come from an interior sequence—A J 10 x x or K J 10 x x. The Ace is in dummy, and South must have the King to justify his vulnerable bid of One No-Trump. Therefore, West had J 10 9 x (x). He could not have been dealt more than five, because six would leave declarer with a singleton, and that again would be inconsistent with his bidding.

East can probably afford to play the Queen, despite the slender risk that West would mistake it for a singleton. But there is more to it than that.

A very important consideration arises at this juncture. Both defenders should constantly keep before them the question : how can we beat the contract? And with every trick, as the situation develops, the estimate should be revised and brought up to date.

115

In the above example, East can see that Spades alone won't thwart declarer. The suit cannot yield more than three tricks and may yield only two. Much will depend on what suit declarer tries to set up. Meanwhile, it looks as if East may need an entry at some stage—to play a Heart through, maybe to cash a Diamond. Who knows? So East wants to retain his Queen—for the time being—and also to tell West that he likes Spades. The correct signal is the eight, which says: " Come on, partner. I like Spades."

Now change East's holding to 8 6 5 2. He should still encourage partner, but now the eight becomes a little too demonstrative. West would probably expect an honour. The five or six is good enough.

With four in partner's suit, it is nearly always right to en-courage. But unless an honour adorns the xs, encouragement should be blended with modesty.

Keep the Spades, but change the situation.

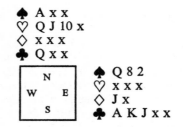

♠ A x x
♡ Q J 10 x
◇ x x x
♣ Q x x

♠ Q 8 2
♡ x x x
◇ J x
♣ A K J x x

West leads the Knave of Spades, and the contract, this time, is One No-Trump. East has no objection to Spades, but his main pre-occupation in life is to get going with the Clubs. Can this heartfelt desire be conveyed quickly to West? Yes. The deuce of Spades will carry the message. West will read: " Don't like Spades. Please think of something else." And —since neither Hearts nor Diamonds look inviting—he will almost certainly switch to Clubs. The point of the hand is that East makes a discouraging signal—not because he dislikes the suit led, but because he likes another much better.

116

The reverse occurs in this situation:

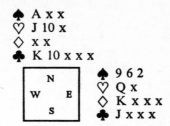

♠ A x x
♡ J 10 x
◇ x x
♣ K 10 x x x

♠ 9 6 2
♡ Q x
◇ K x x x
♣ J x x x

South opened One Diamond and is now in Three No-Trumps. West still leads the Knave of Spades. What should East do? He has no interest in the Spade suit, and this, at first sight, suggests the deuce. But that would call for a switch by West to something else, and East can't want a lead through his honours in the other suits. In fact, he likes Spades *relatively*, in the sense that he likes the other suits less. So he encourages West with the six.

The purpose of signalling is to guide the defence into the most profitable channels. A high card does not *necessarily* show a feature or length in the suit led. A low card does not *always* deny an honour. The idea is not so much to impart specific information as to convey general views on strategy. More often than not, of course, a peter will denote an honour and a deuce will deny it. But that is almost incidental. The prime object of signalling is to *encourage* and to *discourage*.

The Rule of Eleven

Up to now, West has always managed to lead an honour, showing a sequence of one kind or another. Different considerations arise when the opening is a humble x, and this calls for a few words on the mystique of the ELEVEN RULE. The rule is based on the assumption that the x is the *fourth highest card* in the leader's hand. And it enables East to establish how many cards, higher than the one led by West, are held by the other three players. Since his own holding and dummy's are visible to the naked eye, declarer's position can present no mystery.

117

The techique of the ELEVEN RULE calls for nothing more difficult than subtracting West's x from eleven.

The six is led. Six from eleven leaves five. In his own hand and in dummy East sees four cards higher than the six. Therefore declarer has *one*.

You have heard the saying: third hand plays high. That is often true, but the occasions when it is not are too numerous to be called exceptions. Broadly speaking, third hand plays its highest card when dummy has nothing. The purpose is to drive out the highest possible card in declarer's hand so as to promote partner's holding. Alternatively, when declarer does not—or cannot—overtake, East remains on play to lead the suit back *through* declarer.

When dummy has length or honours in the suit led, East cannot rely on ancient adages and proverbs. He must think— and look for guidance to the ELEVEN RULE.

West leads the seven and

Q 8 2

 A 10 3

declarer plays dummy's deuce. Most Easts will play the Ace automatically. The more observant will say later: " My ten would have held the first trick. Still, I couldn't know that, could I?" Indeed, he could. Seven from eleven leaves four, and East can see *all* the four cards higher than the seven. Therefore, declarer has *none*. Therefore, the ten will win the trick.

West leads the six, dummy plays low and East is confronted by this position.

A 10 4

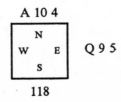 Q 9 5

What card should he play? Apply the ELEVEN RULE. Six from eleven leaves five, and four of the higher cards are on parade—two in East's hand and two in dummy. So declarer has one. If it is the eight or seven, he cannot make more than one trick in the suit in any event. If it is the Knave, he is bound to make two. But what if that one card happens to be the King? Work it out. By playing the nine East confines declarer to two tricks. But the Queen, losing to the King, creates a finesse position against West's Knave. Declarer can now make three tricks. The suit may be distributed like this.

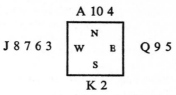

The eleven rule allows East to make a play, which cannot lose, but may win a trick for his side.

West leads the four, and declarer plays the nine from dummy.

Q 10 9

	N	
W		E	K 8 5
	S	

East can tell that South has only one card higher than that led by West. Even if it is only the six, declarer must make one trick. But, of course, that card may be—probably is—something quite different. So what should East do? A moment's reflection will show that it all depends on who has the Ace. If it is with West, declarer won't make more than one trick whatever East plays. He can afford to play badly with impunity. But should declarer have the Ace, it will make all the difference. Now if East follows blindly the " third hand plays high " slogan, his King will fall to the Ace and declarer will make two *more* tricks by taking the marked finesse against West's Knave. So East must not go up with the King, because that play can lose, but cannot gain. At the same time, he wants to encourage partner. The eight is the right card. If West has the Ace, he will know what to do next time.

Even without bringing in the ELEVEN RULE, the lead of the fourth highest gives partner much valuable information. It helps him to COUNT declarer's holding straight away.

The deuce—being the lowest card in the pack—*must* show a four-card suit. The four tells the same story, if the three and the deuce are visible. On the other hand, the lead of the three—followed by the deuce on the next round—definitely proclaims a five-card suit. If West has a card lower than his fourth highest, he must have more than four. And if he has only one lower card, as the three–deuce sequence implies, he could only have started with a five-card suit.

Finessing—Against Whom?

West leads the three, and East sees:

Dummy
J 10 9 5

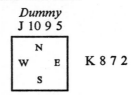 K 8 7 2

What card should he play on dummy's nine? Again the " third-hand-high " doctrinaires would be at fault. On the lead, declarer is *marked* with a singleton. If it is the Ace, playing the King will cost a trick. There is nothing to lose by *not* playing it, because it is impossible to prevent the declarer, whatever he has, from stopping the suit once; twice if he holds the bare Queen. The eight will encourage West, and that is all that is necessary.

West leads the deuce, and declarer plays low from dummy.

J 5 3

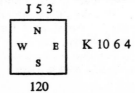 K 10 6 4

East should play the ten. The reason is that if declarer has the Queen, he is bound to make a trick anyway. If West has led from the A Q, the ten is good enough. But if declarer holds the Ace, the King play will cost a trick. Dummy's Knave will remain, sitting pretty, and will jeer at West's Queen.

Occasionally, you will hear someone say: " Never finesse against your partner." That is undoubtedly a noble sentiment, but like so many others, arises from confusion and leads to bewilderment.

This would be a finesse against partner.

7 3 2

```
      N
W         E     K J 6 4
      S
```

Small from West. Now the Knave would be tainted with sin. What is worse, it would be bad technique, for declarer could win a trick with an unguarded Queen. When dummy holds Q x x, the Knave is a finesse—not against partner—but against *dummy*. And that is perfectly right and proper.

Returning Partner's Suit

The next point to arise is: which card should East play *back*, if and when, he gets the chance?

8 7 6

```
      N
W         E     K 10 4 3
      S
```

West leads the deuce, and East's King falls to the Ace. When East is next on play he should lead the three—his *fourth highest*. This time there is no mystique of any kind. It is a straightforward case of enlightening partner. With a double-ton or three (K 10 or K 9 4) the *highest* card is led back. West then assumes that his partner did not have four of the suit, and acts accordingly. Seeing the deuce—or the five, when the four, three and deuce can be accounted for—he knows that

East was dealt four or a doubleton. Sometimes there is room for doubt. But generally speaking, the bidding, declarer's reactions and the general run of play give West every chance to guess right.

Put yourself in West's place.

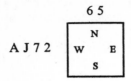

6 5

A J 7 2

He leads the deuce, and partner's Queen falls to the King. East comes in again and plays the nine. Declarer covers and West wins with his Knave. What is the next step? Obviously a short trance. Then a switch. Since partner has only three cards in the suit, declarer has four. West must wait for another lead *through* declarer, who probably has the eight, unless partner started with Q 9 8.

Suppose, however, that East plays back the three. Now West is quite safe in laying down his Ace and cashing the rest of the tricks in the suit. Since East has shown four cards, declarer can have only three, and West need not bother about the eight or anything else.

Could it be that East had a doubleton, after all? Very unlikely. That would give declarer five, and the existence of a five-card suit is generally revealed in the bidding.

In selecting the card to play back—as in playing to partner's lead—the defence should always be inspired by the same motive: to convey across the table, as quickly as can be, an accurate picture of the distribution.

More Unblocking

To the rule, that a defender should play back the fourth highest of partner's suit, there is one important exception. As with some of the earlier hands in this chapter, it is a case of *unblocking*.

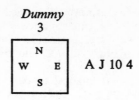

West leads the six, and declarer drops the five on East's Ace. Normally, the four would be the right card to play back, but there is nothing normal in blocking partner's suit, and the danger here is acute. The suit may well be distributed like this:

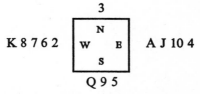

If East returns the four, South's card—whatever it is—will draw the King and the suit will be blocked.

One complete deal will bring the point home:

West leads the five of Spades against Three No-Trumps.

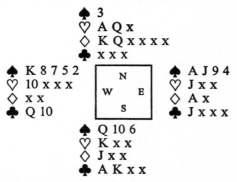

East wins with the Ace and automatically returns the four. Can you see what will happen?

The King will take the second trick, and the next one will be won by declarer's Queen. At trick four, East comes in with his Ace of Diamonds and cashes his Spade. Alas, it is higher than anything West can produce. The Spades are blocked and the contract is unbeatable. The only card that could break it is West's last little x, and there is no way of getting at it.

Return the fourth highest of partner's suit—*unless* there is a danger of blocking it. This arises when the fourth highest is the *only* card low enough to keep communications open with partner. In short: Take care of the xs and the Aces will take care of themselves.

Résumé

(1) The best attack against No-Trump contracts lies in developing the trick-taking capacity of the small cards. Therefore, it is usual to lead from LENGTH.

(2) With a sequence or near sequence of three or more cards, the correct lead is the top (*Q* J 10 9 or *Q* J 9 x or *9* 8 7).

(3) From an interior sequence lead the *second* honour (A *J* 10 x x or K *J* 10 x x or A *10* 9 8 x).

(4) Unless the high-card combination calls for the lead of an honour, open the *fourth highest*.

(5) The lead of the fourth highest by West allows East to apply the Eleven Rule. By subtracting the number of pips from eleven, he can tell how many higher cards than the one led by partner are in the other three hands. And since he can see his own hand and the dummy, he knows how many higher cards are with declarer.

(6) If you want partner to continue a suit, PETER—play a higher card than you need do (a six or five when you have the three or deuce). Play your lowest if you want a switch.

(7) When West leads a small card and dummy has no feature in that suit, East, normally, plays his highest card.

(8) But when dummy has one or more honours, East is correct in finessing against dummy.

(9) In returning partner's suit, lead the top, unless you hold four or more. If you do, play the fourth highest.

(10) But make an exception to the above, when there is a danger that you may BLOCK the suit. Leave yourself a small enough card for partner to overtake after the suit has been cleared.

DEFENCE—CHAPTER VIII

Exercises

(1) The bidding was: One No-Trump—Three No-Trumps.
What do you lead from:

(a)	♠ K J 10 9 x	♡ Q x x	◇ J x x x	♣ x
(b)	♠ K J 10 x	♡ Q x x	◇ Q J 10 x	♣ x x
(c)	♠ A 7 6 4 2	♡ Q x x	◇ Q J 9 x	♣ x
(d)	♠ A J 10 9 x	♡ K J 10 9 x	◇ x	♣ x x
(e)	♠ A Q 10 x	♡ x x	◇ Q J 10 x	♣ x x x
(f)	♠ A K J x x	♡ x x x	◇ Q x x	♣ x x

(2) Bidding as above.   West opens the Queen of Hearts.

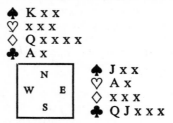

```
        ♠ K x x
        ♡ x x x
        ◇ Q x x x x
        ♣ A x
      ┌─────────┐   ♠ J x x
      │    N    │   ♡ A x
      │ W     E │   ◇ x x x
      │    S    │   ♣ Q J x x x
      └─────────┘
```

What do you play, sitting East?

(3) Bidding as above.   West leads Knave of Hearts.

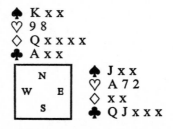

```
        ♠ K x x
        ♡ 9 8
        ◇ Q x x x x
        ♣ A x x
      ┌─────────┐   ♠ J x x
      │    N    │   ♡ A 7 2
      │ W     E │   ◇ x x
      │    S    │   ♣ Q J x x x
      └─────────┘
```

(a) What should East play to the first trick?
(b) What do you suppose is West's holding in Hearts?

(4) Bidding:

North	*East*	*South*	*West*
One Diamond	One Spade	Two No-Trumps	No Bid
Three No-Trumps			

West leads the King of Spades.

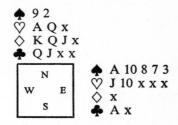

```
        ♠ 9 2
        ♡ A Q x
        ◇ K Q J x
        ♣ Q J x x
                        ♠ A 10 8 7 3
        N               ♡ J 10 x x x
    W       E           ◇ x
        S               ♣ A x
```

(*a*) What card should East play to the first trick?
(*b*) If West continues with the Queen of Spades, what card should East play to the second trick?

(5) Bidding: South, One No-Trump; North, Three No-Trumps.
West leads a small Spade and dummy's Ace wins.

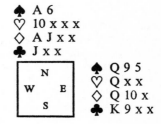

```
        ♠ A 6
        ♡ 10 x x x
        ◇ A J x x
        ♣ J x x
                        ♠ Q 9 5
        N               ♡ Q x x
    W       E           ◇ Q 10 x
        S               ♣ K 9 x x
```

What card should East play?

(6) Bidding:

	South	*North*
	One Club	One Diamond
	One No-Trump	Three No-Trumps

West leads the nine of Spades and declarer plays dummy's Ace.

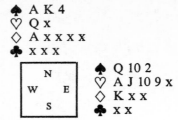

♠ A K 4
♡ Q x
◇ A x x x x
♣ x x x

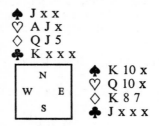

♠ Q 10 2
♡ A J 10 9 x
◇ K x x
♣ x x

What card should East play to the first trick?

(7) Bidding: South, One No-Trump; North, Three No-Trumps.

West leads the four of Diamonds and declarer plays the five from dummy.

♠ J x x
♡ A J x
◇ Q J 5
♣ K x x x

♠ K 10 x
♡ Q 10 x
◇ K 8 7
♣ J x x x

(*a*) What should East play?

(*b*) Assuming that West led a true card, what is declarer's most likely honour holding in Diamonds?

DUMMY PLAY

CHAPTER IX

Suit Management

Kindness to animals is its own reward. Kindness to the cards brings in rich dividends too, and no Chancellor of the Exchequer has yet succeeded in laying hands on them.

No-Trump contracts once more take up the agenda in this chapter. Our concern is with the correct handling of different card combinations. Every suit, in turn, is entitled to courtesy and consideration. No matter how it is divided, take its shape into account, and it will not fail to show proper gratitude.

Our first good deed of the day will be to make Three No-Trumps on this:

♠ J x x
♡ x x
◇ A Q 10 x x
♣ x x x

N
W   E
S

♠ A 9 x
♡ A Q J x
◇ K 9 x x
♣ A x

West opens the four of Spades, Declarer plays low from dummy and East goes up with the King. Does that tell us anything? Why, yes. If he plays the King, he cannot have the ten, for as every good East knows, a finesse against dummy is obligatory in that position. And since West is marked with the ten, the Spades cannot hurt us, so long as we leave them

129

alone. Should West lead one, we will run it up to our nine, and that will be that.

We are over our first hurdle. For as we gather the first trick with the Ace, we know that opponents will be unable to run the Spade suit.

The quest for nine tricks need not take us long. A contribution of five will be made by the Diamonds—regardless of distribution—providing we don't maltreat them. First, we lay down the Ace. If no one shows out, all is well. If one of the defenders does not follow, we know that the other is a snake in the grass with J x x x. A simple finesse removes the fangs.

The Hearts call for just a speck of delicacy. That is why we give them our attention before reeling off too many Diamonds. Should the Heart finesse succeed, we shall want to take it again, and that will require another entry in dummy. Why should we not make an extra trick while we are about it?

The interest of the hand lies in its simplicity. No one should fail to make the contract, but some will—through lack of forethought.

About 10 per cent of the time, a really unlucky player will strike a 4–0 Diamond break. So will the others. But the unlucky one will lay down the King first. Then, if West shows out, he will expect sympathy and commiseration, instead of the dirty look from partner which is all he deserves.

Does it all seem too easy? Then that is what makes it worth stressing, for the situation will recur again and again. And pardonable though it be to go down in a difficult contract, to misplay an easy one is positively infuriating. Much harder, too, to find a convincing alibi when it is all over.

The general rule is: With A K Q 10 9 between the two hands, play high from the hand which has *two* top honours. When declarer and dummy have nine cards between them, nothing can go wrong. If both opponents follow to the first trick, the suit can't break 4–0. And if one of the opponents shows out, he gives the game away. Declarer can " see " the other hand.

Try out the same combination with eight cards:

A Q 10 9

opposite

K x x x

Play the Ace first. If the suit breaks 5–0, you will know which way to finesse. If both opponents follow, you can finesse against either. But you don't know which one, because each, in turn, could have J x x left after the first trick. It will be a case of guessing. The bidding, the opening lead and the play to previous tricks will usually make the guess an odds-on chance in declarer's favour. And should either defender drop the seven or eight on the Ace, that, too, will help. He is less likely to have four of the suit than his partner.

Here there is no guessing:

A Q 10 2

K 7 6 5

If East has J x x x, there is nothing to be done. West's Knave can be caught, provided you *know* about it. The way to take an honest peep is to play the Ace first, then a small one to the King. If East shows out, West need not bother to keep his cards up. Note that you still play high from the hand with the two top honours.

One very small alteration in the pips can make a whale of a difference.

A Q 10 5

K 8 7 6

The eight has appeared behind the King. There is still no way of bringing East to justice if he has been dealt J 9 x x. But perhaps West drops the nine on the Ace. Now the K 8 creates a finesse position against J 4 3 2 with East. Play the Queen from dummy, and if West shows out, finesse. If West played the nine from J 9 x x, just to fool you, it was a good bluff and he deserves to profit by it. More often than not, however, that nine will be genuine.

The principle is the same, but the treatment is a little different here:

A Q 9 2

K 5 4 3

It is a pity that the Knave and ten are both missing, but perhaps we can do without them. Assuming plenty of entries to the South hand (K x x x), how do you set about it?

Lay the King down first. If East shows out, you will be able to catch West's Knave and ten. If East drops the ten or Knave, you play the Ace. Either East follows, and all is well, or he shows out and his partner's 10 x x x—or J x x x—will never live to take a trick, *because* you have taken care to retain Q 9 in dummy. The idea is to develop the suit so as to keep a tenace *over* the missing honour.

Don't End Up in the Wrong Hand

Here is another exercise in good luck. North leads a Spade against Three No-Trumps.

♠ A 10 x	N	♠ J x
♡ A Q 10 3	W E	♡ J 9 2
◇ A J x x	S	◇ x x x
♣ K x		♣ A x x x x

The lead is not unlucky. If you had to play the Spades all on your own, you would not expect to make more than one trick. Now you can't fail to make two. What is the state of the inventory? Two tricks in Spades, the Ace of Diamonds and two top Clubs. The Hearts will have to yield four tricks to bring the total to nine. Work out how you propose to play those Hearts. Yes, you cross into dummy with the Ace of Clubs—the one and only entry—and . . .?

Visualise the various possibilities. If North has the King, nothing matters. If South has the King, doubleton or trebleton, you can afford to play badly. So imagine that South has K x x x. Try the Knave. It wins. Now a small one. The ten holds the trick. All is well—or is it?

You are in *your* hand without a hope of getting into dummy again before the day of judgment. Why did that play go wrong? Because you could not help *overtaking* dummy's second Heart. To keep the lead in dummy, play the *nine* first. Then the Knave. At trick three you are still in dummy. The entry has been saved, and the contract with it.

But how do you play this combination:

J x x

A Q 10

132

The principle is the same, but the Knave is different. This time there is no other card to play. If you lead a small one from dummy, you will have to overtake in your own hand. And you want to *remain* in dummy, to finesse a second time.

In the first example you wanted to lead from dummy three times; in the second example only *twice*. Both times you achieved your purpose by underplaying dummy's card.

Correct timing is the key to this hand.

```
      ♠ K x x x    ┌─────────┐   ♠ A x x
      ♡ A x x      │    N    │   ♡ x x x x
      ◇ A Q 10     │ W     E │   ◇ x x x x
      ♣ A x x      │    S    │   ♣ Q x
                   └─────────┘
```

North leads a Club against Two No-Trumps.

Think it out carefully before touching a card. But *don't* think about the first trick. There is nothing whatever to think about. Hope, not technique, is the order of the day. If you play low from dummy, you will only make one trick— the Ace. South won't put up his King just to oblige you. But if South was not dealt the King, the Queen will hold. Try it. It is a chance to nothing.

Assume that the Queen wins. What card do you play from dummy at trick two?

It must be a Diamond, only a Diamond and nothing but a Diamond. The reason is that the Diamonds must be finessed *twice* and dummy has only one other entry—the Ace of Spades.

Blocking Opponent's Suit

It may be love that makes the world go round, but it is entries that bring contracts home.

```
      ♠ A          ┌─────────┐   ♠ Q J 10 9
      ♡ A x        │    N    │   ♡ 10 x x x
      ◇ A x x x x x │ W     E │   ◇ x
      ♣ K Q J 2    │    S    │   ♣ A 5 4 3
                   └─────────┘
```

North opens a small Heart against Three No-Trumps. South plays the 9 on dummy's x. To hold up or not to hold up? The general rule with six of a suit between the two hands

133

is to hold up once. That will exhaust a defender, who started with a doubleton. But quality comes into it, as well as quantity. That ten in dummy makes all the difference.

One thing we know for certain, North cannot have three honours. With K Q J he would have led the King. It follows that South has one honour, maybe even two. If he has three Hearts in all, we don't much care. And if he has two, the suit will be—must be—blocked. No matter how closely South hugs his cards to his bosom, we can " see " that, if he started with a doubleton, it was something like Q 9 or J 9. Visibility is perfect.

Opponents will get in and doubtless play a Heart—but South will be left high and dry, holding the trick. North cannot overtake, because that will make dummy's ten into a trick at one remove.

So we can take that Ace of Hearts without fear or trepidation. All that remains is to make another eight tricks for our contract. Where do we go for honey? There can be no future in that diaphanous Diamond suit. But the Spades will yield three tricks, *if* we can get into dummy twice—once to knock out the King, and a second time to play off the two winners. Can you see two entries in dummy?

Creating Entries

The correct sequence is this : at trick two the Ace of Spades. Then the King and Queen of Clubs, hoping that no one shows out. But keep your fingers crossed, for the contract depends on those Clubs. To get into dummy *twice* the Knave must be overtaken with the Ace. That is the first entry and allows the Spades to be cleared. Opponents can pick up a Heart trick or two, three if the suit splits 4–3, but that is all. You come in again with the Ace of Diamonds and play what is now your most valuable card—the deuce of Clubs. That three in dummy is the vital link with the two good Spades. It may seem flashy to use a three as an entry, but when all the higher cards have gone, a three is as good as an Ace.

With four of a suit, or more, in each hand, the little xs can do more than take tricks in their own right. They can provide ENTRIES.

North leads a Diamond against Six No-Trumps.

♠ A K x
♡ A K x x x
◇ A K Q J
♣ K

♠ Q x x
♡ x x
◇ x x x
♣ A J 10 9 8

The contract is cold against any distribution that Fate can devise. Declarer needs three Club tricks only, and can afford to lose one. His only difficulty is lack of entries to dummy. Can you see the way out?

At trick two the King of Clubs is *overtaken* by the Ace. The Clubs are cleared and the Queen of Spades remains in dummy for a second entry.

As on the previous deal, an entry is created by OVER-TAKING. Whether the link-up is effected through deuces or Kings is immaterial. What does matter is to realise that a card may be more valuable as an entry than as a straight-forward winner.

In this situation:

A K 4 2

7 6 5 3

The North hand can produce three entries if the suit breaks 3–2. But South must guard jealously his three and dummy's four. Carelessness won't cost a trick in that suit. But it will lead to the loss of an entry, which may be worth several tricks.

The same principle is at work here:

♠ K x x
♡ A 9 x x
◇ —
♣ A x x x x x

♠ Q J x
♡ Q x
◇ K Q J 10 9 x
♣ x x

North opens a Spade against Two No-Trumps and South goes up with the Ace. To revoke would be deplorable, but to follow suit unthinkingly would be only a little less so. Declarer needs two entries in dummy—to set up the Diamonds, and then to get at them. The Heart Queen is an imponderable. Anyone may have the King. But the Queen and Knave of Spades are stone-cold, certain entries. The way to them lies through those little xs in declarer's hand. If he throws one away on the Ace, he will deserve everything partner can say—and think. These two Spade xs must be preserved as LINKS. Therefore, at trick one, the King must be discarded on the Ace. It BLOCKS the golden way into dummy. So get rid of it quickly. UNBLOCK.

Returning Opponent's Suit

All the foregoing hands have hinged on specific plays. Declarer faced concrete problems : to hold up or not to hold up opponents' suits; to create and preserve entries; or to play with the odds in developing different card combinations. Many contracts just do not fall into any such well-defined category; declarer has no hard-and-fast rules to guide him. Let us try one of these amorphous hands.

```
        ♠ J x x
        ♡ K 10 x
        ◇ x x x
        ♣ K Q x x
            ┌─────────┐
            │    N    │
            │ W     E │
            │    S    │
            └─────────┘
        ♠ K 9 x
        ♡ A J x
        ◇ A Q x
        ♣ A J x x
```

West opens a Diamond against Three No-Trumps, and East produces the Knave.

This is the moment for meditation. Declarer can see eight tricks—four Clubs, two Diamonds and two Hearts. Perhaps the Ace of Spades is with East and the King will turn out to be the ninth, decisive trick. Maybe the Heart Queen can be located. Who knows? If the worst comes to the worst, one or other may have to be tried. But no good player will go bald-headed for a fifty-fifty chance, when anything better is available.

How, then, should the hand be played? Work it out, but don't be disappointed if you fail. Only a master would do the right thing automatically.

Take the Queen of Diamonds and play off three Clubs. Note the discards—not because they are of special importance in this case—but because it is always a good thing to do. Now the stage is set for the key play—the Ace of Diamonds. If East follows, play *another*.

The purpose is to put West on play, and the reason is that —whatever he does—he will be wrong.

Since East followed to the Ace of Diamonds, West cannot have more than five. Let us assume that he plays off his winners. Declarer discards one Spade and his last Club. That, incidentally, is why he did not play off *all* the Clubs at the beginning. He had to leave one available for a cheap discard. Dummy's Club remains, of course, and can be cashed at leisure.

Five Diamonds and three Clubs have gone, leaving this five-card position:

♠ J
♡ K 10 x
♢ —
♣ K

N
W   E
S

♠ K x
♡ A J x
♢ —
♣ —

Now you can see why West was predestined to go wrong. Whatever he has, and whatever he leads, declarer must make nine tricks. All West can do is to decide how he will commit *felo de se*. He can present declarer with his ninth trick by leading up to the King of Spades or by playing into his Heart tenace.

Suppose that West has four Diamonds only. Then, it is true, East may win the third Diamond trick. But he is just as unhappy as his partner. A Heart lead will simply find the Queen for declarer. A Spade will fare no better. Declarer will run it up to his Knave. Whatever the position, declarer *must* make a Spade trick—if opponents touch the suit *first*.

What would an anatomy lesson of the play show?

First, the overall plan. Declarer must not touch Spades or Hearts himself. In Hearts he seeks to avoid a guess. In Spades it is essentially a case of *after you, please*. With holdings like K x x opposite J x x or Q x x opposite J x x, whoever goes first incurs a penalty. So let the other fellow do it.

Secondly, technique: To make opponents open up the Spades or Hearts, declarer first removes the Clubs and Diamonds. He must hope that neither defender has four Clubs, because he cannot afford to play off the last one. He will need it if West has five Diamonds. Turn back to that five-card end position. Declarer needs every one of his last five cards (♠ K x; ♡ A J x). So he must retain a Club—to have something to throw away.

Finally, the hand does, after all, illustrate a *specific* play: returning opponents' suit. It is the antithesis of the hold up. Instead of preventing a defender from making the long cards in his suit, declarer *forces* him to cash them.

There are two conditions for employing this technique; declarer must be in a position to *afford* it. He must be sure that neither defender has enough winners to endanger the contract. And there must be a good reason for surrendering the initiative. That reason is nearly always the same: to *force* defenders to open up suits, in which declarer holds tenaces or " untouchable " combinations. This is known as a " Throw In ", and will form the subject of a chapter all to itself. Meanwhile, remember the proverb:

" Don't put off till tomorrow what someone else may be induced to do for you today."

Percentage Plays

We have decided to spare the reader those dreary statistical tables, which bear so sinister a resemblance to the latest issue of the *Board of Trade Journal*. The trouble with statistics is that people try to memorise them, and in a welter of figures, the few that really matter are blurred and fade away.

One of the important things to remember is that when six cards of a suit are out against you, they are more likely to be divided 4–2 (48 per cent of the time) than 3–3 (36 per cent). It seems unnatural, but it is true. . . . With the odds in mind, how do you, sitting South, play

A Q 10 9 x x opposite x in dummy?

The usual procedure is to lead the singleton, then after a huddle, to look at the ceiling for inspiration. If none is forthcoming, declarer selects at random the Queen or the ten, convinced that either card is as good as the other. It is not.

Admittedly, if the suit breaks 3–3, the ten may come off as often as the Queen. But in the more likely event of a 4–2 split, the Queen will be the right card to play. Someone, West perhaps, may have a doubleton Knave, and if that is the case, only one trick need be lost. Losing the ten to the doubleton King will not work the same way. For if West has K x, East must have J x x x and the Knave will still win a trick.

Next time you open with a Three bid you may find yourself with

A J 10 x x x opposite a void.

After the Ace, lead a *small* card—not the Knave. If the suit breaks 3–3, it won't matter. But should the division be 4–2 the x may bring down an honour, and you will retain the J 10 to deal with the Q 9.

The same, of course, applies to J 10 x x x x opposite the singleton Ace.

In case you are unaccustomed to good cards, we present you with a cascade of sparkling brilliants. But don't forget the odds or the facets may slip between your fingers.

♠ x x x x
♡ A x
♢ x x x
♣ x x x x

N
W E
S

♠ A K Q
♡ Q x
♢ A K Q x
♣ A Q x x

West opens a Heart against Three No-Trumps. East wins the first trick with the King and knocks out dummy's Ace. What do you do next?

Either the Club finesse or a 3–3 Diamond break will land the contract. But you can't have your finesse and eat it too, for you will never get into dummy again. So make up your mind now. Which shall it be?

The answer is a Club. Back the finesse, which is a fifty-fifty chance, against a 3–3 split, which will only come off 36 times in a 100.

All this should impress on you the need to expect the un-expected when you and your dummy have *seven* cards in a suit. When you have *eight*, the frequency of a bad break is also rather surprising. No less than 28 per cent of the time one of your opponents will have a singleton. Only two-thirds of the time—or just over (68 per cent)—will you enjoy the *normal* 3–2 division. In short, normality is not so normal, after all.

Taking that as a hint, how do you deal with

A J 10 9 x opposite K x x in dummy?

The King first, then a small one, intending to finesse against the Queen? Quite right—if dummy has an entry. And if not? Do you still lead the King, just in case West was dealt a singleton Queen?

That play is against the odds. If the suit breaks 3–2, it won't matter either way. But if those busy gremlins are at

140

work again, and the division is 4–1, the Queen is far more likely to be guarded three times than to be alone. So you will need to finesse *twice*. To give yourself the chance, leave the King in dummy as an entry. Lead a small one.

Similarly, if for some reason you suspect West of harbouring the Queen, play the Knave first—not the Ace. Should the finesse succeed, you will be able to repeat it, and even three escorts will not avail the Queen.

If a jinx so often takes command when, with your dummy, you hold seven or eight cards in a suit, a friendly leprechaun will generally look after you when you have only six. The odds are nearly two to one (62 per cent) on a gentlemanly 4–3 split.

With nine cards, attempts to seize a shade of odds in the matter of a missing Queen are apt to transcend the realm of luck, which is an art to be acquired, and degenerate into a simple hazard. Half the time the four cards outstanding will split 3–1. Four times in ten they will break 2–2. And once the same defender will hold all four. There you are. There is not much in it.

Finally, it is worth noting what happens when you possess eleven cards, missing the King and the deuce. The uninitiated will play the Ace, like a flash of lightning, and feel deeply aggrieved if the King does not drop. The *cognoscenti* may still pick on the Ace—but at half-speed and with a sense of foreboding. For it is almost an even-money chance, just 52–48 on a 1–1 division.

At times, it helps a lot to know the odds, particularly when six cards are missing. But when the situation is really close, don't worry too much about figures. A cough, a sigh, a shifty look, the vibrations of a plucked eyebrow are often worth more than a decimal fraction.

Résumé

(1) In playing card combinations from which only the Knave is missing, declarer strives to retain tenace positions in both hands. If one opponent shows out, the finesse is taken against the other. The rule is to play a high honour first from the hand with two tops (e.g., the Ace from A Q 9 x opposite K 10 x x x).

(2) But when the nine is also missing, and declarer can finesse in one direction only, he first plays the top (or tops) from the hand *without* the ten (e.g., Ace and Queen from A Q x x opposite K 10 x x).

(3) When declarer takes a finesse which may have to be repeated (J x x opposite A Q 10 or J 9 x opposite A Q 10 x) he must take care not to end up in the wrong hand. This means thinking one move ahead, and planning the leads so that the wrong hand won't be compelled to *overtake* unnecessarily.

(4) When dummy is short of entries, declarer must take care to use each one at the right *time*. Should an entry be knocked out in the early stages, declarer may have to reverse the natural order and develop a short suit before a long one. This will happen when the short suit requires to be played from dummy, while the long one does not.

(5) To create entries declarer may have to UNBLOCK—to discard a high card from his hand, so as to retain small ones, which can be overtaken in dummy (e.g., with K J x opposite Q 10 x declarer creates an additional entry by discarding his King on opponents' Ace).

(6) In certain situations, INFERENCE enables declarer to block opponents' suit at trick one. Since from three honours West would not play an x, the lead of a small card may mark East with an honour. If it is a doubleton, and declarer goes up with the Ace, East cannot unblock without sacrificing a trick. A typical situation is: 10 9 x x opposite A x in dummy.

(7) When declarer hopes to make an additional trick—or tricks—by forcing opponents to play into his tenaces, he

142

sometimes resorts to the opposite of a HOLD UP. He plays *back* the suit opened against him.

(8) In dealing with various combinations, declarer is helped by knowing how the outstanding cards in the suit are *likely* to be divided between the defenders. He must be prepared for " unlucky " breaks, when he and his dummy possess either *seven* or *eight* cards in the same suit.

(9) Holding seven cards of a suit, he will find that 48 per cent of the time the outstanding six cards will be divided 4–2. The 3–3 break is only a 36 per cent chance.

(10) With eight cards of a suit, the odds are 68 per cent on a 3–2 split. A 4–1 division will occur 28 per cent of the time.

DUMMY PLAY—CHAPTER IX

Exercises

(1) North leads a small Spade against Three No-Trumps by West. South plays the Ace of Spades.

♠ K x x		♠ J 10 9
♡ A K Q 10	N	♡ x x
◇ —	W E	◇ A K Q x x x x
♣ A K x x x x	S	♣ x

(*a*) Can any defence or distribution defeat the contract?

(*b*) Which tricks will declarer win in his hand, and which tricks will he win in dummy?

(2) North leads a small Club against West's Three No-Trumps. South plays the King on dummy's nine.

♠ A K		♠ J 10 9 8 7
♡ K J 10 8 2	N	♡ 3
◇ A K 9 5	W E	◇ 6 4 3 2
♣ A 2	S	♣ Q 10 9

(*a*) Assuming that neither defender has a void or singleton in any suit, can declarer make certain of his contract?

(*b*) In what order should declarer play the first six cards from his hand?

(3) North opens the five of Hearts against West's Three No-Trumps.

♠ A x		♠ K J x
♡ 9 7 6 4	N	♡ A 2
◇ A K x x	W E	◇ x x x x
♣ A Q x	S	♣ K x x

(*a*) What card should declarer play from dummy to the first trick?

(*b*) What can declarer infer about South's holding in Hearts?

(4)   ♠ A Q x x   ♠ K 10
       ♡ A K x   ♡ x x x
       ◇ —      ◇ K Q J 10 9 x
       ♣ Q 10 x x x x   ♣ x x

North leads the Queen of Hearts against Three No-Trumps by West.

(a) What card should declarer play from his hand to the first trick?

(b) What card should he play when he takes the lead?

(c) On what will the contract depend?

(5)   ♠ A K x   ♠ x x x
          ♡ Q J x   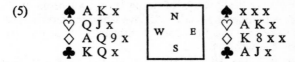   ♡ A K x
          ◇ A Q 9 x   ◇ K 8 x x
          ♣ K Q x   ♣ A J x

After a Three Spades opening from North, East–West reach Six No-Trumps.

How should declarer play the Diamonds?

(6) The contract and the East–West hands are as in (5). But this time it was South who opened the bidding with Three Spades.

How should declarer play the Diamonds?

DEFENCE

CHAPTER X

The Attack Develops

The object of the defence is, of course, to break declarer's heart. There are many ways of doing it, but all begin at the same point—the opening lead. All too often declarer's heart remains unbroken—and his contract unbeaten—because West starts off on the wrong foot.

Hitherto East has been as silent as an oyster in the close season. With nothing to guide him, West led the top of a sequence or the fourth highest of his longest suit. Sometimes there is an R in the month and East bids. Should West *always* lead his partner's suit? And when he does, what sort of card should he select?

Other things being equal, it is *usually* best to lead partner's suit. But other things are not always equal. If South calls Three No-Trumps, after hearing East bid or overbid One Heart, he is clearly prepared for the suit to be opened against him. If East doubles the contract, West has little choice. The double is a COMMAND. West is *ordered* to lead a Heart. Presumably, East's suit is as good as K Q J x x x or A Q J x x, and needless to say, East possesses an entry. So if he does not double, he is unlikely to have that much. Therefore, with a singleton or worthless doubleton, there is a perfectly good temptation not to take partner too seriously. Don't bend over backwards to lead his suit. Can you think of anything better? That is the whole point. With nothing in partner's suit and Q J 10 x x—or Q J 9 x x—and an entry of some sort, forget anything that partner ever said. But well-thought-out forgetfulness must not be confused with amnesia. Without a decent suit, and more especially without an entry, try to oblige partner. And show greater respect for an overbid than for an opening. The reason is that an overbid may have less high card strength, but the suit itself must be more solid—or less threadbare. To open on Q 10 x x would pass muster in a cathedral city. To overbid on anything so flimsy would be considered shocking in Montmartre.

Opponents reach a No-Trump contract after partner has opened the bidding with One Heart. Lead partner's suit with:

(a)	♠	J x x	♡	10 x	◇	Q x x x x	♣	K x x
(b)	♠	K x x	♡	9 x	◇	J x x x x	♣	Q x x
(c)	♠	A x x	♡	x x	◇	J x x x x	♣	Q x x

But lead a Spade from:

(a)	♠	J 10 x x x x	♡	x	◇	K x x	♣	Q x x
(b)	♠	Q J 10 x x	♡	x x	◇	K x x	♣	x x x
(c)	♠	K J x x x	♡	x	◇	K x x	♣	x x x x

In weighing up the situation, be guided by the ENTRY position. There is no future in setting up a suit if you can never get in to make it.

Not leading partner's suit, when you hold three cards in it, calls for something out of the ordinary in the way of excuses. The least would be a suit of your own as good as K Q 10 x x.

Leading Partner's Suit

Having established that it is not necessarily immoral to open, on occasion, something of one's own, let us get back to the majority of cases, which call for the obvious lead of partner's suit.

With a doubleton, always lead the highest. With three, lead the highest, *unless* you have one of the four top honours. It is particularly important to play low from K x x or Q x x. There is no reason in the world to let declarer make two tricks with A J x. He will do, if you open your honour.

Even with J x x, it is best to open the lowest. The suit may be distributed like this.

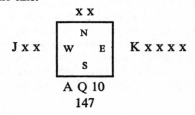

The lead of the Knave will give South an additional trick.

A low one from A x x will pay, when declarer holds, say, Q x x or K J x. In No-Trumps, South is almost bound to have an honour or two in a suit bid against him. But even in a suit contract, it is still correct to play small from K x x or Q x x, though not from A x x.

Occasionally, the bidding may indicate that North holds an honour in the suit. Then open the Knave or Queen, because you want to play *through* dummy. The situation may come about when the bidding follows these lines :

(a)	North	East	South	West
	One No-Trump	Two Hearts	Three Spades	No Bid
	Four Spades			

or

(b)	North	East	South	West
	One Diamond	One Heart	One Spade	No Bid
	Two No-Trumps	No Bid	Four Spades	

North's No-Trump opening on (a) and his Two No-Trumps rebid on (b) indicate that he has something in Hearts. So there is some point in playing the Queen or Knave *through* him.

From two touching honours, lead the top—the Q from Q J x and the J from J 10 x.

With four small xs, it is not wrong to lead the lowest, but it is often more profitable to play the highest. This is the case, especially when you have supported partner. He expects to find you with some length and the lead of a nine or eight, denying an honour, will help him to place the high cards straightaway.

The same principle applies when you open an unbid suit, and also when you switch to a new suit in the middle of the hand. It is rarely wise to lead the lowest of four, unless you have an honour. Conversely, when switching to a three-card suit, headed by an honour, play the lowest. When the danger is that partner will be deceived about one card, it is better to deceive him about an extra x than about a K or Q.

One deal will suffice to illustrate the mechanism of leading partner's suit from a three-card holding, headed by an honour.

North bids One Diamond, East calls a Spade and South Two No-Trumps. North raises it to Three.

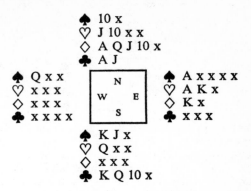

♠ 10 x
♡ J 10 x x
◇ A Q J 10 x
♣ A J

♠ Q x x
♡ x x x
◇ x x x
♣ x x x x

♠ A x x x x
♡ A K x
◇ K x
♣ x x x

♠ K J x
♡ Q x x
◇ x x x
♣ K Q 10 x

West opens his lowest Spade. The Ace of Spades takes the first trick and a small Spade pierces declarer's K J position. He can try to block the suit by going up with the King. That will leave the bare Queen over him. But it won't help much. East comes in with the King of Diamonds, lays down the Heart King and plays another Spade. West puts his partner in with the Ace of Hearts, and two more Spades complete declarer's discomfiture. Three down.

Note that if West opens the Spade Queen, the contract is fool-proof.

Preserving Communications

The chapters on Dummy-Play will have made the reader familiar with the technique of ducking—from declarer's point of view. What is sauce for the declaring goose is sauce for the defending gander. See how it works from East's side of the table.

First listen to the bidding:

North	East (*you*)	South	West
One Diamond	One Spade	Two No-Trumps	No Bid
Three No-Trumps			

149

Partner duly opens the nine of Spades, and you, sitting East, behold the table.

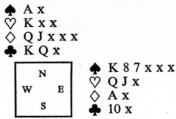

♠ A x
♡ K x x
◇ Q J x x x
♣ K Q x

♠ K 8 7 x x x
♡ Q J x
◇ A x
♣ 10 x

Declarer plays small from dummy. What do you do and why do you do it?

The best way to begin is to shut your eyes and look into declarer's hand. What has he in Spades? Partner's nine denies an honour, so South must have the Q J 10. He may have four, but it is unlikely. With a singleton, partner would have probably found some other lead. One thing is certain. Declarer cannot fail to collect two Spade tricks. The question is how to get hold of four yourself. Unfortunately, you possess one certain entry only. And you need two. So unless partner can help, the whole Spade suit must be written off. Now you can open your eyes. You have seen declarer's Q J 10, so you know that partner started with 9 x in Spades. That x is the key card. Partner must have a chance to use it *before* your Diamond Ace is driven out. Otherwise all is lost.

Try doing the simple, the obvious, the natural thing. Go up with the King of Spades and play another to dummy's Ace. Most Easts would do just that. After which all the Souths concerned would make their contracts. Why? Because that play *kills* partner's x—the key card. That unassuming little x is a *link*—a vital link between West and East. Communications between the two hands depend on it.

To spare that x, don't take the first trick. Peter with the eight, a " come-on " signal, telling partner: " I like the suit very much, but I must duck on the first round, because I am short of entries. I do hope that you can get in quickly and play another Spade while I still have an Ace to my name."

Of course, West is not bound to have an entry, and it is just possible that his nine of Spades was a singleton after all.

Then nothing will break the contract anyway. No defence should ever be based on such an assumption.

Here is the complete deal.

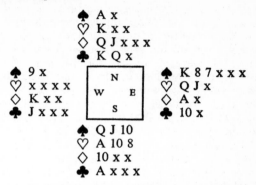

♠ A x
♡ K x x
◇ Q J x x x
♣ K Q x

♠ 9 x
♡ x x x x
◇ K x x
♣ J x x x

♠ K 8 7 x x x
♡ Q J x
◇ A x
♣ 10 x

♠ Q J 10
♡ A 10 8
◇ 10 x x
♣ A x x x

West comes in with the King of Diamonds and plays his second Spade. East still has the Ace of Diamonds and the Spades are set up. As in playing the hand, so in defence, ducking creates an additional entry. Communications between the two hands are open for one extra round.

A very different problem in keeping communications open arises on this deal.

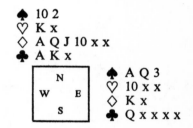

♠ 10 2
♡ K x
◇ A Q J 10 x x
♣ A K x

♠ A Q 3
♡ 10 x x
◇ K x
♣ Q x x x x

The bidding was:

North	East	South	West
One Diamond	No Bid	One Heart	No Bid
Three Diamonds	No Bid	Three No-Trumps	

West opens the six of Spades. What should East play?
Again the " natural " card is the Ace of Spades, and the

151

natural come back, if asked why, will be: "Never finesse against partner" or "Third hand plays high" or "Every cloud has a silver lining", or some equally compelling reason.

The one vital factor, from East's point of view, is that he has an entry and that West almost certainly has not. That King of Diamonds must make an early trick. Apart from that solitary ray of sunshine, prospects are gloomy. West may have the King of Spades, but the odds are against it. Declarer has nothing much in Clubs, and it is unlikely that he bid Three No-Trumps with two unguarded suits.

Anyway, if West has that Spade King, it won't matter whether East plays the Ace or the Queen. But can you see what will happen if South has it? East plays the Ace, then the Queen. Declarer plays low. The third Spade clears the suit, but there is no longer a *link* between the two hands. Communications have been severed. West's two precious Spades will never materialise, because he cannot get in.

If you want the story to have a happy ending, play the *Queen* at the first trick. Declarer dare not duck, because he does not know the position. In fact, he expects West to have the Ace. His only hope—and it is a perfectly reasonable one—is that the Diamond finesse will come off. That would give him eleven tricks.

The four hands are:

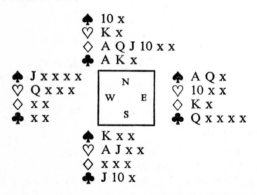

<pre>
                    ♠ 10 x
                    ♡ K x
                    ◇ A Q J 10 x x
                    ♣ A K x
   ♠ J x x x x   ┌─────────┐   ♠ A Q x
   ♡ Q x x x   │   N   │   ♡ 10 x x
   ◇ x x   W │   E │   ◇ K x
   ♣ x x   │   S   │   ♣ Q x x x x
                    └─────────┘
                    ♠ K x x
                    ♡ A J x x
                    ◇ x x x
                    ♣ J 10 x
</pre>

Is East's play of the Queen of Spades just a happy inspiration? Or does it devolve from some recognisable principle?

152

The root of the matter lies in the problem of communications. To make use of twenty-six cards defenders must keep a channel open between them. When either defender sees—or fears—that the other will have no entry, he must take special care to preserve his LINKS—the little xs that will serve to put partner in.

A further consideration is that the play of the Queen can gain, but cannot lose. If West has the King, it will make no difference, but if declarer has it, he is most unlikely to hold it up. To gain on the swings, without losing on the roundabouts, is the essence of good Bridge.

Disrupting Communications

No less important than keeping open your own communications is the task of disrupting declarer's. The general directive should be : Do unto declarer as you would that he did not do unto you.

As West, you lead the Queen of Hearts against Three No-Trumps :

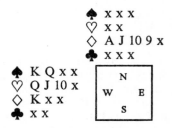

♠ x x x
♡ x x
◇ A J 10 9 x
♣ x x x

♠ K Q x x
♡ Q J 10 x
◇ K x x
♣ x x

Declarer wins and leads a Diamond. Most Wests will play small, invoking the parrot cry : " Second hand plays low." The correct play in this situation from K x x or Q x x (or K x or Q x) is to go up with the honour. If declarer holds a doubleton in the suit, he dare not go up with the Ace. That would kill dummy for ever and ever. Should second hand play low, declarer will finesse. East can take his Queen, but a second finesse will lead straight to four tricks. Even if declarer holds three cards in the suit, playing the King will probably gain a trick. Declarer will be afraid to overtake in case one of the defenders is in a position to hold up the Queen.

153

Set out all four hands and work out the possibilities.

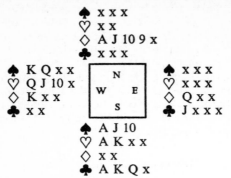

```
                    ♠ x x x
                    ♡ x x
                    ◇ A J 10 9 x
                    ♣ x x x
    ♠ K Q x x         ┌─────────┐      ♠ x x x
    ♡ Q J 10 x        │    N    │      ♡ x x x
    ◇ K x x           │ W     E │      ◇ Q x x
    ♣ x x             │    S    │      ♣ J x x x
                    └─────────┘
                    ♠ A J 10
                    ♡ A K x x
                    ◇ x x
                    ♣ A K Q x
```

By going up with the King at trick two, West *disrupts* declarer's communications with dummy.

But in this position:

$$A J 10 9 x (x) (and no entry)$$

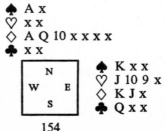

```
              ┌─────────┐
              │    N    │
    K Q x     │ W     E │
              │    S    │
              └─────────┘
```

play low. If you go up with an honour, declarer may duck and catch your other honour next time. A small card on the first round will prevent dummy from making more than two tricks—if declarer has a doubleton. If he has three, you can't do much about it, but ducking will still cost nothing.

Entries to a long suit are declarer's most precious possessions. Therefore, they should be ravaged at the first opportunity.

```
                    ♠ A x
                    ♡ x x
                    ◇ A Q 10 x x x x
                    ♣ x x
                    ┌─────────┐      ♠ K x x
                    │    N    │      ♡ J 10 9 x
                    │ W     E │      ◇ K J x
                    │    S    │      ♣ Q x x
                    └─────────┘
```

South opens a non-vulnerable No-Trump (12–14 points), which North raises to Three. West leads the deuce of Clubs and East's Queen falls to the Ace. At trick two declarer leads a Diamond. West follows, and East takes the Queen with the King. What should he do now?

The King of Spades simply shrieks to be played. That Ace on the table must be removed at all costs. And it must be done immediately—before the Diamonds are set up.

There is one important thing *not* to do. *Don't* play a *small* Spade. South may win in his hand with the Queen and retain the vital entry on the table. Defenders are naturally loth to throw their Kings wantonly into the jaws of hostile Aces. But it is a case of giving up one trick—or four.

Signals

Sometimes doubt gnaws at a defender's vitals. Should he return partner's suit or knock out an entry to dummy? Let us try it out.

♠ A x
♡ J x x x
♢ A Q 10 x x
♣ x x

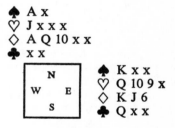

♠ K x x
♡ Q 10 9 x
♢ K J 6
♣ Q x x

Same bidding as last time. Same lead. And again East comes in at trick two with the King of Diamonds. Should he still attack dummy's entry, gallantly sacrificing the King of Spades in the process? Or should he return partner's lead?

It all depends on whether South has three Diamonds or only two. If he has three, he can't be kept out of dummy, anyway. To immolate the King of Spades won't help. And it will waste a valuable tempo.

It is not unusual on such occasions to see East fidget and squirm, trying vainly to guess the position. He can't tell. and that is all there is to it. But West can, and should, put him out of his misery. This brings us to another aspect of

SIGNALLING. To show a doubleton, West plays high–low. With three, he plays his cards in their natural order, starting with the lowest.

Whenever the table has a long suit, East and West signal to each other. Every x carries a message. This way the defenders know how long to hold up their key cards.

Follow the signalling mechanism at work on the last hand.

(a) On declarer's Diamond, at trick two, West plays the deuce. That shows three Diamonds—unless, of course, it is a singleton, which would be just too bad. East does a little elementary arithmetic. He can see eight Diamonds. If West has three, declarer has only a doubleton. So communications *can* be disrupted. Out comes that King of Spades.

(b) West plays the eight. That must be the beginning of a peter, showing a doubleton. Now East knows that declarer has three and that there is no way of stopping him from getting at dummy's Diamonds. Without looking at the King of Spades, he plays back a Club, hoping to beat the contract that way.

As explained in Chapter VIII, the object of signalling is to encourage or discourage partner, and *not* to " show things ". But when there is a long suit about, and it is obvious that there can be no question of encouragement, the same method is used for a different purpose : to inform partner of the distribution. Here is a typical situation.

♠ Q x
♡ x x x
◇ K x x
♣ Q J 10 9 4

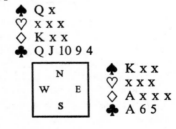

♠ K x x
♡ x x x
◇ A x x x
♣ A 6 5

Bidding :

South	West	North	East
One Spade	No Bid	Two Clubs	No Bid
Two No-Trumps		Three No-Trumps	

West opens the Knave of Hearts. Declarer wins with the Queen and plays the King of Clubs, followed by another. If West has played high–low, East must hold up his Ace once more. But if West did not peter, showing three Clubs, East should seize the trick at once. Now declarer can only have a doubleton and need never get into dummy at all. There is no point in letting him steal a trick for nothing. What is more, East does not want declarer to play the Spades from the table. And that is what he may well do if East ducks—unnecessarily—on the second round of Clubs.

Signalling tells East just what he wants to know: whether declarer has two Clubs or three. It enables him to COUNT.

With four of a suit, the usual practice is still to peter. Partner can usually work out which is which.

Switching

Returning partner's suit is a commendable practice, because it usually pays. But it is not one of the seven deadly virtues, and no stigma attaches to the man who deviates. Like everything else, it calls for the exercise of judgment. Test yours on this deal.

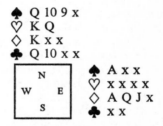

♠ Q 10 9 x
♡ K Q
◇ K x x
♣ Q 10 x x

♠ A x x
♡ x x x x
◇ A Q J x
♣ x x

North raises South's non-vulnerable No-Trump (12–14 points) to Three, and West leads a small Spade. What exactly do you do as East?

Clearly there can be no future for the defence in Spades. Neither is there any point in holding up the Ace. You should reason like this: " West can't have much, but there is just room in his hand for a King—an Ace even. I hope so anyway, for if he has no high card at all, we are sunk. Now what shall I play back? A Heart is quite safe. It will give nothing

157

away. But neither will it do any good. Our one chance is to collect three tricks in Diamonds. So, here she goes."

You play a small Diamond, allowing declarer to win the trick. But now the table's holding is reduced to K x (or x x). If declarer is not in a position to rattle off nine tricks and has to let in West—with the King of Clubs maybe—the contract is broken.

The next example is a little more difficult.

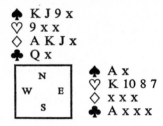

♠ K J 9 x
♡ 9 x x
◇ A K J x
♣ Q x

♠ A x
♡ K 10 8 7
◇ x x x
♣ A x x x

West opens the deuce of Spades against Three No-Trumps and declarer plays dummy's nine. This is the moment for reflection. Afterwards it will be too late.

Obviously a sustained attack on the Spades will not defeat the contract. Should East duck, just to see what suit South goes for himself? Perish the thought. Spades and Diamonds look like yielding him six or seven tricks, and given TIME, he is certain to develop two or three more. That tempo is too precious to lose. So up with the Ace of Spades.

To what suit should East switch? A Club would be bad for several reasons. First, it is tactically wrong to play *up to* an enemy's honour. With K x x declarer would make two tricks instead of one. Secondly, East has no middle cards in the suit, so there is correspondingly less to develop. Thirdly, the Ace of Clubs is valuable as an entry. Hug it closely.

A Heart, then, sticks out a couple of miles. But which one? That is the crux of the hand.

Normally, the fourth highest is the correct lead. But it has been observed already that this does not apply to a sequence; or to an interior sequence, like K J 10 x x. Then the second highest card is led in the hope of trapping the Queen. Sitting over dummy's nine, East's Heart holding should be treated like

158

an interior sequence. Lead the ten. If partner has the Ace or the Queen, it will work out in much the same way. Declarer's Knave can be caught in a pincer movement and East will remain with a *tenace* over dummy's nine.

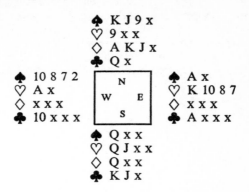

Work out the different possibilities:

(a) If South does not cover the ten, he loses three Heart tricks immediately and is one down in top tricks.

(b) If he covers, West wins with the Ace and returns another Heart. East's seven drives out declarer's second honour and the defence still collect three Heart tricks.

That ten play is rather advanced, not because it is complicated, but because it calls for the exercise of imagination. To exploit a tenace position partner must have the right card. Therefore, assume that he has it. One of the vital ingredients of good defence is wishful thinking. Optimists expect their partners to turn up with good hands. But it takes good players to place their partners with particular cards. Here is another instance.

Q x x

A J 9 2

When West sees that he must somehow grab four tricks quickly to break the contract, he should lead the Knave, hoping—or rather assuming—that East holds K x x. If dummy's Queen goes up, East covers and returns a small one *through* declarer's ten. If the Queen does not go up, West leads a small one to his partner's King.

Of course, these plays don't always come off. But when it looks as if declarer can collect his quota of tricks, it is time to take a chance. More often than not, it will be a case of " Heads you win, tails you don't lose." And what could be fairer than that?

Résumé

(1) In opening partner's suit, play the top from a doubleton or from three small. But lead the lowest of three cards headed by one of the four top honours (e.g., K x x or Q x x).

(2) The above applies to suit contracts as well as to No Trumps. But with this exception: from A x x (x) lead the *Ace* against a suit contract.

(3) Holding four or more cards in partner's suit, it is usual to lead the fourth highest.

(4) When partner opens your suit against No-Trumps, and you have insufficient entries to set it up by yourself, *duck* on the first round. This will allow partner—even if he started with a doubleton—to lead the suit again, should he get in first. Ducking keeps communications open for one extra round.

(5) To prevent or nullify ducking plays by declarer, second hand may have to play high. This situation arises, when the table shows up with no apparent entry, and a suit which invites finesses for split honours (e.g., A J 10 x x). West should play the King from K x or K x x, and the Queen from Q x or Q x x.

(6) When the table is short of entries and declarer seeks to set up dummy's long suit, defenders should *hold up* the controlling card or cards. The purpose is to exhaust declarer of that suit and break up his communications with dummy.

(7) By signalling, defenders can tell each other *how long* the master card(s) should be held up. With a doubleton or four, peter. With three, play the smallest first. This enables partner to count the suit in declarer's hand.

(8) Returning partner's suit is not always the best policy. When dummy shows up with length or strength in that suit, and you can see a more promising line of attack, don't hesitate to switch.

(9) Always defend on the assumption that partner holds the right card—or cards—to break the contract. This is particularly important, when declarer's chances look good, and only specific cards in partner's hand can bring about his defeat.

161

Exercises

(1) Partner, East, opened One Diamond. South bid One No-Trump, and all passed. Sitting West, what do you lead from:

(a) ♠ A Q 4 3 2 ♡ 9 8 7 ◇ J 10 ♣ 4 3 2
(b) ♠ Q 7 6 4 3 ♡ K 4 2 ◇ J 10 ♣ 4 3 2
(c) ♠ Q J 10 6 2 ♡ 5 4 2 ◇ A 2 ♣ 4 3 2
(d) ♠ Q 7 4 2 ♡ 9 7 3 ◇ K 10 4 ♣ 4 3 2

(2) Bidding:

North	East	South	West
One Club	One Spade	Two No-Trumps	No Bid
Three No-Trumps			

West leads the seven of Spades.

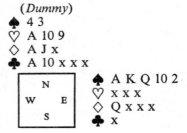

(*Dummy*)
♠ 4 3
♡ A 10 9
◇ A J x
♣ A 10 x x x

♠ A K Q 10 2
♡ x x x
◇ Q x x x
♣ x

What should East play?

(3) South opens Two No-Trumps and North raises to Three. West leads the Knave of Clubs.

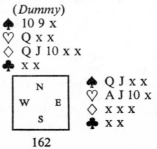

(*Dummy*)
♠ 10 9 x
♡ Q x x
◇ Q J 10 x x
♣ x x

♠ Q J x x
♡ A J 10 x
◇ x x x
♣ x x

Declarer wins the first trick with the Queen, and plays off the Ace and King of Diamonds on which West discards the eight, then the seven. At trick four declarer leads the King of Hearts. What card should East play?

(4) Bidding:

South	West	North	East
One Club	No Bid	One Heart	No Bid
Three Clubs	No Bid	Three Diamonds	No Bid
Three No-Trumps			

West leads the six of Spades.

(*Dummy*)
♠ 4 2
♡ K x x x x
♢ K Q x x
♣ x x

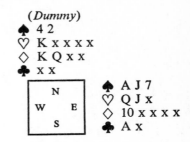

♠ A J 7
♡ Q J x
♢ 10 x x x x
♣ A x

What card should East play?

(5) The contract is Three No-Trumps by South. East bid One Heart over North's opening of One Diamond, and West duly opens the eight of Hearts. Declarer plays low from dummy.

(*Dummy*)
♠ Q J 10
♡ 9 4 2
♢ A K x x
♣ A Q x

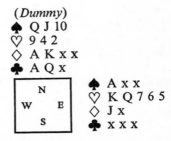

♠ A x x
♡ K Q 7 6 5
♢ J x
♣ x x x

What card should East play to the first trick?

(6) After opening One Heart, South ends up as declarer in Three No-Trumps. West leads the Knave of Spades and declarer plays low from dummy.

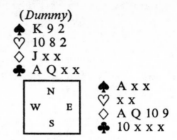

(*Dummy*)
♠ K 9 2
♡ 10 8 2
◇ J x x
♣ A Q x x

♠ A x x
♡ x x
◇ A Q 10 9
♣ 10 x x x

(*a*) What card should East play to the first trick?
(*b*) What card should East play when he gains the lead?

(7) Bidding:

South	West	North	East
One Diamond	One Heart	Two Clubs	No Bid
Three No-Trumps			

Declarer wins the opening Heart lead with the King and plays a small Club.

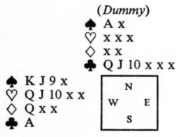

(*Dummy*)
♠ A x
♡ x x x
◇ x x
♣ Q J 10 x x x

♠ K J 9 x
♡ Q J 10 x x
◇ Q x x
♣ A

What card should West play at trick three?

DUMMY PLAY

CHAPTER XI

Reading Defenders' Cards

This chapter is about the supernatural. To be more precise, it is about that which appears supernatural—the knack of dropping singleton Kings, catching Queens and guessing which poker-faced opponent has that all-important Knave.

This is known as card reading, and is much more rewarding than catching an inadvertent glimpse of opponents' cards. It also needs greater skill. But that is by the way.

Like lesser mortals, Bridge players are a lazy lot. They don't bother when they don't have to. If the contract is there anyway, why worry whether East had six Spades or five? Or whether or not that Queen of Diamonds would have dropped?

But often the whole contract hinges on " guessing ", for as someone once remarked, it is easier to play well when you see all four hands.

The expert is in the habit of counting each suit as it develops. He observes that East showed out on the second round of Spades and deduces that West must have had five. He makes a mental note of the 3–3 Heart break. If West also follows to three rounds of Diamonds, he is marked with at most a doubleton Club. It must be so, because the other three suits account for eleven of his cards.

Counting the hand is the natural sequel to tuning-in to the bidding, a process of which much has already been said in our chapters on Defence. The bidding gives indications of who has what and how much. The play to the first few tricks provides clues. By the time half the cards have been played, clues and indications are replaced by hard facts.

Let us try it out in practice.

♠ J x x
♡ x x x x
◇ x x
♣ A Q 10 8

♠ A K x x x x
♡ Q
◇ A x
♣ x x x x

With part-scores of 80 and 90 about, and North–South vulnerable, the bidding takes this form:

East (dealer)	*South*	*West*	*North*
One Heart	One Spade	No Bid	No Bid
Two Diamonds	No Bid	No Bid	Two Spades
Three Diamonds	Three Spades	Four Diamonds	No Bid
No Bid	Four Spades	No Bid	No Bid

West opens the ten of Hearts. Declarer ruffs the second Heart and lays down the Ace and King of trumps. On the second Spade, West shows out.

Take declarer's chair. Gaze into your little crystal and make a prophecy. Will you make that contract? Does it need any guessing or any " luck "? If gazing does not help, throw the crystal away, and COUNT THE HAND.

You have already lost a Heart, and you are bound to lose a trump and a Diamond. So everything depends on not losing a Club. Is that possible? Or rather, is it likely?

Before answering, go over the bidding and the play to the first four tricks. If you have plenty of time, set out the various card combinations, which would enable you to bring

166

in the entire Club suit. West could have the K J bare. Or East could have a blank honour and you could guess which one. Sometimes you see declarer in a long and agonising trance trying to do just that; conjuring up all the possible combinations. It is hard work. And it is nerve racking for dummy. In the present case it is also quite unnecessary. Because, if you COUNT the hand, you will know exactly what to do, and why. Let us try it together. We know that East has three Spades, since West showed out after following to the first round. What else do we know? Think back. East opened One Heart. Then he bid Two Diamonds and Three Diamonds, all on his own. He has clearly shown a five-card Diamond suit. And he bid Hearts first. So he should not be shorter in Hearts than Diamonds. In fact, East should have ten red cards. Add the three Spades and you have his whole hand. Thirteen cards *without* a Club. Knowing that, you can finesse the eight of Clubs confidently on the first round. It is rather spectacular and may bring forth a gasp of admiration—or suspicion—from the onlookers. But for all that, it is simple enough, *if you count the hand*.

There is just an outside chance that we may have miscounted. Perhaps, with four Hearts and five Diamonds, East opened the higher-ranking suit first. The practice has little to commend it, but some players go in for it, so the possibility cannot be ignored altogether. Let us cross-check. If East has four Hearts only, West must have four as well. In that case he would have supported Hearts rather than Diamonds, his partner's second suit. Also, from four, he would have led the fourth highest, not the ten. Since he raised Diamonds, not Hearts, and since he led the ten, it is pretty certain that he started with not more than three Hearts. Therefore East had not less than five.

COUNTING THE HAND is like having a cold bath—difficult and a little frightening, until you get into the habit. Then it comes quite easily and leaves you with a pleasant tingling sensation when it is over.

While we rub ourselves down after that first icy plunge, we can glance at all four hands.

167

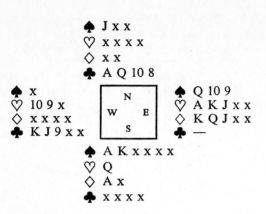

♠ J x x
♡ x x x x
◇ x x
♣ A Q 10 8

♠ x
♡ 10 9 x
◇ x x x x
♣ K J 9 x x

♠ Q 10 9
♡ A K J x x
◇ K Q J x x
♣ —

♠ A K x x x x
♡ Q
◇ A x
♣ x x x x

Locating Missing Honours

The water beckons again.

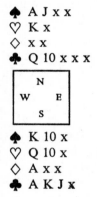

♠ A J x x
♡ K x
◇ x x
♣ Q 10 x x x

♠ K 10 x
♡ Q 10 x
◇ A x x
♣ A K J x

Bidding:

West (dealer)	North	East	South
No Bid	No Bid	No Bid	One Club
One Diamond	One Spade	No Bid	Two No-Trumps
No Bid	Four Clubs	No Bid	Four Spades
No Bid	Five Clubs		

West opens the King of Diamonds.   Declarer wins, draws

trumps and plays a Heart. West, who comes in with the Ace,
cashes the Queen of Diamonds, and seeing his partner drop the
Knave, leads a third Diamond. Declarer ruffs in dummy and
East discards a small Spade.

What now? A Heart and a Diamond have been lost, so all
will depend on guessing who holds that Queen of Spades.
COUNT the points and you will be lucky. What are the
clues? West, who bid One Diamond on the second round,
turned up with K Q 10 x x x in Diamonds and with the Ace of
Hearts. Should he have the Queen of Spades, too? Hardly
likely. With 11 points in top cards and a good six-card suit,
he would have surely opened the bidding. Yet he passed.
That pass is the fatal piece of evidence incriminating East. He
must have that Queen of Spades. The finesse is marked.

Here is another example on the same lines. East, as dealer,
non-vulnerable, opens One No Trump, promising 12–14 points.
South calls Two Spades and all pass.

♠ 10 9 x
♡ J x x
◇ K J x
♣ x x x x

	N	
W		E
	S	

♠ K Q J x x
♡ x x x
◇ A 10 9
♣ K x

West leads the deuce of Hearts. East's Ace and King
capture the first two tricks, and at the next West is back on
play with the Heart Queen. The Club switch is won by East's
Ace, and declarer comes in for the first time with the King of
Clubs. The initiative passes once more to East with the Ace
of trumps, but declarer ruffs the third Club and draws trumps,
finding a 3–2 split.

Nothing to spare now. South has lost five tricks and must make the rest. That means that he cannot afford to be "unlucky" about the Queen of Diamonds. Seat yourself in declarer's chair and do the guessing. Who has the Diamond Queen? Go over the first few tricks and that Queen will cast her shadow on your radar screen. Well, where is she?

Yes, you are quite right. West is the culprit. East has shown up with the Ace and King of Hearts, the Ace of Clubs and the Ace of trumps. That is already one point in excess of a maximum non-vulnerable No-Trump. He cannot have another 2 points up his sleeve.

The next hand is more difficult. If you work it out by yourself, you will be doing really well.

The bidding is the same as before. This time, however, East is vulnerable and his No-Trump should be worth 16–18 points.

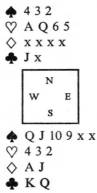

♠ 4 3 2
♡ A Q 6 5
◇ x x x x
♣ J x

♠ Q J 10 9 x x
♡ 4 3 2
◇ A J
♣ K Q

CONTRACT: Two Spades by South.

West opens the deuce of Diamonds, and East's King falls to South's Ace. West comes in once more—with the Queen of Diamonds. East is on play three times—with the two top Spades and with the Ace of Clubs. The trumps break 3–1, the singleton being with West. After drawing trumps, declarer's position is as follows:

♠ —
♡ A Q 6 5
◇ x
♣ —

```
      N
   W     E
      S
```

♠ 9 x
♡ 4 3 2
◇ —
♣ —

South can afford to lose one trick, and one trick only, and prospects are admittedly poor. The odds are against declarer. He will probably go down. But what is his best chance?

Let us COUNT. East has produced 7 points in Spades, 3 in Diamonds and 4 in Clubs, a total of 14. The Knave of Hearts would bring it up to 15. Definitely not enough for a vulnerable No-Trump. Therefore, he must have the King of Hearts. So finessing the Queen can do no good. It is no longer a case of guessing, but of predestination. Is there, then, no hope at all?

Yes, there is one chance. East *may* have a doubleton King. He could have opened a No-Trump on a 5-3-3-2 shape. The King of Hearts, without the Knave, would give him a 17 count. If that is his hand—and it is not particularly unlikely—the contract can still be made. Declarer plays the Ace of Hearts and another, hoping to bring down a doubleton King.

On the last deal, COUNTING the points was enough to ensure success. Declarer was betting on a certainty. This time there is no certain way of making the contract. But there is a certain way of *not* making it—the Heart finesse. All declarer can do is to back the possible against the impossible, and that is always a paying proposition.

The vast majority of Bridge players would finesse that Queen of Hearts and afterwards blame their bad luck. They would argue, and rightly, that other things being equal, a Queen finesse is a fifty-fifty chance. Alas, all too often, other things are not equal. Reading the cards shows where and how they are unequal. Possessed of this knowledge, declarer can play with the odds in his favour. The Principality of Monaco has existed for generations on just that.

Apply the principles brought out by the last hand to the next. It is a teaser, and you are not expected to get it too easily. You have been warned. Now for the springboard.

Any Chance is Better Than No Chance

After an opening of Three Spades by West, North–South reach Six Hearts. The King of Spades is led.

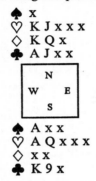

♠ x
♡ K J x x x
◇ K Q x
♣ A J x x

	N	
W		E
	S	

♠ A x x
♡ A Q x x x
◇ x x
♣ K 9 x

That little Club in South's hand provides the only moment of anxiety. After drawing trumps, declarer plays a Diamond, hoping to find West with the Ace. That would provide a winner in dummy to take care of the redundant Club. Unfortunately, East turns up with the Ace and returns the deuce of Spades. Declarer ruffs in dummy, plays off the Diamond honour, ruffs a small one and trumps his last Spade on the table.

By this time he discovers that:

(*a*) West had seven Spades. East showed out on the third round.

(*b*) West had two Hearts. He followed twice.

(*c*) West also had three Diamonds—maybe four. He followed three times.

How does all that help to dispose of that accursed Club?

172

COUNTING has shown at least twelve cards, that are not Clubs, in West's hand—seven Spades, three Diamonds and two Hearts. So he either started with one Club or with a void. If East has Q 10 to umpteen, nothing can be done. But there is just a hope—admittedly a poor one—that West was dealt a singleton honour. If he is in his best form, South will play for this chance, and lay down the Ace. There is a possibility that the Queen will drop and another that the ten will come down. Either will do. Should it be the ten, declarer will play the Knave and *run* it, unless East covers.

COUNTING THE HAND enables declarer to create an opportunity where none would otherwise exist.

Both the last deals illustrate a principle, which has been laid down more than once already in these pages: no matter how bleak the outlook, always *assume* a distribution, which makes the contract *possible*. When all else fails, visualise the card combinations you need and put both your shirts on them.

Finding the Gentleman

The water is not so cold this end. Try it.

♠ x x x
♡ 9 x x x
◇ K x x
♣ A x x

♠ K Q x x
♡ K Q J
◇ A x
♣ K Q 10 x

173

Bidding:

West (dealer)	North	East	South
One Spade	No Bid	No Bid	Two No-Trumps
No Bid	Three No-Trumps		

West opens the Knave of Spades and East plays the nine.

A rapid survey promises fair weather. Any one of four things will bring home the bacon. Should the Hearts or Clubs break or should the ten of Hearts or Knave of Clubs come down, there will be nothing to do except add up the score. Meanwhile, as a matter of routine, scrutinise closely East's nine of Spades. It can't possibly be a peter. So it is undoubtedly a singleton. And this is borne out by the bidding, and the lead, which suggests the top of an interior sequence— presumably A J 10 x x. West *could* have had a four-card Spade suit. But there are so few high cards out that a little shape is to be expected.

Make a mental note: West has five Spades and East a singleton.

Attack the Hearts first. West wins on the second round and plays back a Heart. East shows out.

Make another mental note: West was dealt four Hearts and East a doubleton.

Now the water is getting quite warm. Of course, the odds are that East has more Clubs than West. Therefore, there is a strong temptation to play the King of Clubs, a Club to the Ace and—if the Knave does not drop—to finesse the ten. It is a good chance—but not nearly as good as a certainty.

Lay down the Ace of Diamonds. If West follows, the contract is as certain as the winner of the three-thirty—after the race. Can you see why?

By this time you have counted the hand. Naturally. So you know that West had ten cards (five Spades, four Hearts and one Diamond) that were not Clubs.

Apply the *coup de grace*. Play off the King of Diamonds and all will be revealed. If West shows out, his remaining three cards must all be Clubs. The suit will break 3–3. If West follows, he cannot have more than two Clubs. King, Ace and the ten finesse will—inevitably must—yield four tricks.

Here is another chance to bet—after the race, of course.

♠ Q 10 x
♡ 5 4 3 2
♦ A Q x
♣ A J x

♠ A K J x x x
♡ x x
♦ 10 x x
♣ K 9

CONTRACT. Four Spades.

West leads the King, then the Ace of Hearts. East plays high–low and West leads a third Heart, declarer ruffing East's Knave.

A short huddle is indicated. East was clearly dealt the Queen of Hearts. Otherwise, he would not have petered. Besides West would have played the Queen, if he had it.

A myopic glance at the contract suggests that it will depend on one of two finesses. If West has the King of Diamonds, all is well. If not, maybe West has the Queen of Clubs. Then the second Diamond loser can be discarded. It is a good chance. Three to one on. Your horse is many lengths in front and the bookies are looking pale. But why not wait till it is past the post? It is so much safer.

This time there is no need to count all four suits. Just float on your back and think of the Queen of Hearts. You have placed her in East's hand. How about it?

Draw trumps, ending in dummy, and lead a Heart. As soon as that Queen materialises, throw away a Diamond. It is no good to you. The technical term is " throwing a loser on a loser ". And the advantage is that East will have to lead. With no more Spades or Hearts about, his choice will be limited to playing into one or other of two tenaces—Diamonds or Clubs. Either will do.

The success of the contract can be assured by placing one

card—the Queen of Hearts. Once her whereabouts are known, there is no trouble. And the Queen can be located for a certainty, simply by *noticing* the cards played to the first three tricks.

Betting with the Odds

There is no gainsaying it, guessing is anathema to the expert. He likes to bet on certainties. When nothing is certain, he does the next best thing by manipulating the odds in his favour.

The idea is to back the probable against the improbable. If two Aces are missing, the chances are that the same defender won't have both. When the count shows that West has two Hearts and East five, the odds are that any one specific Heart will be with East, not with West.

Here is an illustration, as simple as it is difficult. Simple, because anyone can do it—if he thinks of it. Difficult, because he won't think of it—unless he is an expert. Even experts don't do these things through sheer brilliance, but because they have acquired certain healthy, and highly profitable, habits. READING THE CARDS is one of them.

West leads the Knave of Spades against Four Hearts.

♠ A x
♡ Q J x x
◇ K J x
♣ K x x x

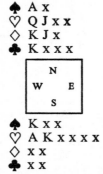

♠ K x x
♡ A K x x x x
◇ x x
♣ x x

If the Ace of Clubs is right, all is well. If not, the contract will depend on guessing the Diamonds. How, then, should we set about it? The man in the street will draw trumps quickly, sway in his chair slowly, and mutter something like : " Well, it's six of one and half a dozen of the other."

But is it?

To the expert there is a vital difference between the Club and Diamond positions. The latter will be the subject of guesswork. The former lends itself only to prayer. The Club must be played *first*, and the reason is that it will provide a *clue* to the Diamonds.

If East has the Ace of Clubs, West will be credited with the Ace of Diamonds. In other words, declarer will go up with the Diamond King, not the Knave. The procedure cannot be reversed, because locating the Ace of Clubs won't help. It is either right or wrong, and that is all there is to it.

Note that good play will not necessarily succeed. East may have both the Aces. But it still pays to back the *best* chance.

Fix the odds on this one.

♠ Q J x x
♡ x x x
◇ Q x
♣ A J x x

N
W E
S

♠ A K x x x
♡ x x
◇ A J x
♣ K 10 x

CONTRACT: Four Spades, reached without interference.

West opens the King and Ace of Hearts, followed by a small one. Declarer ruffs East's Knave, draws trumps and loses the Diamond finesse to West's King. A second Diamond comes back.

Everything now hinges on the Queen of Clubs.

Where is she?

Have you observed the fall of the cards? Then you are in a position to make a pretty shrewd guess. West has pleaded guilty to 7 points in Hearts and to the King of Diamonds—10 in all. East is blameless, except for the Knave and—by inference—the Queen of Hearts. It is more likely that the defenders' high card strength was divided between them 10–5

177

than 12–3. Therefore, the better chance is to play East for the Queen of Clubs.

Inference

To conclude, a nice, cold shower. COUNTING and INFERENCE are so closely bound up that sometimes they overlap.

When a defender shows out, you can COUNT. When he leads a King, and the Queen is in dummy, you INFER that he has the Ace. And when he refuses to lead something, which shrieks to be played, there is another INFERENCE to be drawn. Try it out on this Four Spades contract.

Negative Inference

♠ J x x
♡ J x
◇ A J x x
♣ K Q x x

♠ A K 10 x x
♡ K Q x x x
◇ K x
♣ x

At game-all the bidding went:

South	West	North	East
One Spade	No Bid	Two Clubs	No Bid
Two Hearts	No Bid	Two No-Trumps	No Bid
Four Hearts	No Bid	Four Spades	No Bid

West opens a Heart to East's Ace and ruffs the Heart return. East wins the next trick with the Ace of Clubs and leads back another Club.

Declarer has a surfeit of tricks. Only the uncertain trump position causes him to fidget in his seat. To make the hand he must deal effectively with that Queen of Spades. If East

178

has her, it will be a case of finessing. But if West was dealt Q x x, she will come down tamely on the second round—for West has ruffed once.

Which shall it be?

The COUNT shows that West had one Heart and East five. Clearly the chances are that West is the longer in Spades, and that, in turn, suggests playing for the drop. So far, so good. But there is one conflicting piece of evidence—East's curious behaviour at trick four.

Why did he not lead another Heart to give his partner a chance to ruff again? That Club return seems fatuous. Not a hope that West can trump it. No point in preparing a ruff for himself, since if West gets in at all, the contract will be beaten anyway. When the defence does something palpably senseless—like that Club return—suspicion is the better part of discretion. East must have had a reason, and it could only have been the fear that a third Heart would give the game away. Sitting with Q x x, East would have good cause to fear just that. He knows from the bidding that his partner is left with one trump only and fears that he will be unable to ruff higher than dummy's Knave. That will reveal everything, and the Queen of trumps, naked and defenceless, will be subjected to a fate worse than a guess. She will be finessed for a certainty. To avoid exposing his Queen, East gallantly plays a Club.

If declarer draws the right INFERENCE, he will take the finesse and make his contract. If he plays for the drop, chivalry will score an undeserved triumph and East will tell his wife that he did something very clever.

The moral of the story is that in reading the cards—counting points, placing honours and the rest—you must neglect none of the evidence. The leads that are *not* made are as revealing as the ones that are.

Résumé

(1) To find out how the cards are distributed, experts are in the habit of COUNTING the suits, and the high cards, automatically, as the play develops.

(2) The COUNT, combined with indications given by the bidding—or lack of bidding—can give a picture of the hands, enabling declarer to read the cards of his opponents.

(3) When a defender shows up with all the strength, which his bid—or pass—suggests, declarer should place missing high cards with the other defender, and play accordingly.

(4) To complete the COUNT, declarer may play a card—or cards—for the sole purpose of discovering whether both defenders can follow (e.g., West has shown nine black cards. If he follows to two Hearts, he cannot have more than a doubleton Diamond).

(5) When there are no indications, declarer plays on the assumption that the outstanding high cards are evenly divided. Trying to locate the Ace in one suit, declarer may first play another suit, in which he is missing the Ace. His object will be to GAIN INFORMATION about the probable distribution of honour cards between the defenders.

(6) When one of the defenders has greater length in a suit than his partner, the odds are that any given card will be in that defender's hand.

Exercises

(1)

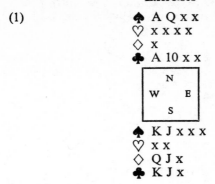

♠ A Q x x
♡ x x x x
◇ x
♣ A 10 x x

♠ K J x x x
♡ x x
◇ Q J x
♣ K J x

Bidding:

West	North	East	South
One Heart	No Bid	One No-Trump	No Bid
Two Diamonds	No Bid	No Bid	Two Spades
Three Diamonds	Four Spades	No Bid	No Bid

The trumps break 2–2.
Can you make certain of the contract?

(2) The contract is Six No-Trumps.

♠ K Q x
♡ A J
◇ A Q x
♣ x x x x x

♠ A 10 x x
♡ K Q x x
◇ K J x
♣ A x

181

West opens the King of Clubs and East shows out on the first round.

Declarer wins and plays off the red suits. West shows out on the third Heart and the second Diamond.

(a) Is it certain that declarer can make his contract?

(b) If West discards four Clubs, which suit should South play?

(3)

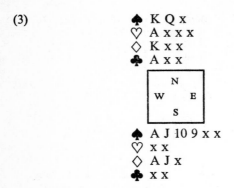

♠ K Q x
♡ A x x x
◇ K x x
♣ A x x

♠ A J 10 9 x x
♡ x x
◇ A J x
♣ x x

The contract is Four Spades. West, who had opened the bidding with Three Hearts, leads the Heart King.

(a) The Diamond finesse fails. How can declarer make certain of his contract?

(b) Which ten tricks will he make?

(4)

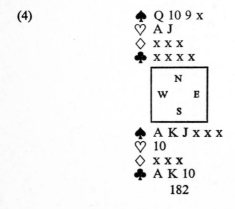

♠ Q 10 9 x
♡ A J
◇ x x x
♣ x x x x

♠ A K J x x x
♡ 10
◇ x x x
♣ A K 10

182

The bidding was:

West	North	East	South
Four Hearts	No Bid	No Bid	Four Spades
No Bid			

West leads the Ace, King and Queen of Diamonds, then the King of Hearts. South draws trumps. West follows to three rounds.

(*a*) Is declarer likely to make his contract?
(*b*) In which hand should he win his third trump trick?
(*c*) How should he play the Clubs?

(5)

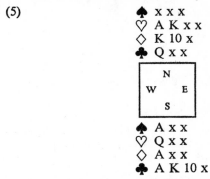

♠ x x x
♡ A K x x
♢ K 10 x
♣ Q x x

♠ A x x
♡ Q x x
♢ A x x
♣ A K 10 x

West opens the deuce of Spades against Three No-Trumps, East follows three times. Playing match-point scoring, declarer tries to make as many tricks as possible. After winning the third Spade, he attacks Hearts, but finds that East shows out on the third round.

What should declarer do next?

(6)

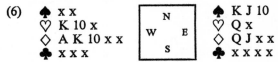

♠ x x
♡ K 10 x
♢ A K 10 x x
♣ x x x

♠ K J 10
♡ Q x
♢ Q J x x
♣ x x x x

Bidding:

North	East	South	West
One Club	No Bid	No Bid	One Diamond
No Bid	Two Diamonds	No Bid	No Bid
No Bid			

North leads the four top Clubs, South follows twice, then discards two small Hearts. West ruffs the fourth Club, draws trumps in two rounds, and leads a Heart up to dummy. The Queen wins. The next trick is a small Heart on which declarer plays the ten and North the Knave. North leads the Ace of Hearts.

Where are the Ace and the Queen of Spades?

(7) ♠ K 10 7
    ♡ A Q J 10 3
    ◇ K Q
    ♣ 6 4 2

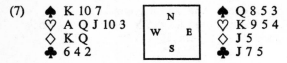

    ♠ Q 8 5 3
    ♡ K 9 5 4
    ◇ J 5
    ♣ J 7 5

Game All.

Bidding:

North	*East*	*South*	*West*
One No-Trump	No Bid	Two Diamonds	Two Hearts
(16–18 points)			
No Bid	No Bid	No Bid	

North leads the King of Clubs, followed by the Ace and a small Club. South wins with the Queen and leads a Diamond, which North takes with the Ace. North leads another Diamond.

Which card should declarer play from his hand, after drawing trumps?

DEFENCE

CHAPTER XII

Reading Declarer's Cards

Sorcery remains the theme in this chapter as it was in the last. If declarer can resort to magic to see our cards, we can do the same to him in defence.

From the first page, of course, we had our suspicions. It was apparent that he eavesdropped on our passes, peeped at our discards, and with malice aforethought, exploited every clue. The last chapter has finally torn the mask from his face. Not content with listening and looking, we now know that he counts, infers and draws conclusions. That is why those doubleton honours fall into his lap. That is why those deep finesses come off as in a dream. In short, that is why he is so infernally lucky.

Fortunately, we can use the same methods. Tuning-in to the bidding has already become a habit. And since, as a rule, declarer's side does more bidding than ours, tapping the wires should help us more than it helps him.

We note what values he has announced. Dummy is on view. When declarer has shown up with all he has promised, we may expect to find partner with the missing cards.

And, of course, we can count the suits, as well as the honours —just as declarer did in the last chapter. Finally, we can draw inferences from his line of play. Taking it all in all, we can base our defence on a pretty good picture of declarer's hand. And with every card played, the details fill in and the picture grows more vivid. From inspired guesswork we go on to read a well-charted map.

Let us read the cards on this deal :

(*Dummy*)
♠ K Q x
♡ J x
◇ Q 9 8 x x
♣ Q x x

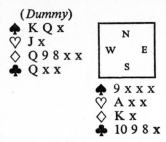

♠ 9 x x x
♡ A x x
◇ K x
♣ 10 9 8 x

Bidding :

East (dealer)	*South*	*West*	*North*
One Spade	No Bid	Two Diamonds	No Bid
Two Spades	No Bid	Three Spades	No Bid
Three No-Trumps			

South makes the obvious lead of the Club ten. North wins with the Ace and returns the deuce. Declarer takes the trick with the King of Clubs and leads a small Heart up to dummy's Knave.

Is everything clear? If you can read declarer's hand at this particular moment, you can break the contract for a certainty. If not, the game is lost.

Let every card tell its story. First, partner's deuce of Clubs. Does it show a four-card suit, a doubleton or three?

With three, partner would have returned the highest, not the deuce. So it is not that.

Had he held four Clubs, he would have also held the Knave. It must be so, for declarer would then have two only, and he has played two Clubs—but not the Knave—already. Besides, if partner had the Knave, he would not have played the Ace at the first trick. A finesse against dummy would be obligatory. So it follows that partner had neither three Clubs, nor four. Consequently declarer must have four himself. And that means three club winners—the King, the Queen and the Knave.

Next comes that little Heart. Why on earth should declarer play a Heart at all? His longest suit is undoubtedly Spades. He bid them twice, showing five cards. Is he missing the Ace? Then, surely the obvious play would have been to clear his

186

longest suit. The fact that a Spade was *not* played carries the most significant message of the hand. Declarer must have A J x x x in Spades and can COUNT eight certain tricks. He is sure of five Spades and three Clubs. That Heart—if he can make it—will be the ninth, fatal trick.

From the bidding we know that East has a stop in Hearts. Without it, he would not have ventured into Three No-Trumps. That stopper is almost certainly K Q x.

By this time, the hand should hold no further secrets for us. Every card can be placed. Work it out. What is declarer's hand? We have already taken a look at three suits. The Spades are: A J x x x or A 10 x x x; the Hearts K Q x; and the Clubs K J x x. That leaves one Diamond and one only. Which one is it? Assuredly not the Ace, for then declarer would have nine tricks on top. And as long as it is not the Ace, we don't care.

Now the defence is crystal clear. That Ace of Hearts must go up like lightning. The King of Diamonds will follow like a peal of thunder, removing declarer's singleton. Then a small Diamond will pierce dummy's Q 9 8 x x through the gizzard. Having read declarer's hand, we know partner's. He started with five Diamonds, headed by the Ace.

COUNTING THE HAND, tuning in to the play, as well as to the bidding, saved the situation just in time. A moment's forgetfulness over that harmless-looking Heart x would have cost the contract.

The fortune teller is here again:

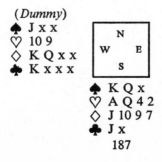

(*Dummy*)
♠ J x x
♡ 10 9
◇ K Q x x
♣ K x x x

♠ K Q x
♡ A Q 4 2
◇ J 10 9 7
♣ J x

Bidding:

East (dealer)	South	West	North
One Club	No Bid	One Diamond	No Bid
One Heart	No Bid	Two Clubs	No Bid
Two No-Trumps	No Bid	Three No-Trumps	No Bid

South's first source of worry is that he is too good. Holding 13 points himself, he cannot expect partner to have more than one or two. North will never get in, so the only consideration is not to help declarer. The Knave of Diamonds is the obvious lead.

Declarer wins with the Queen on the table and runs the ten of Hearts to South's Queen.

Dummy has been visible for the past twenty seconds, and South must now do his READING and COUNTING.

What is declarer's hand? Let us take it suit by suit.

In Spades he must have the Ace. Without a stop of some sort, he would not have bid No-Trumps.

His Hearts look very much like K J to four. The bidding suggests it and the play bears it out.

We know about the Ace of Diamonds, because partner did not play it. Besides, and this applies in equal measure to Spades and Clubs, partner just cannot have as much as an Ace.

Declarer's Club holding presents, at first sight, an element of uncertainty. Is it A x x x or A Q x x? In point of fact, he is unlikely to have the Queen. That would give him a count of 18. Too much. With 18 his rebid would have been Two No-Trumps rather than One Heart.

Now we come to distribution, and here everything points to a 4–4–3–2 pattern—the most frequent of all.

Declarer must have at least four Clubs, for a " prepared " Club opening on a three-card suit is not made on strong hands. If he has five Clubs, nothing matters much anyway. The contract is unassailable.

In Hearts, he cannot possibly have more than four.

In Diamonds and Spades, declarer holds five cards, and we know from the play that the Diamond is not a singleton. Therefore he can have no more than three Spades.

Now we have the COUNT. All the relevant passages in declarer's hand have been read and we can put the question:

how does he propose to make the contract? The answer, no doubt, is that he intends to collect three Diamonds (he may even hope for four), two Hearts (three if the finesse had come off), three Clubs and the Ace of Spades.

The next question is: can he be stopped, and if so, what is the best chance?

See if you can find a way, and bear in mind that declarer has not seen your hand and does not know that all the high cards are over him.

There is no certain method. Nothing even that can be described as an odds-on chance. But by far the most promising card to play is that small Spade, away from the K Q. Hope that partner has the ten. That will be half the battle. If declarer also has the nine, victory will have been snatched from the jaws of defeat. With the nine in his hand, no declarer would be likely to play dummy's Knave. Even without the nine, only a good player would think of it.

That ten of Spades is just about the only contribution to be expected of partner—apart from the Queen of Clubs. If all goes according to plan, the ten will drive out the Ace and the defence will take two Spades, two Hearts and a Club. Declarer cannot get home without bringing in the Clubs. He must lose one trick in the suit, and it will be the setting trick.

The deal illustrates the advantage of reading the cards at the first opportunity; and the importance, stressed more than once in these pages, of *visualising whatever combination of cards is needed to break the contract*.

COUNTING the hand set the stage for success. But it was the ethereal ten of Spades which clinched it.

Let us take another look through the backs of the cards.

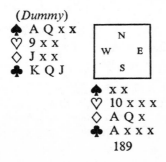

(*Dummy*)
♠ A Q x x
♡ 9 x x
◇ J x x
♣ K Q J

♠ x x
♡ 10 x x x
◇ A Q x
♣ A x x x

189

Bidding:

West	North	East	South
One No-Trump	No Bid	Two Spades	No Bid

South leads his fourth highest Heart and sees dummy go down with a minimum non-vulnerable No-Trump—13 points. North's Queen falls to East's Ace and declarer draws trumps in two rounds with his King and Knave. Next comes a Club and . . . ?

What was in declarer's hand?

Five Spades, headed by the K J, stand out conspicuously. The fifth trump is as vivid as the rest, for self-respecting players do not bid four-card suits over their partners' No-Trumps.

In Hearts we can distinguish the Ace and Knave, though the light is too bad to see whether there is a little x beside them. The outlines of that Knave are especially clear. Partner put the Queen on the first trick, and of course he would play the *lowest* of touching honours.

So far, the picture is not very encouraging. Declarer can take five Spades, the Ace of Hearts and—GIVEN TIME—two Clubs. That is all he needs, and he is nearly there already. Can the defence beat him to it? Are there six tricks to be gathered before eight are lost?

First, answer this question: What has declarer in Diamonds? Quite right. Nothing. He has already produced 9 points and a five-card suit. Add a King and he would not be playing the hand in a part score. The defence, then, can count on five tricks—three Diamonds, the Ace of Clubs and the King of Hearts. A little hope and imagination—the same formula as on the last deal—may cause a sixth trick to materialise out of nothing.

All hinges on whether declarer had three Hearts or the A J bare. If it is a doubleton, there is no hope—just as there is no hope if he has only two Diamonds. But if he started with A J x . . .

Play off the three Diamonds, leaving partner on play with the King. Now let him do the bright thing. He knows the position. A small Heart, away from his King, will give declarer a nasty guess. If he plays low, South will win with

190

the ten and shoot back a Heart to the King.   With the nine in dummy, it is an even-money chance.   Or is it?

It is always good to make declarer guess, for he is bound to take wrong views every now and again.   But as we saw in the last chapter, good players are more likely to make the right guess than the wrong one on a hand like this.

An expert declarer will reason: " South has already produced 10 points—the A Q of Diamonds, and the Ace of Clubs. North's share has been 5—the Queen of Hearts and the King of Diamonds.   Why should South have so much more of the good things of life than his partner—13 points, if he has the King of Hearts, to only 5?   In the absence of any evidence to the contrary, I will assume that the outstanding strength is divided more evenly, and that North has the King of Hearts. So up with the Knave."

For all that, North and South will have produced the best defence, and one that would succeed against most declarers, at least half the time.

The worst defence would be to omit reading declarer's hand.   If South does not *know* that his partner must have the King of Diamonds, he will probably play a Heart.   And then it will be all up.   The defence will fail even against a bad declarer.

To beat the next hand South must add FORETHOUGHT to the usual ingredients of CARD READING and IMAGINATION.

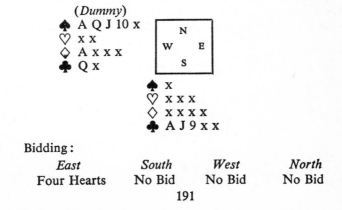

(*Dummy*)
♠ A Q J 10 x
♡ x x
◇ A x x x
♣ Q x

N
W   E
S

♠ x
♡ x x x
◇ x x x x
♣ A J 9 x x

Bidding:

East	South	West	North
Four Hearts	No Bid	No Bid	No Bid

South leads his singleton Spade. Declarer wins in dummy with the Knave and plays a trump. Partner produces an unexpected Ace and gives South his ruff.

That is two tricks, the half-way mark. Where should South look for the other two?

Ninety-nine players out of a hundred, and the other one, too, sometimes, will lay down the Ace of Clubs and look immensely pleased if partner encourages with the ten. They will hope for two Club tricks, forgetting that it would be a luxury which they neither need nor deserve.

Unless declarer has two Clubs—without the King—this play cannot succeed. He will trump the second Club and it will be all up. But the contract is always beaten, so long as declarer has even one Club. The setting trick will be a second Spade ruff. That is where the FORETHOUGHT comes in. South should lead a *small* Club, not the Ace.

It is true that if declarer holds the singleton King he will make an extra trick. But then nothing will help, anyway. Declarer must have enough winners once he gets going.

The very fact that East opened Four Hearts from hand should put South on his guard. Seven probable Hearts and at least three Spades—for the King did not fall on the second round—account for ten cards in declarer's hand, leaving only three for the minor suits.

Of course, it is tempting to cash that Ace of Clubs. But even temptation must be resisted sometimes. Count the hand, and you will know whether to yield—or whether declarer has a singleton.

Despair, not temptation, is the enemy on the next deal.

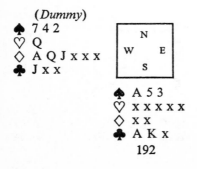

(*Dummy*)
♠ 7 4 2
♡ Q
◇ A Q J x x x
♣ J x x

♠ A 5 3
♡ x x x x x
◇ x x
♣ A K x

Bidding:

East	South	West	North
One Heart	No Bid	Two Diamonds	No Bid
Two Spades	No Bid	Three Diamonds	No Bid
Three Spades	No Bid	Four Spades	No Bid

Did you listen carefully? Then you should have a pretty good idea of East's distribution. He bid and rebid Spades, which should show a five-card suit. But he first called Hearts, and that indicates that he had more Hearts than Spades. So before the first shot is fired, South knows that declarer holds eleven cards in the majors.

On the natural lead of the King of Clubs declarer drops the Queen. What next?

The average player will finger various cards, utter subdued lamentations and switch to something else. His argument will be that to play the Ace would make the Knave good on the table, and that is something which outrages every decent instinct.

Be outraged but play the Ace. Never mind about that Knave. Declarer's Hearts are all winners, so there is nothing he can usefully discard. But if he started with two Clubs, he may be able to park one on the Ace of Diamonds.

Is that quite clear? We know that East had six cards in Hearts and five in Spades. If he was dealt a doubleton Club, he cannot have a Diamond. With Q x in Clubs, any good player will drop the Queen. It costs nothing, and it may confuse the defence. At the second trick South must clear up the position. It is now or never, and it would be fatal to be hypnotised by that meretricious Knave.

Suppose that declarer did false card with the Queen and now follows to the second round of Clubs. Can you see the way to break the contract?

Any one of those five Heart xs will ensure victory. Reading declarer's hand makes partner's an open book. He can only have a singleton Heart, and the Ace of trumps guarantees the entry needed to give him a ruff. We know that he can over-ruff the table, for even if declarer's Spades are K Q J 10 9, partner will have the eight.

It is easy to go wrong if you don't COUNT the hand. It is

193

especially easy to fall from grace at trick two by failing to take
the second Club. But that would be a policy of despair, for
unless declarer can follow suit, the contract is untouchable.

Here is another case for earphones and reading glasses.
Just for a change, West will hold the closed hand.

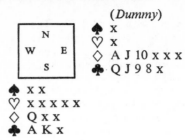

(*Dummy*)
♠ x
♡ x
◇ A J 10 x x x
♣ Q J 9 8 x

♠ x x
♡ x x x x x
◇ Q x x
♣ A K x

Bidding:

West	North	East	South
One Spade	No Bid	Two Diamonds	No Bid
Two Hearts	No Bid	Three Clubs	No Bid
Three No-Trumps			

North leads the ten of Spades. Declarer wins with the Ace
and plays the ten of Clubs. North's card is the seven.

If you have acquired the habit of COUNTING the hand,
you will know already at least eleven cards in West's hand.
The majors account for eight or nine, for he bid them both.
And since he has three Clubs, he cannot have more than two
Diamonds. How do we know that he has three Clubs, no
more and no less? That seven reveals the secret—to all those,
at least, who read Chapter X. North is signalling to show a
doubleton. His seven cannot be a singleton. If it were,
West would have four Clubs, in which case, the contract would
not be Three No-Trumps.

Having discovered—with partner's help—the distribution
of the Club suit, South holds up on the first round. That is
not difficult. The next step requires confidence—confidence
by South in his ability to read the cards correctly. After
winning the second Club, South should lead a small Diamond
—yes, right into that long and powerful suit in dummy. It
needs nerves of steel—the first time. Afterwards, it is just

habit. As West cannot have more than two Diamonds, he is not in a position to profit by the lead. And unless he has the doubleton King (the King alone would make no difference) that dummy, with two potential Club tricks, will be killed stone dead and despatched to the mortuary.

If North turns up with the King, the defence will have achieved two objectives: a Diamond trick will be set up, and communications between declarer and his dummy will be severed.

One minor point should be noted. When South comes in again, with his Queen of Diamonds perhaps, he should play a Heart, not a Spade. North's lead is almost certainly the top of a sequence, something like 10 9 8 x x (x). But he is marked with three Hearts. Why? Because West has four. With five he would have surely rebid them. If declarer's Hearts are A Q 10 x or K J x x, partner will appreciate a thrust through the soft underbelly. North can probably play a Spade himself.

A reconstruction of declarer's hand would show that he must have been dealt something like this:

♠ A K Q J x ♡ A Q x x ◇ x ♣ 10 x x

The five-card Spade suit is no certainty. He could have four. The answer to that question will emerge when West reveals whether he has one Diamond or two. With a singleton he will doubtless win the first trick with the Ace. With a doubleton he will be tempted to duck, just in case North has both the King and Queen. But that thirteenth card—Spade or Diamond—will be the only issue in doubt after North's play to the second trick.

COUNTING the hand resembles a jig-saw puzzle. As each piece is added, the others begin to fit naturally into their proper places.

We have held pretty good cards so far, and it is only fair that, for a change, we should deal ourselves an occasional Yarborough. So let us conclude this chapter in a blaze of gloom, if only to show that there is glamour in adversity.

Confronted by a collection of melancholy xs, the average player is apt to lose interest. He is wrong. Partner may have a useful hand, and Bridge is essentially a partnership game.

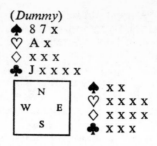

(*Dummy*)
♠ 8 7 x
♡ A x
♢ x x x
♣ J x x x x

♠ x x
♡ x x x x
♢ x x x x
♣ x x x

After opening Two Spades, South finally plays the hand in
Six Spades. West leads the King of Diamonds, to which
declarer plays low. The Queen of Diamonds is won by the
Ace, and the Ace and King of Hearts are followed by a Heart
ruff in dummy. Thereafter South plays off six solid trumps,
from the Ace to the nine, without pausing for breath. Those
six leaden Spades feel like eight, at least, to the defenders.
That is always the way. But there is no reason to be dejected.
Declarer has not put his cards on the table, so presumably he
is in some doubt. Obviously West has features of interest.
Otherwise the small slam would be on ice. It is East's
bounden duty to help partner. He cannot expect to win a
trick. But he may enable West to win two by giving him a
COUNT on the hand.

The mere fact that everything of value to the defence is
with West must make it difficult for him to discard. He can
let go his Hearts. That is easy, because if South had a fourth
Heart, he could have ruffed it with impunity. Dummy's eight
and seven of trumps cannot be over-ruffed, and both defenders
can see it early on. But West may not know whether to hang
on to his Clubs or to his Knave of Diamonds. This is where
East is called upon to manipulate his Yarborough with skill.
His first two discards should be Diamonds. Then he can start
on the Clubs. West can count, and he will draw the obvious
deduction. He will say to himself: " To give me a COUNT
on the suit, partner discarded his Diamonds. He could find
only two. Therefore he started with no more than four.
Dummy and I had three each, leaving three for declarer.
Consequently the one card I must keep to the end is that
Knave of Diamonds."

196

Had East discarded *three* Diamonds, West would know that South had no more, and he would keep his Clubs.

Here is the complete deal:

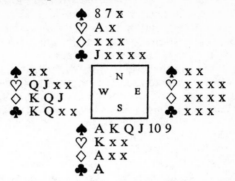

```
                    ♠ 8 7 x
                    ♡ A x
                    ◇ x x x
                    ♣ J x x x x
     ♠ x x                          ♠ x x
     ♡ Q J x x         N            ♡ x x x x
     ◇ K Q J       W     E          ◇ x x x x
     ♣ K Q x x         S            ♣ x x x
                    ♠ A K Q J 10 9
                    ♡ K x x
                    ◇ A x x
                    ♣ A
```

Put yourself in West's place and imagine how grateful you would be to partner for telling you what to keep.

The moral is this: COUNT the hand yourself. And help partner to COUNT it. Gang up on declarer from both sides. The maxim that it is unsporting to shoot sitting birds does not apply to declarers.

Résumé

(1) In defence, as in dummy-play, each trick should help to build up a mental picture of the complete deal.

(2) By noting the fall of the high cards, a defender learns how much *more* strength may be expected from declarer. What is left is likely to be with partner.

(3) Counting the suits reveals the distributional pattern. Declarer is not expected to have length (five cards or more) in a suit, which he has not mentioned in the bidding.

(4) Every discard is a clue. Therefore, each defender should discard constructively, so as to provide partner with clues to help him in reading the hand.

(5) Having read the cards, the defenders should seek to read declarer's mind. By deducing from his line of play how he intends to make his contract the defenders may discover the best way to break it.

Exercises

(1)

(*Dummy*)
♠ Q J 10 x
♡ Q x x
◊ K x
♣ K x x x

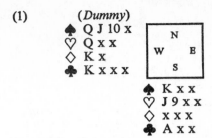

♠ K x x
♡ J 9 x x
◊ x x x
♣ A x x

Bidding:

East	*West*
One Heart	One Spade
Two Diamonds	Two No-Trumps
Three Diamonds	Three Hearts
Four Hearts	

South leads the Ace of Clubs against Four Hearts by East. All follow. What should South lead at trick two?

(2)

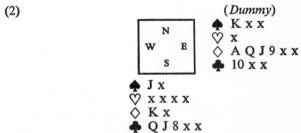

(*Dummy*)
♠ K x x
♡ x
◊ A Q J 9 x x
♣ 10 x x

♠ J x
♡ x x x x
◊ K x
♣ Q J 8 x x

Bidding:

West	*East*
One Heart	Two Diamonds
Two Hearts	Three Diamonds
Three No-Trumps	

North leads the deuce of Spades. Declarer wins with the Ace and runs the ten of Diamonds. What card should South lead after winning the trick with his King?

(3)   (*Dummy*)
♠ K 10 x
♡ A K 10 x
◇ 10 9 x
♣ Q 10 x

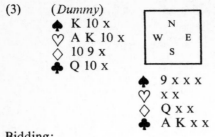

♠ 9 x x x
♡ x x
◇ Q x x
♣ A K x x

Bidding:

West	North	East	South
One No-Trump	Two Spades	Four Hearts	No Bid

Declarer ruffs the opening Spade lead, draws trumps—North showing out on the second round—and lays down the King of Diamonds. Crossing to dummy with a trump, declarer plays the ten of Diamonds and runs it. What card should South play when he comes in with the Queen of Diamonds?

(4)   (*Dummy*)
♠ Q J x x
♡ A x x
◇ K J x
♣ Q x x

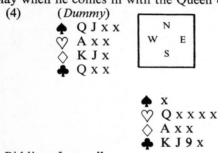

♠ x
♡ Q x x x x
◇ A x x
♣ K J 9 x

Bidding: Love all.

East	West
One No-Trump	Three No-Trumps

(East's No Trump promises 12–14 points.)

Declarer takes the opening Heart lead with the Knave, and plays off four Spades—the A K from his hand—ending in dummy. The sixth trick is a small Diamond from the table on which declarer plays the Queen.

What card should South lead when he comes in with the Ace of Diamonds?

(5) (*Dummy*)

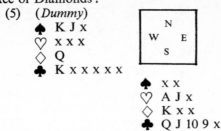

♠ K J x
♡ x x x
◇ Q
♣ K x x x x x

♠ x x
♡ A J x
◇ K x x
♣ Q J 10 9 x

Bidding: North–South game.

East	West
One Spade	Two Clubs
Two Diamonds	Two Spades
Three Spades	Four Spades

South opens the Queen of Clubs. Declarer plays low from dummy and ruffs in his hand. Then he plays a small trump to the table and runs the Queen of Diamonds. What card should South play, when he wins the trick with the King?

(6)

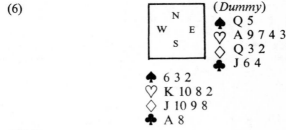

(*Dummy*)
♠ Q 5
♡ A 9 7 4 3
◇ Q 3 2
♣ J 6 4

♠ 6 3 2
♡ K 10 8 2
◇ J 10 9 8
♣ A 8

Bidding:

West	East
One Diamond	One Heart
One Spade	Two Diamonds
Two No-Trumps	Three No Trumps

North leads the deuce of Clubs. What card should South return after winning the first trick with the Ace?

DUMMY PLAY

CHAPTER XIII

Playing Safe

Losing with bad cards is only monstrous. Losing with good ones is humiliating. It happens often enough, of course, and public opinion puts the blame fairly and squarely on " bad breaks ". The purpose here is to apply a cure for unlucky distributions.

The first step is to forget such expressions as " How could I guess that all the Spades would be in one hand? " or " Why should I expect Mrs. Jones to ruff my Ace of Diamonds? " People who say such things are notoriously unlucky. What is so much worse, their bad luck is likely to continue.

The Time for Pessimism

It has been observed already that Wishful Thinking is sometimes the only possible approach to difficult contracts. To get home, the cards must be distributed in a certain way. Therefore, assume that they are so distributed. The corollary is that Black Pessimism is often the right attitude to take up, when the contract seems to present no difficulty. Foreboding is then the order of the day.

What is the outlook on this?

(*You*)	(*Dummy*)
A K 9 x x	J x x

Imagine a rollicking grand slam in which that is your trump suit. With an air of perfect insouciance you bang down the Ace and—unless something startling happens—you follow with the King. If you need all five tricks, you just have to hope that someone has a doubleton Queen.

Now go to the other extreme. You need three trump tricks only, and entries abound all over the place. This time, you can't fail. Even if all the missing cards are in one hand, three tricks are certain.

But what if you need four tricks? This is where pessimism comes into its own. You put on dark glasses and visualise an unlucky break. To guard against a singleton Queen, you play the Ace. Two small xs make their appearance and you are little wiser than before. Still, if you think it out, you can't miss. A small one towards the Knave will triumph over every adversity.

```
              J x x
            ┌───────┐
            │   N   │
Q 10 x x    │ W   E │    x
            │   S   │
            └───────┘
              A K 9 x x
```

Whatever West does, he makes one trick only.

```
              J x x
            ┌───────┐
            │   N   │
   x        │ W   E │    Q 10 x x
            │   S   │
            └───────┘
              A K 9 x x
```

Here the Knave loses to the Queen. But then South re-enters dummy and finesses against the ten.

Of course, playing it that way means giving up the chance of making all five tricks by dropping a doubleton Queen. That is the essence of a SAFETY PLAY.

SAFETY PLAYS are made to guard against bad distributions—to ensure the *required* number of tricks at the occasional expense of an *extra* trick. Declarer thinks only of the tricks he needs for his contract and gives up deliberately the chance to make more.

Strictly speaking, the term is applied to the development of a suit. But the same principle holds good for the treatment of entire hands.

Certain card combinations occur frequently, and their correct treatment has become standardised. In every situation a SAFETY PLAY can be worked out at the time. But it helps to know the more common recipes by heart and to reserve available brain-power for other, less-well-defined occasions.

Several standard SAFETY PLAYS have crossed our path already. The time has come to look at some of the others. And the best way is to put each one in its natural setting, with the whole pack spread out to cast the shadows of real life. For the main difficulty with SAFETY PLAYS is to spot them —at the time. A split-second later, the whole thing is always absurdly simple.

Let us go. Our mission is not to fail on the *easy* contracts, which is not always quite so simple as it sounds.

We start with an infrangible Four Spades.

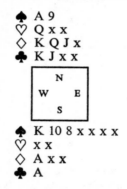

♠ A 9
♡ Q x x
◇ K Q J x
♣ K J x x

N
W   E
S

♠ K 10 8 x x x x
♡ x x
◇ A x x
♣ A

West leads the King of Hearts, followed by the Ace and a third Heart. Dummy's Queen holds.

The unlucky player discards a Diamond from his hand, lays down the Ace of trumps and emits his habitual groan when East shows out. How could he possibly tell that West would have all four Spades?

A moment's pause will show that he should have thought of that one thing and of nothing else. The reason is that nothing else could beat him. To find all four trumps with West was the only danger. Therefore, it should have been his sole preoccupation.

The correct play is to lead a small Spade towards the Ace. To save time, the Queen of Hearts can be ruffed. The important consideration is that the first trump should be played by

204

declarer, not by dummy. If West follows with an x, cover with the nine—and relax. You are home.

The point of the hand is to make a SAFETY PLAY—to envisage a bad break and to guard against it. As always, a small premium must be paid on the insurance. Good play confines declarer to ten tricks. A poor player can make eleven, if the trumps happen to break 2–2.

In the next example West opens a small Spade against Three No-Trumps and the ten drives out declarer's Ace.

♠ Q 9 7 x
♡ A K x x x
◇ A K
♣ x x

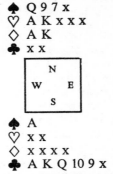

♠ A
♡ x x
◇ x x x x
♣ A K Q 10 9 x

This deal may help to demonstrate the difference between theory and practice. Confronted by a problem on paper, most declarers will succeed in making the contract. In real life the majority will go down—some of the time. Yet no one should ever go wrong; not once in a thousand years. Four Club tricks are needed, and four only. And it is brutally clear that South has no side entry. What, then, is the danger? That the Clubs will break 4–1 or 5–0 and that he will be unable to win the fourth, decisive trick in Clubs. To avert that piece of bad luck—which, incidentally, will occur nearly a third of the time—declarer plays the ten of Clubs away from his hand. Or better still, he enters dummy and finesses the ten on the first round. After that, all is plain sailing. Dummy retains a small Club to give declarer his entry to the others. This, again, is a SAFETY PLAY and will cost one trick part of the time. Five No-Trumps can be made against a 3–2 Club break. By giving up the luxury of that eleventh trick, declarer ensures his contract against an unfavourable distribution.

Spot the SAFETY PLAY on this hand.

♠ A K x		♠ 10 x x
♡ K J x x	N	♡ A x x
◇ A 7	W E	◇ J 9 6 5 2
♣ A K x x	S	♣ x x

The contract is again Three No-Trumps. North leads a small Diamond and South goes up with the Queen on dummy's deuce. What is the best line of play?

Clearly the ten of Diamonds is with North, so it is a good idea to play up to the Knave on the table. Whatever North has—or does—the Diamonds will yield two tricks. Imagine that North wins with the King and—noting partner's deuce of Spades—switches to a Club.

Any suggestions about that SAFETY PLAY? Declarer's aim is to make three Heart tricks, and if the finesse is right, or the suit breaks 3–3, it will present no problems. But what if the finesse is wrong and the doubleton Queen wins? You can guard against it, and that is where the SAFETY PLAY comes in. Declarer leads the King of Hearts, and then the Ace. If North has a doubleton Queen, it drops. If South has the Queen—which means, of course, that the finesse would have succeeded in the first place—West still makes three Heart tricks by leading the third round from dummy.

Had West needed four Heart tricks, he would have had to finesse and to hope for a 3–3 break as well. But since he can afford to lose one trick, he pays it as a premium to give himself the best chance of not losing two.

The next example is another standard SAFETY PLAY which will be found in every text-book.

x x x x

A Q 10 x x

Assuming entries all over the place, how do you set about this combination to make four tricks?

To get at the answer, try making five tricks. You finesse against the King of Spades and hope for a 2–2 break. Many declarers follow the same practice if they need four tricks only. Should the Queen finesse lose, dummy is re-entered

and an x is led towards the A 10. If East plays low, declarer
goes into an agonising huddle. He is between the devil and
the deep blue sea. To finesse again—or to drop the Knave?
That is the hideous question.

The correct play is to lay down the Ace at trick one. If all
follow, a small one is played from dummy towards the Q 10 x x.
If either the King or the Knave make their appearance (the
two outstanding xs were absorbed on the first trick), there is
no further problem. Of course, East may show out. But
then nothing can be done about it. SAFETY PLAYS ensure
against bad luck, not against Fate itself. The purpose in
laying down the Ace is to guard against a blank King—and
against the subsequent trance.

A Small Premium on a Large Policy

North opens the Queen of Spades against Six Diamonds.

An exhilarating contract, isn't it? A happy ending to an
evening's Bridge—so long as you don't mess it up. Just
because the hand is so simple, it is worth giving it an extra
thought. Can anything go wrong? Not really. Still, it is
just possible. North may have a void in trumps. No reason
why he should, of course. But these things do happen, and
that is what makes this deal a bad one for " unlucky " players.
The lucky ones take the first trick in dummy and cover South's
five of trumps with the eight. Then they add up the score.
If North follows, he cannot help taking the trick. But his side
can take no other, since the Diamonds now break. If North
shows out, the eight wins. Needless to say, if South plays the
nine or ten, declarer covers. He is safe. Either North follows
and the trumps break 3–1 or 2–2, or he shows out and gives
the game away.

Of course, declarer can make all thirteen tricks if the trumps
break 2–2 or if North holds the bare Queen. But what is 20
points compared with a slam? Look after the pounds, and

the pence will look after themselves. That is the essence of all SAFETY PLAYS.

If Bridge were played with one suit only, the correct technique for almost every situation would have been standardised long ago. Fortunately, there are three other suits to make life more interesting. Methods for dealing with whole hands cannot be formulated in advance. But the SAFETY PLAY approach needs no formula. It is simply a case of looking for the danger spot and avoiding it, if possible.

Tackle the examples that follow in the same way as those that have gone before. A little forethought; a little pessimism —when you can afford it; and occasionally, a little ingenuity.

North opens proceedings with Three Diamonds, and West finds himself eventually in Six Spades.

South follows with the deuce of Diamonds to North's Queen, and declarer's King wins. The Ace of Spades comes next and North shows out. Annoying, but there it is. The contract is, of course, unbeatable. But it requires a particle of forethought to make it. Have you drawn up a plan?

Almost anything will do—except an ill-starred attempt to cash the Ace of Diamonds. You cannot cash it. South will ruff it and there will be nothing unlucky about it. North's bid shows at least six Diamonds, so there is no such thing as " I couldn't tell ". As good a play as any is to concede a Diamond—a small Diamond—at once. The next one is ruffed with the King of Spades. Then declarer takes the marked finesse against the Knave of trumps, re-enters dummy and finesses again. All very simple, when you think of it.

Alternatively, play the second Diamond from dummy. South can ruff a loser if he likes. If he doesn't, a small Diamond is ruffed with the King and the finesses against the Knave are taken as before. The only loser will be the last Diamond.

Avoidance Play

In the following example there is no need to be unlucky either. Avoid the pitfalls and Fortune will smile.

♠ K J x
♡ 10 x
◇ K x x
♣ K Q J x x

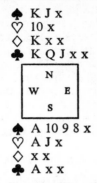

♠ A 10 9 8 x
♡ A J x
◇ x x
♣ A x x

A small Heart is opened against Four Spades. East plays the Queen. Most Souths will succeed, but some will be unlucky. If Fortune is in one of her spiteful moods, it is possible to lose a trump, a Heart and two Diamonds. Playing SAFE will circumvent misfortune. The first consideration is to keep out West—to prevent him leading through the King of Diamonds. Therefore, duck the first Heart, in case West holds the King. But that is not all. West may have the Queen of Spades, so the finesse is taken into East's hand. By this time, most of the premium has been paid. Just one instalment remains outstanding. If Fortune was really peevish, she dealt West, Queen to *four* Spades. Bearing that in mind, declarer must not play the Ace first. The ten is led and ducked in dummy. East can take the trick—with a singleton Queen maybe—but he is unlikely to do further damage. Whatever he plays, South draws trumps and makes his Clubs.

Can anything go wrong? Let's see. East may have a singleton Club, and if so, he will lead it, hopefully, at the second trick, when he is in with that Queen of Hearts. Should that happen, South can take out a different insurance policy. He will play off the Ace and King of trumps, and set about the Clubs. Unless the Spades break 4–1, he will be in no trouble.

209

If East started with a singleton Club, West had four, and this will give declarer plenty of time to discard a Diamond—both Diamonds, in fact—before West can turn really nasty. If East ruffs a Club with the Queen of trumps, South doesn't care. A Diamond from East cannot hurt him.

Declarer's object throughout is to guard against bad luck. According to the tactics of the defence, he decides which particular piece of bad luck is the most likely to befall him. There is nothing safe in allowing the defence to ruff one's winners. South should bear this in mind, when he suspects East or West of leading a singleton. SAFETY is still a top priority. More than ever. But as far as the trump suit is concerned, it precludes too much ducking and finessing. When a ruff is feared, the best policy usually lies in a couple of rounds of trumps—a papa–mama game.

Swapping Losers

What is the SAFETY PLAY on this?

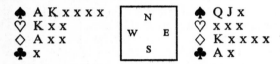

♠ A K x x x x ♠ Q J x
♡ K x x ♡ x x x
♢ A x x ♢ K x x x x
♣ x ♣ A x

North opens the King of Clubs against Four Spades. The contract looks eminently sensible and the odds are well in declarer's favour. That is the ideal moment for pessimism to assert itself. What can go wrong? The answer is that North may have the Ace of Hearts, and South may come in with a Diamond to make a thorough nuisance of himself.

This time, the insurance policy costs nothing at all. Once more, it is a case of holding up an Ace for a few seconds. Don't take that King of Clubs. Let it ride. North can lead another Club if he likes—or he can switch. Whatever he does, West draws two rounds of trumps, discards a Diamond on the Ace of Clubs and plays three rounds of Diamonds, ruffing the third one high. If the suit breaks 3–2—and the trumps are no worse than 3–1—it is all over bar the congratulations. Declarer enters dummy with the Queen of Spades and cashes two good Diamonds.

210

Declarer had a losing Diamond from the start. He chose to lose a Club instead—to make sure that South should not gain the lead.

All these plays revolve around the same principle—the principle of looking for snags and taking all available precautions to guard against them.

By way of a change, let us have a SAFETY PLAY for a part-score contract.

After an opening Spade bid by South, West becomes declarer at Two Hearts.

North opens the nine of Spades.

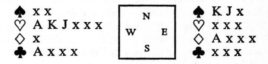

♠ x x   ♠ K J x
♡ A K J x x x   ♡ x x x
◇ x   ◇ A x x x
♣ A x x x   ♣ x x x

South's Spade Queen wins the first trick and a trump comes back, won by declarer's King. Prospects are pleasing, so a little suspicion will not be out of place. Looking at his losers, declarer can see two Spades, a Heart maybe and two or three Clubs.

At the third trick declarer leads a small Club. South wins and returns another trump. What should declarer do to make certain of his contract? A perfect SAFETY PLAY is available, and it calls for nothing more complex than finessing against the Queen of Hearts. This has nothing to do with the probable distribution of the trump suit. West does not greatly care whether his Knave holds or not. He is home either way. If North wins with the Queen, the Hearts will have broken and the eighth trick will be a Club ruff in dummy. If North shows out, declarer will make all his six trumps, and in that case he can afford to lose three Clubs.

The next example is a good deal more difficult. Have a shot at it, but don't be disappointed if you fail. We are back in the slam business, and North opens a Heart against Six Spades. What is the procedure?

211

Elimination

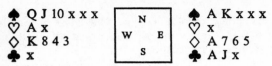

♠ Q J 10 x x x
♡ A x
♢ K 8 4 3
♣ x

♠ A K x x x
♡ x
♢ A 7 6 5
♣ A J x

Once more the contract looks too easy for words—though not for SAFETY PLAYS. As always when the heavens are smiling, ask yourself the eternal question: can anything go wrong? It seems unlikely, but there is no law against a 4–1 Diamond break. If it is Q J 10 9, you have had it. But it may be Q J 10 2. In fact, the odds are that the deuce will not be a singleton. Can you cope with such a situation?

Let us experiment together. At the second trick we ruff a Heart in dummy. Then comes a trump, the Ace of Clubs, a Club ruff, another trump and yet another Club ruff. By this time, our Clubs and Hearts have all gone, and so have opponents' trumps.

Now we lead the three of Diamonds. Whatever North produces, we duck. Can you see what must happen? If North's Diamond was the deuce, South must overtake. A Heart or Club will give us a ruff and discard, and that will be the twelfth trick. If South had a singleton, he will have nothing else to play.

If North started with a singleton—other than the deuce—the defence will fare no better. Either he will be left on play to give us a ruff and discard or South will overtake. Then he, in turn, will find himself in a predicament. His Diamond holding will be Q J 2, the ten having been used to overtake his partner's nine. Now the lead of the Queen will give West a finesse position.

The next illustration involves the same technique—forcing opponents to be nice. The contract is Four Spades.

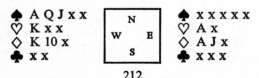

♠ A Q J x x
♡ K x x
♢ K 10 x
♣ x x

♠ x x x x x
♡ A x
♢ A J x
♣ x x x

212

North opens a Heart. A lesser man would lead a trump or a Diamond and put West out of his comparative misery. But not North.

The " normal " play is to win with dummy's Ace of Hearts and finesse the Spade. If it fails, there is a fifty-fifty chance of guessing the Diamond. If that fails, too, there is a perfectly good case of bad luck. Alternatively, declarer can adopt a SAFETY PLAY and probably make the contract, luck or no luck. At trick two he leads a Club. Then—after another Heart, perhaps—he leads a second Club. Opponents lead a third Heart or switch to trumps. Declarer wins with the Ace of Spades and ruffs his last Heart in dummy. Then he trumps dummy's third Club in his hand and exits with a Spade. As long as the trumps break 2–1, all is well. With no more Clubs or Hearts about, opponents are in a fix. They must either give declarer a ruff and discard or play into his Diamond tenace.

Note that with ten trumps between the two hands the correct play is to finesse. The odds are that the King will not be singleton. But the SAFETY PLAY gives a better chance. It fails when South has K x x in trumps, and then only if declarer misguesses the Diamond. That will not occur more than about 5 per cent of the time.

The last two illustrations involve the principle of elimination. Declarer stripped his hand, and dummy's, of two suits, compelling opponents to give him a ruff and discard or to lead into a tenace. That is always a pleasant thing to do, but it transcends the realm of SAFETY PLAYS and impinges on another sphere—the world of End Plays and Throw Ins. And that must await development in the next chapter on Dummy-Play.

Résumé

(1) The purpose of SAFETY PLAYS is to guard against unlucky distributions.

(2) The SAFETY PLAY is a form of insurance and involves payment of a premium. To give himself the best chance of the required number of tricks, declarer abandons the hope of an overtrick.

(3) The term SAFETY PLAY is used to describe the treatment of a suit. But the insurance principle, on which it is based, applies to the development of entire hands.

(4) While *all* contracts should be studied from the SAFETY angle, this approach is most needed on hands that look easy. It is then that declarer can usually *afford* a SAFETY PLAY.

(5) SAFETY PLAYS take many forms, but some features are especially prevalent. One of the most frequent is the deep finesse or the duck—when there is no side entry to a long suit. (A K Q 10 x opposite x x). Also—

(6) Laying down an Ace or an A K—instead of finessing—to guard against singleton or doubleton honours.

Exercises

(1) North leads the Queen of Clubs against Six Spades.

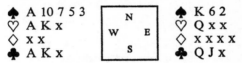

♠ A J 8 7 4   ♠ K 9 2
♡ J x x   ♡ A K Q
◇ Q J x x   ◇ A K x
♣ x   ♣ A x x x

What is the right way to play the trumps?

(2) North leads the Knave of Hearts against Four Spades.

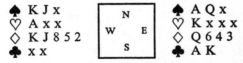

♠ A 10 7 5 3   ♠ K 6 2
♡ A K x   ♡ Q x x
◇ x x   ◇ x x x x
♣ A K x   ♣ Q J x

How should declarer play the trumps?

(3) North leads a Club against Five Diamonds.

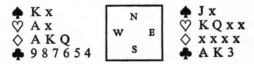

♠ K J x   ♠ A Q x
♡ A x x   ♡ K x x x
◇ K J 8 5 2   ◇ Q 6 4 3
♣ x x   ♣ A K

What card should declarer play from dummy at the second trick?

(4) North leads a Spade against Five Clubs. South wins with the Ace and returns another Spade.

♠ K x   ♠ J x
♡ A x   ♡ K Q x x
◇ A K Q   ◇ x x x x
♣ 9 8 7 6 5 4   ♣ A K 3

How should declarer play the trumps?

(5) North opens the Knave of Diamonds against Three No-Trumps.

♠ K x
♡ K x x
◇ K x x
♣ A K 9 8 x

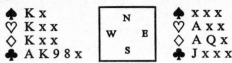

♠ x x x
♡ A x x
◇ A Q x
♣ J x x x

(a) Can declarer make certain of the contract?
(b) How should he play the Clubs?

(6) North opens the deuce of Spades against Six Diamonds.

♠ A x
♡ A K Q
◇ A Q 9 7 6 2
♣ A x

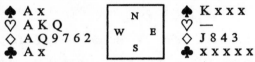

♠ K x x x
♡ —
◇ J 8 4 3
♣ x x x x x

Declarer wins the trick in dummy. What card should he play next?

(7) North leads the six of Spades against Three No-Trumps. Declarer takes South's Queen with his King.

♠ K J x
♡ x x x x
◇ A Q x x
♣ K 8

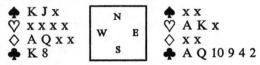

♠ x x
♡ A K x
◇ x x
♣ A Q 10 9 4 2

(a) Assuming that neither opponent has a void in any suit, can declarer make certain of the contract?
(b) What card should he play at trick two?

(8) North leads a small Spade against Three No-Trumps by West. South covers dummy's Queen with the King and declarer wins.

♠ A J x
♡ A x x x
◇ 6 5
♣ A J x x

♠ Q
♡ x x x
◇ A K J 7 4 3 2
♣ x x

At the second trick West leads a Diamond to which North plays the eight.

216

(*a*) Can declarer at this stage be certain of the contract?

(*b*) What card should he play from dummy to the first Diamond?

(9)

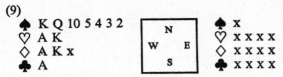

♠ K Q 10 5 4 3 2
♡ A K
◇ A K x
♣ A

♠ x
♡ x x x x
◇ x x x x
♣ x x x x

West is in Four Spades.

North leads the Queen of Clubs.

What card should declarer lead to the second trick?

DEFENCE

CHAPTER XIV

Leads, Signals and Discards

X marks the spot in this chapter. So far, things have been too friendly altogether. Whenever it has been their turn to play, those two gallant defenders, East and West, have torn to ribbons one contract after another. But there has been no ill feeling. Now a new element—X—enters our lives. That is the conventional symbol for a double, and there is no doubt that it raises the temperature and adds zest to the onlookers. What is more, a double affects the run of the play. No longer do the defenders *hope* to defeat the contract. They *expect* to do it. And that makes a difference.

First comes the opening lead. If it is the doubler's turn, he is not entitled to a great deal of sympathy, for he must have foreseen the problem when he doubled. If East doubles, West's position is more uncertain. He feels that something constructive is expected of him, but what it is he does not always know. To lay down a series of inexorable rules is, fortunately, quite impossible. If Bridge could be completely standardised, it would lose its charm, and there would be no bad players, which means that there would be no good ones either. For all that, partner can be guided by certain principles —and misguided by others.

Leads after a Double

If East bids a suit, and subsequently doubles opponents, he expects West to lead his suit.

If West bid something, while East has said nothing, other than " double ", West should lead his own suit.

That is the general idea, but it is not a law of the Medes and Persians. From a holding headed by the A K or K Q J, in an

218

unbid suit, West is entitled to lead the King. Nine times out of ten, he should do just that. A double does not call for the unnatural, and it does not preclude the normal lead on any hand, at any time.*

When the defenders have bid different suits, no ready-made rule applies. A singleton in partner's is the obvious lead against a suit contract. But with A K J in his own suit, West still opens the King, if only to have a look at the table. Do the obvious, and you won't be far out.

By way of a generalisation, it should be noted that a penalty double often suggests shortage in partner's suit. With length in it, the expectation is that opponents will be short. That is a bad time to double, because some of partner's high-card strength is liable to vanish on the way to the starting post.

This factor carries most weight when partner has X-ed a part score contract. And its influence is least pronounced in the case of a sacrifice by opponents. Then the double is almost automatic, and that is not a good moment to draw rigid inferences about partner's distribution.

As mentioned above, if East calls something, and later doubles No-Trumps, he definitely wants West to lead his suit. But even here discretion is the better part of fanaticism. Take this sequence:

East	*South*	*West*	*North*
One Spade	One No-Trump	No Bid	No Bid
X	No Bid	No Bid	No Bid

West holds:

♠ K x   ♡ 10 x x   ◇ Q 10 x x x   ♣ J x x

The fourth highest Diamond is the right lead. This time, East's double shows one thing only: that he has a good hand. To apply a double is the one way he has of doing it, and though he must be prepared for a Spade lead, he does not demand it unconditionally. That King of Spades may turn out to be an invaluable entry for bringing in the Diamonds, and declarer may be put out to find it in an unexpected quarter.

Now for a misguiding principle. From time immemorial—the Ape Age, no doubt—the myth has flourished that a double

---

* An important exception will be noted in Chapter 20.

of No-Trumps by East is a ukase for the lead of a suit bid by North. West, according to this legend, must not think or even fidget. His bounden duty is to pick the highest card he can find in North's suit and fling it on the table. That sort of thing may be magnificent, but it is not Bridge.

Certainly, East may have doubled Three No-Trumps, because he thought that his cards were in the right place. That, in turn, implies something useful in the suit—or suits—bid under him. If North bid two suits, and East holds A Q in one of them and K J in the other, he may well take a sanguine view of his prospects in defence, for he knows that South will have trouble in setting up dummy. But that is no reason for helping declarer and attacking East's entries from the word go. Those high cards represent not only tricks, but TIME. They constitute an assurance that South will have to let the defence come in a few times, before he can develop nine tricks. Meanwhile, East–West should set up something of their own. Those stoppers in North's suit(s) provide the opportunity. South will probably have to drive them out. But don't do it for him. Let him do it in his own time.

This does not mean that West should be reluctant to open North's suit in response to partner's double. Far from it. But he should not do so blindly for often enough something better may present itself.

The sequence is:

South	West	North	East
No Bid	No Bid	One Diamond	No Bid
One Spade	No Bid	Three Diamonds	No Bid
Three No-Trumps	No Bid	No Bid	X

It is practically impossible to construct a hand for West on which he should lead a Diamond. A Heart or Club is the obvious opening. Later, it may be proper to play through the Diamonds. But to set about establishing dummy's six or seven-card suit, from the first trick, is a policy which will nearly always help declarer.

Turn to this bidding:

South	West	North	East
—	—	One Diamond	No Bid
One Heart	No Bid	One Spade	No Bid
Two No-Trumps	No Bid	Three No-Trumps	X

West holds:

♠ 10 9   ♡ J x x x   ◇ 10 x x x   ♣ Q x x

This time, the ten of Spades does look like a good lead, and there is reason to believe that East will lick his chops at the sight of it.

The bidding suggests that North–South have between them at most seven Spades. That leaves East with four or five. The unbid suit is Clubs, but Q x x is an unprepossessing holding, while the ten–nine combination in Spades makes an ideal basis for the attack on dummy's shorter suit.

Deal again:

West	North	East	South
No Bid	One Diamond	No Bid	One No-Trump
No Bid	No Bid	X	No Bid
No Bid	No Bid		

West holds:

(1) ♠ J x x x   ♡ J x x x   ◇ 10 x   ♣ K J x
(2) ♠ K x x   ♡ Q x x x   ◇ 10 x x x   ♣ Q x

A Diamond is a reasonable lead on the first hand, but not on the second. Both times East is likely to produce something in North's suit. But on hand (2), West has too many Diamonds himself to find length with his partner. With a doubleton, it is different, Add a fifth Heart or Spade to hand (1), and again West should leave the Diamonds strictly alone. The fourth highest of his longest suit becomes the right lead.

The better West's hand, the more he has by way of entries, the less should he be inclined to attack the suit bid over him. If every double is treated as a command, East will have to restrain himself far too often, and many profitable penalties will be missed. The occasions on which East has a good hand and expects to defeat a No-Trump contract are more numerous—especially at rubber Bridge—than the specific cases in which he has length and strength in North's suit, and wants it opened at all cost. Other things being equal, lead North's suit. When they are not equal, use your judgment.

Trump Signals

To the novice all cards below the ten look much the same. The expert fondles his pips with the loving care bestowed by the jeweller on his carats. Every single one makes a difference. The technique of petering, discussed in earlier chapters, has already shed light on this aspect of the game. A close relative of the peter is the trump signal. The idea is the same: to convey information by inverting the natural order in the play of seemingly unimportant cards. Holding the deuce, three and four of trumps, a defender *normally* parts with the deuce first. As far as taking tricks is concerned, it does not matter. All three cards are equally useless. But it is natural to let go the lowest before the highest. Therefore, there must be some reason for dropping the deuce *after* the three-spot. This sequence implies the desire to RUFF something, and it shows *three* trumps.

By following to trumps in the wrong order, so to speak, a defender draws his partner's attention to a shortage in another suit. At the same time, he tells him that he owns a third trump with which to ruff.

Off we go:

Bidding:

South	West	North	East
One Heart	One Spade	Two Diamonds	No Bid
Two Hearts	No Bid	Four Hearts	No Bid

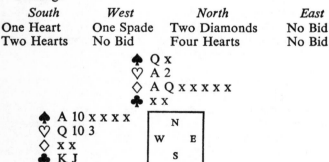

```
              ♠ Q x
              ♡ A 2
              ◇ A Q x x x x x
              ♣ x x
♠ A 10 x x x x      N
♡ Q 10 3        W        E
◇ x x
♣ K J                S
```

West opens the Ace of Spades, observes partner's nine and continues. South wins on the table, dropping his own Knave under the Queen, while East's deuce confirms that he was dealt a doubleton. Now comes the Ace of trumps, followed by the small one. South's Knave falls to West's Queen, and . . .

One moment. In what order did East play his trumps? Was it the four, and then the six? If so, he can't have another trump—that is, if he knows about trump signals—so it will do no good playing a third Spade. The Club is the best chance. Should East turn up with the Ace, the contract will be pulverised immediately. Even if he can do no better than the Club Queen, he may make up for it by holding the King of Diamonds. That will do just as well, so long as a trick in Clubs is set up quickly. This line of defence succeeds if South's hand is:

(1) ♠ K J x   ♡ K J x x x x   ◇ K x   ♣ Q x or
(2) ♠ K J x   ♡ K J x x x x   ◇ J x   ♣ A x

But, perhaps East played high–low in trumps—first the six, then the four. That means that he started with THREE trumps. So he has one left. A third Spade is led and ruffed by East. This time, the contract is beaten as long as East has the King of Diamonds. Declarer's Clubs can be as good as A Q. His hand may be:

(3) ♠ K J x   ♡ K J x x x   ◇ J x   ♣ A Q x

Note that the first line of defence will present South with the contract on hand (3), while the second line will give it away on hands (1) and (2).

If West must guess whether declarer started with five trumps or six, he is doomed to go wrong some of the time. Trump signals eliminate the guesswork.

Some players—a minority—play high–low always to show three trumps, regardless of the position in the other suits. The general practice is to signal only when a ruff is contemplated. Outside the ranks of the Bridge elite, the convention is not widely known. But it is well worth mastering, for when the occasion arises, it saves the defence many a headache —and sometimes presents declarer with a veritable migraine.

The McKenney or Suit Preference Signal

No form of signalling is abused so enthusiastically, so persistently or so brutally, as the McKenney. Known in America as the Lavinthal, this is now as common as flying

223

saucers. From a statistical point of view, it would have been better for the majority of rubber Bridge players if they had never heard of it. But they have. And it is a useful mechanism, even though a good many mechanics drive it too hard.

The McKenney comes into operation when a defender follows to a suit with an unnecessarily high card or with a suspiciously low one.

Spades are trumps. East, who bid Hearts, throws the King on West's Ace. The King, mark you. Not the eight or the ten, but the King. Slightly shattered by this piece of ostentatiousness, West asks himself: "Why did he do it? If he wanted me to continue, he could have encouraged me without going to such extremes. Perhaps, he has something else in mind. I wonder."

West is perfectly right. Since East bid Hearts, he could have certainly produced a peter without bringing in the King. So it is not a peter. It is a signal. An unnecessarily *high* card calls for a switch to the *higher ranking* suit. A suspiciously low one, shows interest in the *lower ranking suit*. Trumps, of course, are excluded.

East's King of Hearts clamours for a Diamond. The deuce would suggest Clubs. The implications are sometimes less clear when the signaller plays low. Ostentation can rarely be mistaken. Excessive modesty may lend itself to misunderstanding.

Let us examine both at close quarters. Bidding:

West	North	East	South
One Spade	Two Hearts	No Bid	Four Hearts
No Bid	No Bid	No Bid	

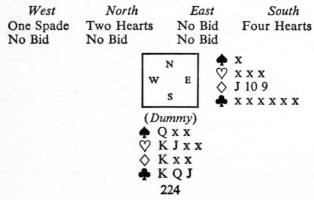

```
              N            ♠ x
        W           E      ♡ x x x
              S            ◇ J 10 9
                           ♣ x x x x x x
       (Dummy)
        ♠ Q x x
        ♡ K J x x
        ◇ K x x
        ♣ K Q J
```

East's Spade lead is an immediate success. West wins the first trick with the Ace of Spades and gives his partner a ruff. The defence needs two more tricks, and dummy is depressingly good. The only hope is that West has another Ace to come in with for one more ruff. Since he is without the King of Spades, he must surely have another Ace. But is it Clubs or Diamonds? If West is McKenney-blameless, East must guess. There is no indication whatever and no reason to expect success more than half the time.

The McKenney (or Lavinthal) suit signal works like a charm. At trick two, West leads the *deuce* of Spades—a suspiciously low card. If he simply did not want to waste anything, he could have returned the five or the seven or something equally trivial. Why the deuce? Because he wants East to put him in again with the Ace of Clubs—the *lower* ranking suit.

Had West wanted a Diamond, he would have played the Knave of Spades or the ten—an unnecessarily high card.

Here is another illustration:

Bidding:

South	North
One Heart	Four Hearts

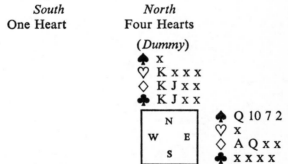

(*Dummy*)
♠ x
♡ K x x x
◇ K J x x
♣ K J x x

♠ Q 10 7 2
♡ x
◇ A Q x x
♣ x x x x

West leads the King of Spades. Left to his own devices, he will then sit and ponder and ruminate. But he won't know whether Clubs or Diamonds are his best bet. They look alike in dummy, and West may have the same holding—a doubleton or trebleton—in both.

East holds the answer to the riddle, and to convey it to his partner, he drops the *Queen* of Spades. It can hardly be a

225

singleton, and a peter, in that position, would be devoid of meaning. Besides, petering with Queens is not fashionable in the best circles. So it is—it must be—a suit preference signal, calling for a switch to Diamonds. And if West has a doubleton Diamond, the contract is beaten. Reverse East's holding in the minors and he would drop the deuce, asking for a Club.

The singleton-on-the-table situation lends itself especially to McKenneys, and the next example is on the same theme.

West leads the Ace of Spades against Six Diamonds.

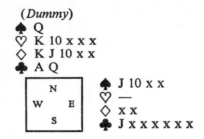

(*Dummy*)
♠ Q
♡ K 10 x x x
♢ K J 10 x x
♣ A Q

♠ J 10 x x
♡ —
♢ x x
♣ J x x x x x x

East should feel very, very happy. He knows that the slam will be beaten. The Spade Ace will take the first trick. The second will be a Heart ruff. To make sure, East plays the Knave of Spades on his partner's Ace. Surely, that is an *unnecessarily* high card and will be correctly interpreted by West. Had East intended to peter, he could have found something less flamboyant than the Knave.

With a singleton on the table—and whenever it is *obvious* that partner will switch—an ostentatious discard is a McKenney.

But don't overdo it. That is where we came in, and we had better go back to the beginning. Occasions for suit preference signals are comparatively rare. When they occur, they should be unmistakable. For the rest of the time, forget that McKenney—or Lavinthal—ever existed. If in doubt, treat partner's card as a peter or as a request to switch or as an expression of general apathy.

Use the McKenney when the occasion arises, but don't look for it on every hand.

On Not Petering

The same advice holds good for all forms of signalling.
The inexperienced defender likes the role of a human semaphor,
petering and McKenneying at every turn. He wants to show
his features, oblivious of the fact that partner may be unable
to profit by the information.

The purpose of signalling is not to show high cards, but to
indicate to partner the best line of defence. If partner is not
in a position to take action, don't signal. Desist. The
knowledge that you hold a King or an Ace may help declarer.
Locating the missing cards is his problem, and he does not
deserve any help. Let him find out for himself.

Put on South's spectacles and look at it from his angle.

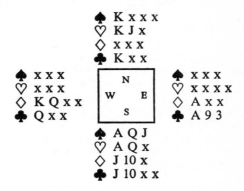

```
                ♠ K x x x
                ♡ K J x
                ◇ x x x
                ♣ K x x
♠ x x x          ┌─────────┐          ♠ x x x
♡ x x x          │    N    │          ♡ x x x x
◇ K Q x x        │ W     E │          ◇ A x x
♣ Q x x          │    S    │          ♣ A 9 3
                └─────────┘
                ♠ A Q J
                ♡ A Q x
                ◇ J 10 x
                ♣ J 10 x x
```

West opens a small Diamond against Two No-Trumps, and
the defence collect four tricks before South can get a look in.

What is the worst possible discard East could make on the
thirteenth Diamond? Obviously the nine of Clubs. If West
believes him and switches to the Queen of Clubs, it will be all
over at once. And even if he does not, the defence will fare
no better, for declarer will notice the nine and will play
accordingly.

Without assistance, the contract will depend on guessing
the Club position. The wanton peter saves declarer the guess.

The moral is : signal to partner, not to declarer.

And never waste an important card for the pleasure of signalling with it. Throw away what you don't want. A good partner will understand that you want what is left—the suit you have kept.

West opens One No-Trump, non-vulnerable, and East raises him to Three. North leads the ten of Clubs.

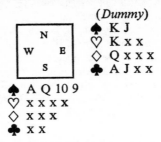

(*Dummy*)
♠ K J
♡ K x x
♢ Q x x x
♣ A J x x

♠ A Q 10 9
♡ x x x x
♢ x x x
♣ x x

Declarer turns up with the K Q of Clubs and runs the suit putting South to two discards.

The defence must be based on the assumption that North has an entry in one of the red suits, and that he will come in before West can rattle off nine tricks. To make him play Spades, South discards his lowest Diamond, then his lowest Heart. That is the equivalent of a peter in Spades, which South cannot afford.

Now for a different situation. Once again, the contract is Three No-Trumps. No suit was mentioned in the bidding, and North opens a small Heart.

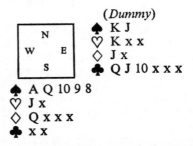

(*Dummy*)
♠ K J
♡ K x x
♢ J x
♣ Q J 10 x x x

♠ A Q 10 9 8
♡ J x
♢ Q x x x
♣ x x

South's Knave falls to declarer's Queen, and the next two tricks are won by the King and Queen of Clubs. A third

228

Club is led from the table. By now, it is clear that North has the Ace and that only a Spade switch can defeat the contract. This time, South peters in Spades. A low Diamond could be misunderstood, for when all is said and done, North could place South with the Ace of Hearts. A small Heart would also be ambiguous, leaving North to choose between Spades and Diamonds. With five Spades, South can *afford* to peter.

Discards

A good rule in discarding is to keep the winners and to throw away the losers. There are exceptions. Some will come under the microscope in Chapter XVI. But by and large, hold on grimly to the cards needed to break the contract.

This sort of thing happens frequently at rubber Bridge:

Bidding:

North	*East*	*South*	*West*
One Club	No Bid	One Diamond	One Spade
No Bid	No Bid	Three No-Trumps	No Bid
No Bid	No Bid		

West leads the King of Spades.

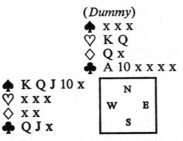

(*Dummy*)
♠ x x x
♡ K Q
♢ Q x
♣ A 10 x x x x

♠ K Q J 10 x
♡ x x x
♢ x x
♣ Q J x

South wins the second round of Spades with the Ace, and runs six Diamonds.

West should assume that East has the missing Spade. If South had it, he would have probably held up the suit once more. What, then, should West throw on the Diamonds? The first three discards are easy enough, for the Heart midgets are no good to anyone. How about the fourth discard?

In real life, many a West will be mesmerised by dummy's

229

Clubs. Fear of that long suit on the table will blur his vision, and he will let go a precious Spade. Afterwards he will say : " How stupid of me," but it will be too late.

The point West should bear in mind is that if South has the King of Clubs—or the Ace of Hearts, for that matter—he is home in a canter. Counting declarer's tricks, he can see six Diamonds and two black Aces. Therefore, partner must be credited with the King of Clubs, and a small Club can be discarded. The Spade—every Spade—is vital, for all three will be needed to break the contract.

In discarding, try to count declarer's tricks. When that is not enough, be guided by the inferences to be drawn from his play.

Inferences from Play

The bidding is as uninformative as ever. A non-vulnerable South opens One No-Trump and North puts him up to Three. West leads a Heart, and East's Queen holds the trick.

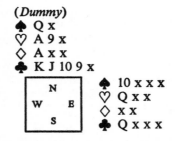

(*Dummy*)
♠ Q x
♡ A 9 x
♢ A x x
♣ K J 10 9 x

♠ 10 x x x
♡ Q x x
♢ x x
♣ Q x x x

Another Heart is won in dummy, and this is followed by the Ace and a small Diamond. West captures declarer's Knave with the Queen and leads a third Heart. South takes the trick with the King and plays off the King and ten of Diamonds, discarding a Club from dummy. West follows both times, but East must throw something away. What should it be?

This is no time for squirming and wriggling. Antics of that sort can only help declarer. East should discard two Clubs without the least sign of discomfort. The one thing that stands out about the hand is that South is missing the

230

Ace of Clubs. With so useful a suit on the table, he would have surely attacked it first, before the Diamonds, if he had the Ace. And since he has no points in Clubs, he is bound to be pretty good in Spades, almost certainly as good as A K. If he has four of them as well, East's ten may be the key card. In Clubs the Q x will be as good as Q x x x. If the Queen takes a trick at all, the contract will be broken, and if South guesses correctly—going up with the King—he will have collected nine tricks and the Queen won't matter either way. No doubt, declarer should have attacked the Clubs immediately. That is neither here nor there. Declarers sometimes have lapses, and the defenders are there to take advantage of them.

East can do nothing, actively, to defeat the contract. But by discarding correctly, he can give declarer a chance to go wrong. There is such a thing as winning passively; it consists in allowing the other side every opportunity to lose.

Résumé

(1) A penalty double does not demand *unconditionally* the lead of a particular suit. Generally speaking, West should open a suit bid by himself or by East.

(2) If neither defender has bid, West will often do best to lead his own suit.

(3) When East doubles a No-Trump contract, it is reasonable to infer that he has some strength in the suit—or suits—called by North (the prospective dummy). If West is short in that suit, it often turns out to be the most effective lead. But the double is not an absolute command for that opening, and if West has a promising suit of his own, he should not hesitate to play it.

(4) To tell partner that he wants to ruff, and also that he has three trumps, a defender signals by following high–low in trumps.

(5) The McKenney or suit-preference convention comes into operation when a defender makes an *unnecessarily* high or a *suspiciously* low discard. The high discard calls for the play of the *higher* ranking suit, and the low discard for the *lower* ranking suit. The trump suit is disregarded.

(6) A situation, which lends itself to the McKenney, arises when a defender leads a suit for his partner to ruff. By selecting an unnecessarily high or low card, he indicates his entry for giving partner another ruff.

(7) A McKenney suit-preference signal should be always unmistakable. When in doubt, assume that partner is petering—or discouraging—and ignore the convention.

(8) Never peter unnecessarily. Bear in mind that the information you disclose by signalling may be of greater value to declarer than to partner.

(9) Avoid using potential winners as signals. Throw away what you do not want led, leaving partner to infer that you are interested in the suit which you have kept intact.

(10) Try to count declarer's winners and strive to retain enough set-up tricks to defeat the contract. Unguard a suit, when it is apparent that unless partner can stop it on his own, the contract is unbeatable.

DEFENCE—CHAPTER XIV

Exercises

(1) Bidding:

South	North
One Diamond	One Heart
One No-Trump	Three No-Trumps
No Bid	

East doubles.
What should West lead?

(a) ♠ J 10 9 x   ♡ x   ◇ K J 9 x x   ♣ x x x

(b) ♠ 10 x   ♡ x x   ◇ K J 9 x x   ♣ J 10 9 x

(c) ♠ J 10 x   ♡ Q J 10 8   ◇ J 10 x x   ♣ x x

(d) ♠ x x x   ♡ J 10   ◇ K 10 x x   ♣ J x x x

(2) Bidding:

North	East	South	West
One Diamond	One Spade	Two Hearts	No Bid
Four Hearts	No Bid	No Bid	No Bid

(*Dummy*)
♠ A J x
♡ A x x
◇ A Q J x x x
♣ x

```
        N
   W         E
        S
```

♠ Q 10 x x x x
♡ K x
◇ K x
♣ K x x

West opens the King of Spades. South wins in dummy and leads the Ace and another trump. West follows with the four, then the deuce.

What card should East play when he comes in with the King of Hearts?

233

(3) Bidding:

East	South	West	North
Four Spades	Five Diamonds	No Bid	Six Diamonds

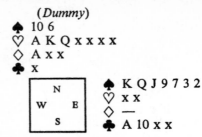

(*Dummy*)
♠ 10 6
♡ A K Q x x x x
♢ A x x
♣ x

```
        N
    W       E
        S
```

♠ K Q J 9 7 3 2
♡ x x
♢ —
♣ A 10 x x

West leads the Ace of Spades. What card should East play?

(4) Bidding:

North	East	South	West
One Club	No Bid	One Heart	One Spade
Two Hearts	No Bid	Four Hearts	No Bid

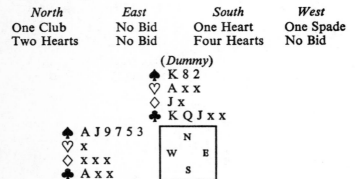

(*Dummy*)
♠ K 8 2
♡ A x x
♢ J x
♣ K Q J x x

♠ A J 9 7 5 3
♡ x
♢ x x x
♣ A x x

```
        N
    W       E
        S
```

West opens the Ace of Spades and East drops the Queen. What card should West lead to the second trick?

(5) Bidding:

East	South	West	North
One Spade	No Bid	Two Spades	X
No Bid	Three Diamonds	No Bid	No Bid
No Bid			

234

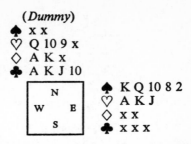

(*Dummy*)
♠ x x
♡ Q 10 9 x
◇ A K x
♣ A K J 10

♠ K Q 10 8 2
♡ A K J
◇ x x
♣ x x x

West leads the Ace of Spades.　What card should East play?

(6) Bidding:

South	West	North	East
One Club	No Bid	One Diamond	One Heart
One No-Trump	No Bid	Three No-Trumps	No Bid
No Bid	No Bid		

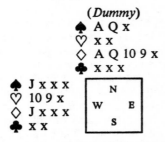

(*Dummy*)
♠ A Q x
♡ x x
◇ A Q 10 9 x
♣ x x x

♠ J x x x
♡ 10 9 x
◇ J x x x
♣ x x

West opens the ten of Hearts, which holds.　The nine is overtaken by East's Knave, which also holds the trick.　South takes the King of Hearts with the Ace, discarding a Club from dummy.　Next he plays the Ace, King and Queen of Clubs. East drops the six, then the five.　What should West throw on the third Club?

DUMMY PLAY

CHAPTER XV

End Plays

" Will you be good enough to cut your throats? " That is what declarer says, in effect, when he performs an End Play. The question is purely rhetorical. No alternative is open to the defence, and it is just a matter of selecting a sharp instrument.

The point arises: how can opponents be persuaded to embark on self-destruction? The answer is that all ways of escape must first be cut off. That is why the end play comprises, strictly speaking, two phases. First comes the elimination or strip-play. Then the throw-in. Because declarer would like defenders to lead Spades, he begins by stripping the hand of the other three suits. Then, when the stage is set, he THROWS IN one of the opponents. The idea is to force the defence to be thoroughly obliging—to present declarer with a ruff and discard or to lead up to a tenace.

Once or twice, the vague contours of the End Play have already passed across our horizon. That was only a preview to whet the appetite. Here is the real thing.

The Elimination Technique

This is how it works out in practice :
West is in Six Spades. North leads a Club.

♠ A K x x	N	♠ x x x x x
♡ K Q x	W E	♡ A x x
◇ A J x	S	◇ K 10 x
♣ K x x		♣ A x

Declarer plays two rounds of trumps and notes that one of the opponents shows out the second time. But the contract is safe. A second round of Clubs, and a Club ruff, are followed by three rounds of Hearts. Then, declarer leads a Spade and puts his hand down. It does not matter who has that third Spade or what he does when he gets in with it. The luckless defender can do one of two things : play into the Diamond tenace, or give declarer a ruff and discard by leading a Club or Heart. He is stymied, because he has no EXIT CARD. It is that which characterises a successful END PLAY. A defender can play no card without injuring his own interests and benefiting declarer. He has no WAY OUT. Hence the term—EXIT CARD.

The next deal involves a slight variation. It would be a pity to change the scenery, so the contract remains Six Spades by West, and North again leads a Club.

♠ K Q x x x	N	♠ A x x x x
♡ K 9 x	W E	♡ A 10 x
◇ Q x x	S	◇ A K x
♣ A x		♣ x x

Playing the hand in honest, straightforward fashion, declarer will go one down like a gentleman, conceding a Heart and a Club. Partner will say, " Hard luck " or " I did not ask you to bid a slam ", according to his nature and inclinations. And that will be that.

This time, victory cannot be guaranteed. For all that, West can give himself a good chance. He draws trumps, plays off the Diamonds and leads a Club.

Take a close up of what has happened. Declarer has removed his own Diamonds and Clubs, and opponents' Spades. The defence must now lead Hearts, the very thing declarer wants. That is why he went to all that trouble with the other suits. If he has to attack Hearts himself, he will lose a trick—unless he happens to find the Q J bare. But if the other side has to open up the Hearts, declarer may land all three tricks. He can play for split honours, or if an honour is led, he can play the same defender for both Queen and Knave. This time, the strip play does not ensure the contract. But it creates a good chance where virtually none existed before.

Whenever declarer faces a card combination which he does not want to open up himself, he tries, if possible, to end play

237

his opponents. With K 9 x opposite A 10 x, the advantage of not taking the initiative is obvious. The same applies to holdings like: Q 10 x or K J x opposite A 9 x, and A 10 x opposite J x x. Sometimes, forcing the defence to take the first step is worth a certain trick to declarer (as with K J x opposite A 10 x). Sometimes, it only gives him a better chance of not losing a trick or of losing one trick instead of two (as with Q 10 x opposite A 9 x). The end play also yields a certain trick with K 10 x or Q J x opposite x x x. To avoid making the first move in a particular suit, declarer eliminates the others. That is the underlying motif of the END PLAY.

Loser on a Loser

Can you apply this technique to the next example? Imagine that you were dealt the hand at rubber Bridge and that an admiring gallery is watching your every move.

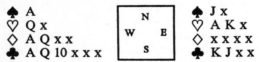

♠ A   ♠ J x
♡ Q x   ♡ A K x
◇ A Q x x   ◇ x x x x
♣ A Q 10 x x x   ♣ K J x x

North opens the King of Spades against Six Clubs.

How do you fancy your chances? Make your plan. You can assume a normal lead. For the rest, you need not expect any lucky breaks. The contract is cold. Did you . . . draw trumps, discard one Diamond x on dummy's third Heart, and another on the Knave of Spades? Good. You have end played North, and the slam bonus is yours.

You discarded a *loser* on a *loser*, and you elected to lose a Spade, not a Diamond, because you wanted North to be on play. North had no EXIT CARD. That is why you THREW HIM IN.

Of course, if the King of Diamonds is on the right side, the slam is a certainty from the word go. But the winners at Bridge are not the players who bring off finesses. They are the players who don't take finesses when they can do without.

Here is another example of the loser-on-a-loser technique. But it is a good deal more difficult than the last hand, and calls for precise timing.

238

North leads the Queen of Hearts against Four Spades. Anyone can make the contract if the Club finesse comes off. Good play gives fair prospects of success even if it does not.

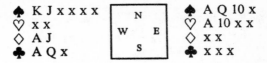

♠ K J x x x x   ♠ A Q 10 x
♡ x x   ♡ A 10 x x
◇ A J   ◇ x x
♣ A Q x   ♣ x x x

Declarer ducks the first Heart, takes the second and loses the Knave of Diamonds to North's King (or Queen). He does not " finesse " the Diamond, because there is nothing to finesse. He gets rid of it, and he takes care to keep South out of the lead. For the same reason, declarer ducked the first Heart. He wanted it out of the way, and he also did not want South to have an entry, later, with the Heart King. A Club from South is the very thing to avoid.

By now, preparations are nearly complete. Two Hearts and one Diamond have gone. North's best return is another Diamond or a trump, but it does not really matter. West enters dummy, and ruffs the third Heart. If South had three, the King drops. West now lays down the Ace of Diamonds—if it is still about—and draws trumps, ending in dummy. This is the position:

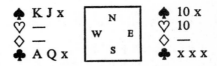

♠ K J x   ♠ 10 x
♡ —   ♡ 10
◇ —   ◇ —
♣ A Q x   ♣ x x x

Can you see what is going to happen? Dummy leads the ten of Hearts, and declarer discards that useless little Club. If North started with four Hearts, he must win the trick and lead into the A Q of Clubs—or give declarer a ruff and discard. If South had four Hearts, declarer has lost nothing, though in that case he will need the Club finesse for his contract.

In addition to eliminating the red suits, declarer threw a loser on a loser. Instead of losing a small Club, he preferred to lose the ten of Hearts. That was to put North on play at the psychological moment—when North had no safe EXIT.

Avoiding a Finesse

Can you avoid a finesse on this deal?

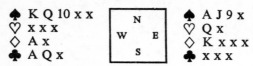

♠ K Q 10 x x		♠ A J 9 x
♡ x x x		♡ Q x
◇ A x		◇ K x x x
♣ A Q x		♣ x x x

North leads the King of Hearts against Four Spades, and switches to a trump.

It looks as if the contract won't be made if the King of Clubs is offside. But this is one of those occasions when no stone should be left unturned and no avenue must remain unexplored.

West's best line is to lead a Heart. Let North play another trump if he likes. Suppose that the trumps break 2–2. Declarer plays off the Ace and King of Diamonds and ruffs a small one in his hand. Now the last Heart is trumped on the table and the stage is set for the THROW IN—with dummy's fourth Diamond. If South shows out, all is over. West discards his little Club and puts his hand on the table. North is well and truly end-played. Again he has the choice of leading into a tenace (A Q of Clubs) or giving declarer a ruff and discard.

If South has the long Diamond, West is no worse off than before. The Club finesse is still there.

The A Q of Clubs have established Squatters' Rights in this chapter. Let us keep them intact. But it is about time for a new trump suit. Four Hearts is the contract, and North leads the King of Diamonds.

♠ K x x		♠ A x x
♡ A Q x x x		♡ K x x x x
◇ x x		◇ A J
♣ A Q x		♣ x x x

Declarer wins, draws trumps and plays three rounds of Spades. Against bad defence, no skill is required. North wins the third Spade, cashes his Diamond and leads into the

Club tenace. Or else, South takes the Spade and brightly returns a Diamond, end-playing his partner.

Against good opposition West will have to display a certain technique. *South* will win the third Spade, and return a Club. Declarer must not finesse. He can compel North to do it for him. Winning the Club return with his Ace, West puts North on play with a Diamond, and it is the same old story for poor North—a ruff and discard or a lead up to the Queen of Clubs.

An Early End Play

More often than not, the throw-in is executed when only a few cards remain to be played. Hence the term " End Play ". But there is no rule about it, and in practice the same technique can be put into operation at an early stage of the proceedings. Neither is it essential to carry the stripping process very far. Here is quite a common situation :

North opens a Diamond against Three No-Trumps.

    ♠ A K x   ♠ Q J x x
    ♡ A J 9   ♡ 10 x x x
    ♢ A Q 10   ♢ x x
    ♣ A J x x   ♣ 10 x x

On the lead, West can see eight tricks. An early end play will ensure the ninth.

After winning the first Diamond with whatever may be necessary, West plays off four Spades, discarding a Club, and takes a finesse in Hearts. He does not mind what happens next. He is home. A red card gives him his ninth trick at once. A Club takes a little longer, but achieves the same result. Providing that the Spades have been eliminated, North is helpless. He cannot exit safely in any one of three suits.

No-Trumps do not lend themselves so readily to End Plays as suit contracts. Firstly, ruffing enables declarer to strip the hand more easily. And when the elimination has been completed, he can gain a trick in two different ways : a lead into a tenace or a ruff and discard. In a No-Trump contract the second possibility does not arise.

241

An impressionist's view of a typical End Play hand would show : a lot of trumps, two short suits easy to eliminate; and an " untouchable " tenace. Something like this :

	N	
♠ A K x x x x		♠ Q J x x
♡ K x	W E	♡ A x x
◇ A Q 9		◇ x x x
♣ A x	S	♣ K x x

We are back in slamland, and North opens anything but a Diamond against Six Spades.

Declarer eliminates Hearts and Clubs. Then, from dummy, he leads one of those unstrippable Diamonds. Whatever South puts up, he covers. North finds himself in the mess in which he has floundered—through no fault of his own—from the first page of this chapter. He can play into the Diamond tenace or concede a ruff and discard.

It is not a difficult hand, as end plays go, but there is room for carelessness. There may be three trumps in one hand, and a thoughtless declarer may draw them all automatically. To remove opponents' trumps looks neat and tidy. And with ten Spades between the two hands, it seems eminently safe. But if West looks ahead, he will see, at once, that he cannot afford to draw more than two rounds of trumps. He will need two Spades in dummy for the end play. Having stripped the Hearts and Clubs, declarer will find himself in his own hand. Only a trump can take him back to dummy. And when North has been given the lead with the Diamond, there must still be a trump left on the table. Otherwise, of course, he will exit with a Heart or Club, and all the elimination will have been wasted.

The moral is that end plays must be planned from the beginning.

North leads the nine of Spades against Five Diamonds. Three No-Trumps would have been a better contract, but that is neither here nor there.

	N	
♠ A x x		♠ 10 8 7
♡ K x x	W E	♡ A J
◇ K Q x x		◇ A x x x x
♣ A x x	S	♣ K J x

242

Declarer wins the first trick, draws trumps and returns a Spade. The nine suggests that North led the top of nothing. Therefore, South should have all the high Spades that matter. He can cash two winners, but whatever he does next will seal his fate. He has the choice of leading into one of two tenaces or giving West a ruff and discard.

Declarer can bring about the same result by eliminating Hearts before putting South in with a Spade. It is not necessary, because the purpose of an end play is to *force* opponents to lead something nice and profitable. On this hand, a Heart lead is as nice and profitable as a Club.

Perhaps an End Play

And now for an END PLAY that may not be an End Play at all.

West leads a trump against an injudicious contract of Six Diamonds.

♠ x x x x x
♡ A J
♢ K x x x
♣ A x

♠ A x x
♡ K Q x
♢ A Q J x x
♣ K x

Declarer sees two Spade losers staring him in the face. Can he do anything about it? Try a strip-tease. Draw trumps. Eliminate Hearts and Clubs. Now play the Ace of Spades and another. If either defender has K Q alone, the slam is in the bag. It is an honest END PLAY, and that is all there is to it. But the same happy result may be achieved against an unwary defender with K x. He may omit to throw his King on the Ace.

Of course, if dummy's Spades are headed by the ten—or

better still, by the Knave—the East–West problem is more acute. There may or may not be a way out, according to the position of the honours. Declarer does not know. But to discourage too much forethought on the part of the enemy, he should play his Ace of Spades as soon as possible—before his strip play arouses suspicion. Then, maybe, a defender will forget to unblock.

Smother Play

A rare member of the Throw-in group bears the title of Smother Play. So seldom are its features seen at the Bridge table that the family likeness is apt to be overlooked. Yet it is quite unmistakable.

West leads the nine of Clubs against Six Hearts

♠ K x x
♡ A K Q
◇ A Q x
♣ J x x x

♠ A x
♡ 10 9 x x x
◇ K x x
♣ A K x

A Club loser is pretty certain, doubly so on the lead. But the rest of the picture is promising—until East ejects a Spade on the second round of trumps. That marks West with J x x x, and the barometer needle lurches towards Stormy Weather.

Can declarer do anything about it? Let us face it. The contract looks impossible. But did not someone once say: " If it is difficult, it will be done at once; if it is impossible, it will take a little longer "?

The End Play technique shows the way. Everything depends on West's distribution—whether or not his hand can be stripped.

244

Let us try it out, hoping fervently that West does not ruff anything as we unstitch him.

First come the two top Spades, and a Spade ruff. Then the three Diamonds. Finally, the King of Clubs (the Ace went on the first trick) and a small Club.

If West follows throughout, all is well. The position will be :

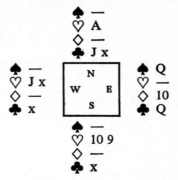

East wins the Club, but his return takes for declarer that untakable trump finesse.

This rare type of Throw-in, which compels East to smother his partner's guarded honour, may also occur when the trumps are divided like this :

```
        A x x                      A K x
       ┌─────┐                    ┌─────┐
       │  N  │                    │  N  │
K x x x│ W  E│ x  or  Q x x x     │ W  E│ x
       │  S  │                    │  S  │
       └─────┘                    └─────┘
      Q J 10 9 8                  J 10 9 8 x
```

To succeed, the Smother Play requires a fair measure of good fortune. West must be strippable. And in the two-card end game, East must not have a card to which dummy will follow. Everything must be just right. But then one of the secrets of luck is to grab it with both hands, when it comes within range.

Résumé

(1) The purpose of an END PLAY is to *force* the defence to make a lead which will benefit declarer.

(2) The first stage in the process is to " strip " the hand—to eliminate the suits which the defence can play without helping declarer.

(3) The second stage is the throw-in, giving the lead to the defence at the right moment.

(4) If the end play has succeeded, the defender who has been thrown in, will have no safe EXIT card. He will be obliged to play into a tenace or—in a trump contract—to present declarer with a ruff and discard.

(5) Sometimes, an end play will succeed whichever opponent is thrown in. More often, it is necessary to throw in the defender who sits over declarer's—or dummy's—tenace(s).

(6) Completing the elimination of the hand, declarer may be able to throw a loser on a loser, knowing—or hoping—that the trick will be taken by the defender whom he seeks to end play.

DUMMY PLAY—CHAPTER XV

Exercises

(1) The contract is Five Diamonds, North opens the Ace of Hearts and switches to a trump.

♠ A Q 10　♡ x x　◇ K Q x x x x　♣ K x
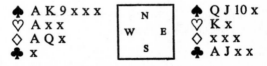
♠ x x x　♡ K　◇ A J x x x　♣ A x x x

(*a*) Can the contract be made if the K J x of Spades are over declarer's A Q 10?

(*b*) How should West play the hand?

(2) The contract is Six Clubs by West. North leads a Diamond.

♠ A Q　♡ A Q 9　◇ x x　♣ A Q x x x x
♠ x x　♡ x x　◇ A K x x　♣ K J 10 9 x

(*a*) If the trumps can be drawn in one round, what will be the position when six cards are left?

(*b*) Will declarer or dummy be on play at that stage?

(*c*) What suit should declarer lead at trick eight?

(*d*) If the next hand plays low, what card should be played by the third hand at trick eight?

(3) The contract is Six Spades. North leads the King of Clubs. The trumps are divided 2–1.

♠ A K 9 x x x　♡ A x x　◇ A Q x　♣ x
♠ Q J 10 x　♡ K x　◇ x x x　♣ A J x x

(*a*) What should be the last five cards?

(*b*) What cards, in declarer's hand, and in dummy, will make up the ninth trick?

(4) South opens the bidding with Three Diamonds, after which East–West reach Six Spades. North leads a Heart.

♠ A K Q x x
♡ x x
◇ J x x
♣ A K x

♠ J x x x x
♡ A K x
◇ A x x
♣ x x

(a) If trumps break 3–0, what should be the last four cards?

(b) Where will the lead be at that stage?

(c) What card should be led to the tenth trick?

(5) The contract is Three No-Trumps. North opens the Queen of Diamonds to which South does not follow.

♠ A Q x
♡ K x
◇ A K 10 x
♣ A x x x

♠ K J 10 x
♡ x x
◇ x x x
♣ K x x x

(a) What should be the last six cards?

(b) What East–West cards should make up the next trick if South reveals four Clubs and four Spades?

(6) The contract is Four Hearts. North leads the Queen of Clubs.

♠ x x x
♡ A K Q J
◇ K 9 x
♣ A K x

♠ Q 10 9
♡ x x x x x
◇ A J x
♣ x x

(a) If trumps break 3–1, what should be the last seven cards?

(b) What card should be led to the next trick?

(c) What are declarer's chances?

DEFENCE

CHAPTER XVI

Countering End Plays

One of the arts of defence lies in preventing declarer from playing too well. The may-the-best-man-win attitude is eminently praiseworthy—so long as you are the best man. Not otherwise. Declarer, of course, may have an inflated idea of his own worth. Then he must be deflated at once. To do that, you must first discover what is in his mind, much as you would do at noughts and crosses. If he is bent on a cross-ruff, you play trumps. If he seeks to set up dummy's long suit, you attack the entries. Every poison has its antidote, and that applies to all forms of venom exuded by declarer.

All who have digested the previous chapter will be familiar, by now, with the technique of the Throw-in. It is an advanced form of warfare and calls for modern equipment. Declarer's plan of campaign is briefly as follows : to eliminate from your hand all the cards you could lead without loss to yourself, and to leave you only such cards as he wants played for his own benefit. Against all your better instincts, you are forced to be a philanthropist. Then somebody says : " Well played "—to declarer.

Sometimes the victim of an end play cannot avert the blow. But often enough, the tables can be turned on declarer, and then the " Well played " is addressed to you.

A Finesse That Is Not

Keep wide awake and you will earn the applause on this deal.

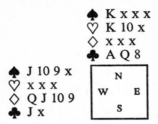

♠ K x x x
♡ K 10 x
◇ x x x
♣ A Q 8

♠ J 10 9 x
♡ x x x
◇ Q J 10 9
♣ J x

The bidding does not help. South opens a non-vulnerable No-Trump and North raises to Three.

You, West, lead the Queen of Diamonds and find East with K x x. South wins on the third round and attacks Hearts. East produces the Ace and returns another Heart. Declarer leads three rounds of Spades, ending in the closed hand, and cashes the rest of the Hearts. By this time, he has shown up with A Q x in Spades, Q J x x in Hearts and A x x Diamonds.

He has collected seven tricks, and this is the position.

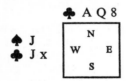

♣ A Q 8

♠ J
♣ J x

Now South leads the three of Clubs, and if you have fallen asleep, it is all over. East has nothing left but Clubs, and if you somnolently play that x, South will insert dummy's *eight*, END PLAYING East. Whether he likes it or not—and, in fact, he won't like it a bit—he will have to lead from his King *into* dummy's A Q of Clubs.

Waking up rudely, you may say: " How could I guess that South would finesse the eight? " And perhaps you will add : " It is all very well upbraiding me, as if I could see all four hands. But what happens if I go up with the Club Knave and declarer has the nine? Won't East be end played just the same, having to lead away from his ten?"

The first point to note is that South did not "finesse" the eight at all. He threw in East, which is a very different matter. As for the nine and ten, forget about them. If South had either, he could not lose the contract. Therefore, it was right to assume that East had both.

All this, of course, could not have happened a trick or two earlier. East had a Spade or a Heart to return. With only three cards left, he had not. A vigilant West will know that. Noticing one suit after another vanish from partner's hand, he will realise that East can have no safe EXIT card—nothing that he can lead without benefiting declarer. In short, he is wide open to an end play. Therefore, that Knave of Clubs must go up like greased lightning—TO PROTECT partner.

Getting Out of the Way

Now let us break a slam contract:

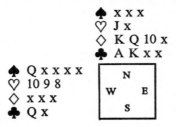

```
            ♠ x x x
            ♡ J x
            ♢ K Q 10 x
            ♣ A K x x
♠ Q x x x x    ┌─────────┐
♡ 10 9 8       │    N    │
♢ x x x        │ W     E │
♣ Q x          │    S    │
               └─────────┘
```

Bidding:

South	West	North	East
One Diamond	No Bid	Two Clubs	No Bid
Three No-Trumps	No Bid	Six Diamonds	No Bid

West opens a small Spade. East's Knave loses to declarer's Ace, and three rounds of trumps follow rapidly. Noting East's small Heart on the third Diamond, West stirs his grey matter and ruminates.

South has shown up with a four-card trump suit. In Spades his Ace deceived no one, for he is marked with the A K 10. East must have played his highest Spade, and it happened to

251

be the Knave. With J 10, he would have played the ten. Seven of declarer's cards have been revealed.

After the trumps, come the Ace and King of Hearts, and then a Heart ruff in dummy. The next trick is the Ace of Clubs, and since South follows, eleven cards in his hand can be registered at Somerset House. The other two are almost certainly Clubs, for if a Heart lurked among them, declarer would have surely tried to get another ruff out of dummy.

As West prepares to follow to that Ace of Clubs, he knows everything. What, then, should he do about it? Any views?

Let us go back for a moment to noughts and crosses. To foil declarer, first pierce his innermost thoughts. What is he up to? Clearly, he hopes to set up the long Club for a Spade discard. And if that is his idea, his next play will be a small Club from dummy. It must be so, for the only entry left on the table is the King of Clubs, and South will need it later—to get at the long Club or to lead a Spade through East. Now West knows the future as well as the present, and like all the best seers, he can predict his own unhappy fate. That small Club—which is destined to follow the Ace—will fall to his own Queen, and he will be well and truly END PLAYED. With nothing but Spades left, he will have to lead into South's K 10, and that ten of Spades will be the twelfth trick.

To parry the blow, West must get out of the way. No one can throw him in, if he has nothing to be thrown in with. There is a curse on that Queen of Clubs, and she must go at once, on the Ace. Another split second and it will be too late.

It is true that South may have the Knave. But if that is the case, the slam is infrangible, and it won't matter much whether the twelfth trick is a Spade or a Club.

By allowing himself to be end played, West surrenders unconditionally. By getting rid of that fatal Queen, he retains a chance—and a pretty good one, at that—of breaking the contract.

There are several stages in the defence against an end play.

The first is to see it coming. Suspicion grows as declarer strips the hand and safe EXIT cards become fewer and fewer. Next, the defender looks for his Achilles heel—or partner's. What is the target, the suit—or the card—which lends itself to an end play? Having found it, in good time, the defence seeks appropriate counter measures. Usually this means playing or discarding an unnecessarily high card, and maybe even throwing away a winner.

Whether it is a case of protecting partner or of refusing to be end played oneself, the principle is the same: make sure that only the defender with a safe EXIT card is put on play.

Playing Off Winners

The next deal is a variation on the same theme:

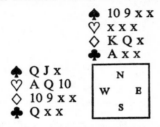

West leads a Diamond against Four Spades. South wins with the Ace and lays down the two top Spades, East showing out the second time. A Diamond to the table is followed by a Heart on which declarer plays the Knave.

West must play off his Queen of Spades immediately. This is not a case of drawing two trumps for one, but of avoiding an end play. *One* more Diamond looks safe, because there is still one left on the table, and South can cash it any time he likes. But if West is then thrown in with a trump, he will be forced to give declarer a ruff and discard; to play away from his Queen of Clubs; or to lead from his Heart tenace.

When a defender holds a " good " hand—high cards in several suits—he is especially vulnerable to the end play, and it becomes more necessary than ever to think ahead. There is no talisman against good cards, but an honest, old-fashioned cure is to PLAY OFF winners if circumstances permit. With fewer high cards left, there is less danger of being thrown-in.

Declarer's hand on the last deal was:

♠ A K x x x   ♡ K J x   ◇ A x   ♣ K J x

Note that he could have made a certainty of the End Play by

253

cashing dummy's third Diamond and leading a trump, before touching Hearts. Alas, bad declarers are too often wasted on defenders who don't deserve them.

Always Retain an Exit Card

This time, declarer will do his level best, but that, of course, is no reason for letting him get away with it.

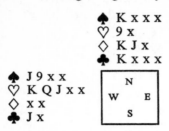

♠ K x x x
♡ 9 x
◇ K J x
♣ K x x x

♠ J 9 x x
♡ K Q J x x
◇ x x
♣ J x

South is in Six Diamonds. West leads the King of Hearts, taken by declarer's Ace. Three rounds of trumps are followed by the Ace and another Spade. East keeps pace with the Diamonds, but discards a Club on the second Spade. South plays the Ace of Clubs, another to dummy's King, and ruffs a third one in his hand.

Meanwhile, West has to throw things away. On the third trump he can park a Heart, but then he must find something else to discard on the third round of Clubs. Four cards are left. What should they be? The J 9 of Spades, obviously, and . . .?

The answer is that one of the remaining two must be a small Heart. The other does not matter a bit, for it will have to be discarded on declarer's last trump. If South knows his business, he will play that thirteenth Diamond without a moment's pause. But by then the damage may have been done. If West hung on to his Queen of Hearts, he trapped himself for good and all. With three cards left, he will be forced to win a Heart trick and to lead *away* from his J 9 of Spades into the Q 10. That is why he must get rid of the big Hearts and keep an x.

How, why, and above all, when should West foresee this

254

denouement? Dare he let go his top Hearts without a clue about the ten?

In real life, a defender often sees the danger, when it is too late, after he has parted with his precious x's.

The alarm bell should have rung when East showed out on the second Spade. That was a warning to West, that come what may, he must never allow himself to be thrown in to lead Spades into the Q 10. It is true that the Heart ten may be with declarer. But then the contract is unbeatable. West can see, that if he retains a Heart honour—the END PLAY is certain. The ten of Hearts is not. And that is all there is to it.

Breaking Up an End Play at Trick One

A good defender should be something of a criminologist. He should look for clues everywhere, and he should ask himself: what is declarer's motive?

Apply the Scotland Yard technique on this deal:

♠ K J x
♡ A x x
◇ A Q 10 x
♣ x x x

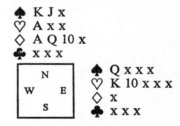

♠ Q x x x
♡ K 10 x x x
◇ x
♣ x x x

South is in Five Diamonds, and West leads the Queen of Hearts. Declarer ducks in dummy.

At everyday rubber Bridge, East will give a come-on signal in Hearts and await developments.

But if East is a criminologist, he will view declarer's play to the first trick with suspicion. Why did not South take the Heart Queen with the Ace? There must be a reason. What can it be?

The probable explanation is that South wants to keep East out of the lead.

Turning over the next page in declarer's mind, East will guess why it is that South is anxious to keep him out. Dummy's three wretched Clubs speak for themselves. If East gets in, he will attack Clubs. And that is what declarer is obviously trying to avoid.

By this time, East knows exactly what to do. He overtakes the Queen of Hearts with the King and plays a Club through the closed hand. Declarer hates it, so it must be right. And at trick one, the End Play position is broken up.

Here is the complete deal:

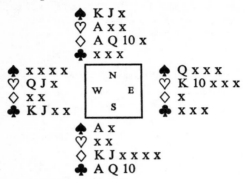

♠ K J x
♥ A x x
♦ A Q 10 x
♣ x x x

♠ x x x x
♥ Q J x
♦ x x
♣ K J x x

♠ Q x x x
♥ K 10 x x x
♦ x
♣ x x x

♠ A x
♥ x x
♦ K J x x x x
♣ A Q 10

If West is allowed to hold the first trick, the contract is unbeatable. South eliminates Spades and Hearts, draws trumps, and throws West in with a Club. West has no safe EXIT card.

East cannot be expected to foresee all that at the first trick. But declarer's play presents him with a precious clue, and he should make the most of it.

Of course, Three No-Trumps—even Four—is a far better contract than Five Diamonds. But South was probably unhappy about Hearts, while North could see no way of stopping the Clubs. It is an old story, and an End Play should not be allowed to avert the old, unhappy ending.

Ruffing Partner's Trick

Defending with a blizzard calls for both fortitude and skill. Too many players lose interest, and bemoan their fate, instead of concentrating on declarer's.

For a change, we will play the next deal with all four hands

256

exposed. But it must be clearly understood that we are West, and that out of our thirteen desultory cards we must find one to break the contract.

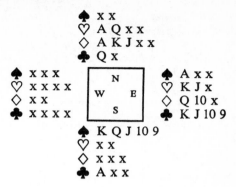

Bidding:

East	South	West	North
One Club	One Spade	No Bid	Three Diamonds
No Bid	Three Spades	No Bid	Four Spades

Declarer ducks the first Club, and East promptly switches to a small trump, his best defence. South wins, plays the Ace of Clubs, ruffs his last Club in dummy, and proceeds to lead out the Ace, King and another Diamond.

The man of the moment is West. It is for him to make or break the contract. If he wallows in melancholy, forgets partner and thinks only of how bad a card-holder he is, declarer is home.

There has been no elimination, and no End Play in the true sense of the word, yet East—if he is left on lead—will suffer all the unhappy after-effects of the throw-in. Whatever he does, declarer will make ten tricks. East must be saved from himself, and West is the man for the rescue operation. Those miserable xs carry within them a secret weapon, a trump which can ruff the Queen of Diamonds and switch the lead from one side of the table to the other. West can take the trick. True, it is partner's trick already, but it is worth two—in West's hand. In East's hand that Diamond Queen is like a bomb, which will explode at any moment. Grabbing it manfully, West can remove the fuse, by playing a Heart. It is as simple as that. The Heart suit is frozen, and East can unfreeze it. To vary the metaphor, West can shoot at goal and East can't. That is why West must seize the ball.

In the best circles, ruffing partner's tricks is looked upon as a solecism. But when partner is predestined to play the wrong card—having no right cards in his hand—decorum must give way to expediency.

End Playing Dummy

Here is an example, which allows either side to End Play the other.

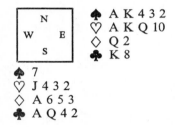

♠ A K 4 3 2
♡ A K Q 10
♢ Q 2
♣ K 8

♠ 7
♡ J 4 3 2
♢ A 6 5 3
♣ A Q 4 2

Bidding:

East	South	West	North
One Spade	No Bid	One No-Trump	No Bid
Three Hearts	No Bid	Three No-Trumps	No Bid

North leads the Queen of Spades. Declarer ducks, but takes the Knave of Spades and leads the Queen of Diamonds.

At this stage, most Souths will go up with the Ace automatically, then sit back and meditate. The best defence is to meditate first—then there will be no urge to go up with the Ace.

In the first place, South should know quite a lot about declarer's hand. West is marked with eight (or nine) cards in the minors. He cannot have more than three Hearts, for if he had, the contract would be Four Hearts, not Three No-Trumps. And he cannot have three Spades, for then he would have given East preference—Three Spades over Three

258

Hearts. Even if West is the sort of player whose bidding does not inspire exaggerated confidence, North's attack on the Spade suit, and declarer's play to the first trick, supply corroborative evidence.

From shape, South turns to strength. West must have the K J of Diamonds and the Knave of Clubs. As likely as not, he has the tens to go with them. That only gives him 5–6 points, and he can hardly have less.

The second consideration is declarer's plan of campaign. Presumably, he hopes to make three Diamonds in his hand, and five top tricks in dummy. If he gets as far as that, the ninth trick will just fall into his lap. South will be END PLAYED automatically. At some stage, he will have to lead Clubs or Hearts, and neither will do him any good. Even if West plays Clubs himself, the position won't improve, for it will give the defence only four tricks—one Spade, one Diamond and two Clubs. To break the contract, South must make his Heart, as well as two Clubs.

Having meditated, South duly ducks the first Diamond. His object is to cut off declarer from his dummy. Should a second Diamond follow, South will win and apply the End Play technique to dummy. The Ace of Clubs will be followed by a small one, locking West on the table. Sooner or later, he will have to concede a Heart—or let North enjoy himself with his Spades.

Stripping Dummy

Apply the same technique once more:

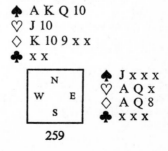

♠ A K Q 10
♥ J 10
♦ K 10 9 x x
♣ x x

♠ J x x x
♥ A Q x
♦ A Q 8
♣ x x x

259

Bidding:

North	East	South	West
One Diamond	No Bid	One Heart	No Bid
One Spade	No Bid	Two No-Trumps	No Bid
Three No-Trumps			

West opens the Queen of Clubs. South ducks, but wins the Club Knave with the Ace and proceeds to run the Knave of Diamonds.

East can count nine tricks against him. Fortunately, he can also see good prospects of five for his own side.

On the bidding, South is marked with the King of Hearts. In fact, his Two No-Trump bid must consist of the A K in Clubs, the King of Hearts and the Knave of Diamonds. Theoretically, he can pick up three Diamond tricks, three Spades, two Clubs and a Heart.

East's main concern is to prevent declarer from turning theory into practice. And the way to do it is to win the first Diamond and lead a small Heart.

South is helpless. If he goes up with the King, he will lose two Hearts and two Diamonds, in addition to the first Club. If he runs the Heart up to dummy—which is more than probable—he will never live to cash his King of Clubs. Whatever he does, East will End Play dummy. First he will cash the Ace of Hearts, then he will play off the Ace of Diamonds. Finally, he will throw in dummy with his other Diamond and wait patiently for a Spade.

Observe that the Heart must be led at once. If South has time to set up his Diamonds first, he will be in a position to go up with the King of Hearts from his hand and cash his Club, before crossing over to the table. Here and there, an altruistic East will return a Club to set up " Partner's suit ". In good defence there is no room for such pathetic loyalty. West cannot possibly have an entry. Therefore, he can put his suit away in moth-balls.

East's Heart lead is a piece of strip play by the defence. The purpose is not to develop the suit, but to remove it from dummy. Which only goes to show that every dog has his day, even the dog in the manger.

Résumé

(1) The threat of an END PLAY begins to materialise, when declarer strips the hand, and safe EXIT cards become fewer and fewer.

(2) When it is apparent that a defender is in danger of being THROWN IN, his partner should endeavour to protect him.

(3) Protecting partner may call for the unusual play of a high card—secondhand—to prevent ducking by declarer.

(4) It may be necessary to ruff or overtake partner's trick—because he has no safe EXIT card and must not be allowed to remain on play.

(5) When a defender has reason to fear that he will be END PLAYED himself, he should endeavour to play off his winners. That will reduce declarer's opportunities of throwing him in.

(6) When the threat of being END PLAYED is acute, a defender should not hesitate to discard winners in his danger suit—the suit in which he fears a THROW-IN. Partner may have the card(s) to hold that suit.

(7) The defence may be able to use the END PLAY technique against declarer or his dummy. This calls, first, for the elimination of the cards which provide a means of communication between the two hands. Declarer is then locked in his own hand or in dummy, and is forced to play away from his high-card combinations.

DEFENCE—CHAPTER XVI

Exercises

(1) West, who had opened the bidding with One Club, leads the King of Hearts against Four Spades.

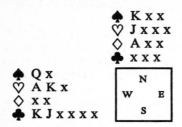

```
              ♠ K x x
              ♥ J x x x
              ◇ A x x
              ♣ x x x
♠ Q x              ┌─────────┐
♥ A K x            │    N    │
◇ x x              │ W     E │
♣ K J x x x x      │    S    │
                   └─────────┘
```

East plays low, and South drops the ten. At the second trick, West switches to a Diamond, East's Queen falling to South's King. Declarer leads the Queen of Hearts to West's Ace and the Diamond return is taken on the table. Declarer discards a Club on the Knave of Hearts, and leads a trump to his Ace.

What should West do to give himself the best chance of breaking the contract?

(2) West leads a Diamond against Six Spades.

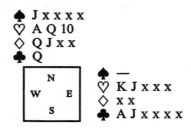

```
              ♠ J x x x x
              ♥ A Q 10
              ◇ Q J x x
              ♣ Q
   ┌─────────┐      ♠ —
   │    N    │      ♥ K J x x x
   │ W     E │      ◇ x x
   │    S    │      ♣ A J x x x x
   └─────────┘
```

South wins the first trick with the Queen, lays down the Ace and King of Spades—on which West drops the five and the Queen—and then leads three more rounds of Diamonds, ending in dummy.   To the seventh trick he leads the Queen of Clubs.

What card should East play?

(3) Bidding:

East	South	West	North
Three Hearts	Four Spades	Five Hearts	Six Spades

West leads the Queen of Clubs against Six Spades.

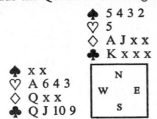

♠ 5 4 3 2
♡ 5
◇ A J x x
♣ K x x x

♠ x x
♡ A 6 4 3
◇ Q x x
♣ Q J 10 9

Declarer wins in his hand with the Ace, lays down the Ace of trumps—on which East shows out—leads the King, and crosses over to dummy with the King of Clubs.   The fourth trick is another Club, ruffed in the closed hand.   South now leads the deuce of Hearts.

What card should West play?

(4) West leads the Queen of Clubs against Six Hearts.

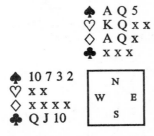

♠ A Q 5
♡ K Q x x
◇ A Q x
♣ x x x

♠ 10 7 3 2
♡ x x
◇ x x x x
♣ Q J 10

South wins with the Ace, draws two rounds of trumps—East throwing a Club the second time—and enters dummy with the Queen of Diamonds.   Next he ruffs a Club, goes back to dummy with the Ace of Diamonds and trumps dummy's last Club in his hand. The eighth trick is declarer's King of Diamonds, to which all follow. Then he leads the eight of Spades.

What card should West play?

(5) Love all. Bidding:

West	East
One No-Trump	Three No-Trumps

North leads the Queen of Hearts against Three No-Trumps by West.

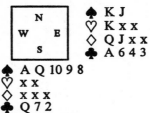

```
                    ♠ K J
         N          ♡ K x x
    W         E     ◇ Q J x x
         S          ♣ A 6 4 3
    ♠ A Q 10 9 8
    ♡ x x
    ◇ x x x
    ♣ Q 7 2
```

West wins the first trick with the Ace of Hearts in his hand and plays four rounds of Diamonds. North discards two small Spades. Declarer then plays the King of Clubs and another to dummy's Ace, North playing the eight and the ten.

What should be South's last six cards?

(6) Bidding:

North	East	South	West
One Club	One Heart	Two No-Trumps	No Bid
Three No-Trumps	No Bid	No Bid	No Bid

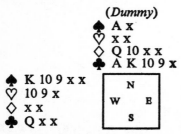

```
                    (Dummy)
                    ♠ A x
                    ♡ x x
                    ◇ Q 10 x x
                    ♣ A K 10 9 x
    ♠ K 10 9 x x
    ♡ 10 9 x          N
    ◇ x x         W       E
    ♣ Q x x          S
```

West opens the ten of Hearts.

264

Declarer wins the third round of Hearts with the Ace, crosses to dummy with the Ace of Clubs and runs the Queen of Diamonds, followed by the ten. On the third round of Diamonds East plays the King and South the Ace.

What should West retain as his last six cards?

DUMMY PLAY

CHAPTER XVII

Deceiving Defenders

One of declarer's greatest assets is that he has no partner. Dummy, aptly named *le mort* in French, cannot react, except on the emotional plane. Its feelings need not be considered and declarer can let himself go, without a thought for all those tiresome obligations, which normally restrict self-expression. During his term of office, declarer need suffer no inhibitions. One of his prerogatives is to tell lies, for only the enemy is there to believe them. Partner, dead for the time being, remains immune. To capitalise this licence to the full, the astute declarer will study the art of lying. Falsehood by itself is not enough. Which falsehood? How much of it? And when? These are questions which take up the greater part of this chapter.

The defenders try to signal to each other with almost every card. Holding K Q, West leads the King. The Queen lead would fool East, and unlike dummy, East is very much alive. But if South holds the K Q, he can please himself, and naturally he selects the card which is most likely to confuse the enemy.

A King in a Nine's Clothing

Here is an instance of deception in its most primitive form, widely practised, yet often successful.

♠ K Q 10 9   ♠ A J x x
♡ x   ♡ K Q x x x
◇ K Q J 10 9   ◇ x
♣ A x x   ♣ x x x

North opens a Club against Four Spades. Declarer can see four losers and tries a simple ruse to bluff his way out. After taking his Ace of Clubs, he leads the *nine* of Diamonds. If North has the Ace, he may not want to " waste " it on so small a card, and if he does not, West will be out of the wood. The play of the King would give North no chance to go wrong. The unassuming appearance of the nine may induce him to make a mistake.

Conversely, if declarer wants to drive out an opposing Ace quickly, he leads the King from, say, K Q J.

The general rule is : lead the highest of a sequence if you want opponents to take the trick, and the lowest if you hope that they will hold off.

And what is the policy if a suit is opened by the defence, and declarer has the choice of winning the trick with one of two touching honours?

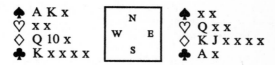

♠ A K x   ♠ x x
♡ x x   ♡ Q x x
◇ Q 10 x   ◇ K J x x x x
♣ K x x x x   ♣ A x

North opens a small Spade against a dubious Three No-Trumps. The Hearts are wide open, and West fears the worst.

South plays the Knave of Spades. Should West win with the Ace or the King? Many players put on the Ace automatically. Theirs not to reason why, theirs but to lie and die. A little thought will show that this particular lie can only hurt the liar. The idea in playing the Ace, of course, is to make South think that his partner has the King. But that is just what he won't think. He will reason that if West could only stop the suit once, he would hold up his Ace for a round or two, hoping to sever communications.

The King is much less revealing. North *may* be leading from the Ace, and if he is, West probably cannot afford to hold up his King. That is how it will appear to South, and should he turn up with the Ace of Diamonds, he may well return a Spade. If West flaunts the Ace on the first trick, South is far more likely to be suspicious and to switch to Hearts.

Or perhaps, North leads the Queen, dummy has nothing of note and West sits with the A K. If he goes up with the Ace, he exposes the whole bag of tricks. The King leaves room for doubt. North's lead could have been from A Q J x x (x).

Holding the A K of a suit, with which he hopes to see opponents persist, declarer should win the first trick with the King. In this situation the truth is more confusing than a falsehood.

Calculated Extravagance

Subtlety comes into its own in the next example:

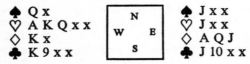

♠ A Q x   ♠ x x
♡ J x x   ♡ x x
◊ K J x x   ◊ A Q x
♣ A x x   ♣ Q J 10 x x x

West is in Three No-Trumps. North's lead of a small Spade is propitious, but dummy is not. If the Club finesse fails, the defence will surely switch to Hearts and the contract will be doomed.

South plays the Knave of Spades, and declarer wins the trick with the—Ace! He looks at it this way: if he wins with the Queen, and the Club finesse fails, North will see the futility of going on with Spades. With all those Clubs staring him in the face, his only hope will lie in grabbing four more tricks, before West can regain the initiative. Hearts alone offer that chance, and he will not hesitate to lead away from an A Q or a K J or whatever he has. But the play of the Ace " marks " South with the Queen of Spades, and North's natural play—if he comes in with the King of Clubs—will be another small Spade to put his partner in with that mythical Queen.

Holding A K J, in a similar situation, declarer should take the ten with the *King*, not the Knave.

Here is another subterfuge to put off the defence.

♠ Q x   ♠ J x x
♡ A K Q x x   ♡ J x x
◊ K x   ◊ A Q J
♣ K 9 x x   ♣ J 10 x x

North opens the King of Spades against Four Hearts, and West can see four possible losers. To dissuade North from cashing his Ace of Spades, West drops the Queen. If there is a switch, declarer parks his little Spade on dummy's third Diamond and concedes two Clubs. He is home, regardless of his luck with the Clubs.

Of course, North may suspect a trap when he sees that Queen. But he can't be sure, and many a defender in that position will be reluctant to risk the Ace—in case West is telling the truth.

The Ruff Presumptive

To induce the defence to open up trumps, declarer sometimes simulates an urge to ruff.

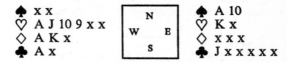

♠ x x
♡ A J 10 9 x x
◇ A K x
♣ A x

♠ A 10
♡ K x
◇ x x x
♣ J x x x x x

North opens the King of Spades against Four Hearts. West wins in dummy and returns the ten. This is a distinct hint that he wants to ruff one or more Spades in dummy and may tempt opponents to lead trumps. That, of course, is what declarer wants them to do, for it will help him to find the Queen. Conversely, if the defender who wins the trick shuns trumps, West may deduce that he is timid about leading away from that Queen. It is not much to go by, but it may be an indication.

Delicate false carding is required to upset the signals of the defence. No blatant lies, just a little gentle distortion.

Petering by Proxy

North opens the King of Hearts against Four Spades.

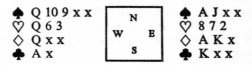

♠ Q 10 9 x x
♡ Q 6 3
◇ Q x x
♣ A x

♠ A J x x
♡ 8 7 2
◇ A K x
♣ K x x

It appears, at first sight, that the contract will depend on the trump finesse. But when South follows to his partner's King with the four of Hearts, West decides to give himself an extra chance. He plays, not the three, but the six. North may be induced to take a wrong view and to see a come-on signal in South's four. And for all North knows, a Heart continuation is the one way to break the contract. False cards cannot hoodwink everyone every time. But even an occasional success justifies deception. There is really nothing to lose. To confuse defenders—to make them doubt and wonder and guess—is a good thing in itself.

When only the Truth Deceives

But be careful not to set the signals against yourself. To tell lies carelessly is worse than not to tell lies at all.

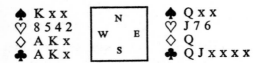

♠ K x x		♠ Q x x
♡ 8 5 4 2	N	♡ J 7 6
◇ A K x	W E	◇ Q
♣ A K x	S	♣ Q J x x x x

North leads the King of Hearts against Three No-Trumps, and South plays the three spot. West's only hope of deceiving North is to tell him the truth. Can you see why?

If North has all three top Hearts, nothing will matter anyway. But conceivably, the Hearts are divided:

North: A K 10 9   *South:* Q 3

With that Knave on the table, South dare not unblock. He is most unhappy about the three and wishes heartily that it had a few more pips on it. But it has not, and there is nothing he can do about it. If—through force of habit—West false cards with the four, he makes it appear that South's three is the beginning of a peter. In fact, he does for South the one thing the luckless man cannot do for himself—encourage North to continue with Hearts.

The deuce, on the other hand, may well obscure the picture for North. It confirms that South played his lowest Heart and suggests—wrongly, of course—that he wants a switch to some other suit.

Precisely the same reasoning applies to this situation.

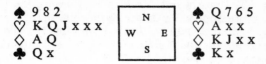

♠ 9 8 2
♡ K Q J x x x
◇ A Q
♣ Q x

♠ Q 7 6 5
♡ A x x
◇ K J x x
♣ K x

After a Spade bid by North, East–West reach Four Hearts. As soon as the King of Spades is led, West wishes that he had contracted for Three No-Trumps. South cannot have more than two Spades, so he will ruff the third one, and the Ace of Clubs will be the setting trick.

Lo and behold, South plays the three of Spades. It can only be a singleton, but North does not know it, and may well place the singleton with West. If declarer false cards—just because he always false cards, on principle—North cannot go wrong. If South has the deuce, he must be signalling for more. And if West is foxing and has the deuce himself, it will still be safe to lead the Ace of Spades. The only way to conceal the truth is to produce that deuce and leave North guessing.

In short, false carding should never be automatic. It requires forethought, like any other play, and should be worked out a move or two ahead.

Pretending to Finesse

Declarer often has to resort to deception when he hopes to " steal " a trick unobtrusively.

♠ Q J x
♡ A K Q
◇ J x
♣ A J x x x

♠ K 10 x x
♡ x x x
◇ x x x
♣ K Q x

Luckily for West, North opens a small Heart against Three

No-Trumps. South's Knave is taken by the King—not the Ace, needless to say—and West adds up the accounts. He can make eight tricks any time he likes, but before he can set up the Spades, North–South may discover that they own a lot of Diamonds. That rules out the idea of running the Clubs. Too much information will pass across the table in the discards. West's best hope is to pilfer a Spade trick quickly. To do it unobserved, he leads the Knave with the alleged intention of finessing against the Queen. North may hold up the Ace.

A more daring fraud sometimes succeeds in this situation :

North : ♠ A x   *South :* ♠ Q x

South can see no way of avoiding a Spade loser. He leads the Queen boldly, pretending to finesse. Holding the King, but not the Knave, West may decide not to cover.

A Lie to Nothing

There are times when the simplest type of fraud is the most effective. Declarer is confronted by this position.

North : J 10 9   *South :* A Q x

West leads the suit, and East plays low. South overtakes the Knave with the Queen, conveying the impression that he started with A Q bare. If West gets the chance, he may lead the suit again, hoping to drop the Ace. This innocent subterfuge may give the defence an awkward guess—especially in a No-Trump contract—and it costs nothing.

One of the oldest forms of deception consists in tempting the opposition to crash their honours. This is most likely to succeed in the trump suit, though only against mediocre opposition.

The suit is divided :

North : J 10 9 x   *South :* Q x x x x x

Declarer leads the Queen. An unwary West, sitting with K x,

pounces on her, felling East's singleton Ace. Of course, he ought to know better. With A Q x x x x South would finesse or lay down the Ace, just in case the King is bare. But sometimes West does not think of it—till the post-mortem.

A Bare-faced Swindle

Nothing succeeds like success—except impudence. Try it here:

♠ J x		♠ A Q 10 x
♡ A K J x x	N	♡ Q 10 x
◇ J x x	W E	◇ x x x
♣ A K x	S	♣ x x x

After a non-vulnerable No-Trump from South, East–West reach Four Hearts. North leads a Club, and declarer surveys his dubious prospects. Since South is marked on the bidding with the King of Spades, there are four inevitable losers—three Diamonds and a Spade. To escape the inescapable, declarer leads the Ace of Spades, then a small one. South may not go up with the King. Some womanly instinct may tell him that unless West held a singleton, he would finesse. So he ducks, deciding that the Knave must be with North.

After winning a trick with his Knave, declarer re-enters dummy with a trump, sets up a third Spade and is home.

The same technique can be used in cases of this sort:

North : A Q x x   *South :* J 10

In a side suit, at a trump contract, South leads the Knave, expecting West to cover if he has the King. If West plays low, declarer assumes that the King is over dummy. He goes up with the Ace and leads a small one. Again East may hold back the King, placing South with a singleton.

Plausibility

Next to effrontery, plausibility is the main ingredient in successful fraud.

West leads the ten of Hearts against Six Spades.

♠ K J x
♡ A Q x
◇ K Q x x
♣ A x x

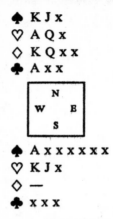

♠ A x x x x x x
♡ K J x
◇ —
♣ x x x

Declarer surveys his prospects pleasurably. Since a Club was not opened, there can be no trouble. Opponents will make the Ace of Diamonds, but no one can stop South parking his two Club losers on the King and Queen, and that will be that.

Alas, West shows out on the Ace of trumps, and what looked like a certain slam promises to be just another hard-luck story. Or is there still a hope?

To a declarer of fertile mind a neat ruse against East may present itself. Crossing over to dummy, he will lead a small Diamond. East may hold the Ace, without the Knave behind it. Then doubt will tear at his heart-strings. He will know that something piscatorial is afoot. But what? South may have the bare Knave of Diamonds. East does not know. If he suspects the wrong subterfuge and goes up with the Ace, declarer is home.

274

Plausibility is again the motif on the next deal:

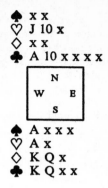

♠ x x
♡ J 10 x
◇ x x
♣ A 10 x x x x

♠ A x x x
♡ A x
◇ K Q x
♣ K Q x x

Bidding:

West (dealer)	North	East	South
One Diamond	No Bid	One Heart	Double
No Bid	Two Clubs	No Bid	Two No-Trumps
No Bid	Three No-Trumps	No Bid	No Bid
No Bid			

West opens the nine of Hearts, and this time declarer sees nothing remotely pleasing about his prospects. Dummy's ten is covered by East's Queen and the writing appears on the wall. For his ninth trick South must look to the K Q of Diamonds, and before he can get there, West will come in with the Ace to lead through dummy's J x of Hearts. If West has two Hearts only, holding up the Ace will sever communications. But East did not rebid his suit over Two Clubs, as he might have done with six of them, so it is more likely that he has five and West three.

What, then, is the solution? Once more, the only hope is to hoodwink East. Just as in the previous example declarer pretended to have the bare Knave of Diamonds, so this time he fosters the illusion of a third Heart in his own hand. He ducks the Queen, hoping that East will ruminate on these lines: " Evidently, partner has a doubleton and declarer A x x. Otherwise his play makes no sense. Another Heart from me will give South a trick for nothing. My best return is, surely,

275

the ten of Diamonds through declarer." And that, of course, seals the contract.

In the tactical sense, deception is the complement to card-reading. Instead of placing the cards of his opponents, declarer relies on their inability to place his. That is why the best time to bait a trap is early in the game, while a haze of uncertainty still hangs over the table, and before the clash of cards reveals who has what and how much.

Defence Against the Defence

At times the defence does the bamboozling—and it is then up to declarer not to be hoodwinked too easily. Far too often, a guileless West falls into this sort of trap.

♠ Q J x x   ♠ A K x x
♡ Q 7 2   ♡ 9 5 3
◇ Q x x   ◇ K J 10 x
♣ A Q J   ♣ K x

He finds himself in Four Spades. North leads a Diamond. South wins with the Ace and returns the four of Hearts. Most declarers play low, and most of the time it makes little difference. But once in a while it costs the contract. That is when South underplays the A K. West should not even hesitate. However unlikely it may seem that the Queen will hold, he must try it. The play cannot lose, for North will certainly be able to beat dummy's nine without using up one of the two top honours—if he has one.

Résumé

(1) Since declarer has no partner to mislead, he need never play TRUE cards—lead the highest of a sequence or follow with the lowest x.

(2) In deciding which card to play, declarer seeks to confuse opponents, to obscure their signals to each other, and to create a false impression about his own holding.

(3) Though, in principle, declarer should avoid telling the truth, false cards must not be played automatically. In some situations, honesty is the least revealing policy.

(4) Holding the A K, in No-Trumps—and welcoming a continuation of the suit—it is rarely correct to win the first trick with the Ace. The defenders are unlikely to believe that declarer would part so quickly with his only stopper.

(5) When West opens a suit which declarer fears, and East plays low—because he has a singleton, or cannot afford to peter—declarer should follow with his *lowest* card. A false card in this position would help the defence.

(6) The opposite holds true when declarer wants a defender to persist with a suit. He false cards to convey the impression that the other defender is beginning a peter.

(7) To " steal " a trick—to induce the defence to hold up on the first round of a suit—declarer may pretend to take a finesse (i.e., he leads the Knave from Q J x opposite K x x)

(8) To deceive the defence, declarer may play unnecessarily high in winning a trick (e.g., King from A K J or even Ace from A Q x). The purpose is to discourage a switch by the defence to another suit in which declarer has no certain stopper.

Exercises

(1) The contract is Three No-Trumps by West.

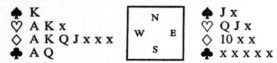

♠ 10 9   ♠ A K J 2
♡ A x x   ♡ x x x
◇ A K x x   ◇ x x x
♣ A K x x   ♣ x x x

How should West play the Spades to give himself the best chance of making four tricks?

(2) North leads a trump against Six Diamonds by West.

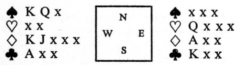

♠ K   ♠ J x
♡ A K x   ♡ Q J x
◇ A K Q J x x x ◇ 10 x x
♣ A Q   ♣ x x x x x

Declarer plays the Ace of Diamonds and draws the last trump crossing over to dummy's ten.

Which card should he play from dummy at trick three?

(3) North leads a small Spade against One No-Trump by West.

♠ K Q x   ♠ x x x
♡ x x   ♡ Q x x x
◇ K J x x x ◇ A x x
♣ A x x   ♣ K x x

South plays the Knave. What card should West play?

(4) North leads the deuce of Hearts against Three No-Trumps by West.

♠ A J 10 8   ♠ K 9 4
♡ K x x   ♡ A x x
◇ A J x   ◇ x x x x
♣ K x x   ♣ A x x

How should West play the Spades?

(5) North leads the Ace of Spades against Five Diamonds by West.

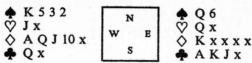

```
        ♠ K 5 3 2          ┌─────────┐          ♠ Q 6
        ♡ J x              │    N    │          ♡ Q x
        ◇ A Q J 10 x       │ W     E │          ◇ K x x x x
        ♣ Q x              │    S    │          ♣ A K J x
                           └─────────┘
```

South plays the four.   What card should West play?

(6) North leads the King of Hearts against Five Clubs.

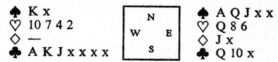

```
        ♠ K x              ┌─────────┐          ♠ A Q J x x
        ♡ 10 7 4 2         │    N    │          ♡ Q 8 6
        ◇ —                │ W     E │          ◇ J x
        ♣ A K J x x x x    │    S    │          ♣ Q 10 x
                           └─────────┘
```

South follows with the three.   What card should West play?

(7) North leads the King of Spades against Six Hearts by West, South following with the deuce.

```
        ♠ A J 10           ┌─────────┐          ♠ x x
        ♡ A 10 9 x x x     │    N    │          ♡ K J
        ◇ K Q J            │ W     E │          ◇ A x x
        ♣ A                │    S    │          ♣ Q x x x x x
                           └─────────┘
```

What card should West play after winning the first trick?

(8) North leads the eight of Diamonds against Three No-Trumps.

```
        ♠ K Q J            ┌─────────┐          ♠ 4 2
        ♡ K J 7 5 3        │    N    │          ♡ Q 6
        ◇ A 3              │ W     E │          ◇ Q 9 5
        ♣ 5 4 2            │    S    │          ♣ A K Q J 8 7
                           └─────────┘
```

The bidding was:

East	South	West	North
One Club	One Diamond	One Heart	One Spade
Two Clubs	No Bid	Three No-Trumps	No Bid
No Bid	No Bid		

What is declarer's best plan of campaign?

279

DEFENCE

CHAPTER XVIII

Deceiving Declarer

Declarer has no monopoly in prevarication. The advantage of numbers is with us, the defenders, for we can tell two lies to his one. Against that, we run the risk of deceiving each other. The ideal, of course, would be to mislead declarer all the time, and partner never. Even Lincoln admitted, by inference, that some of the people could be fooled all the time. May not one of these people be declarer?

Since, as a rule, we cannot afford to bamboozle partner in the process, the best time to hoodwink declarer is when our worse half is immune. At times, partner cannot be fooled, because he is in no position to use the information, whether it be true or false.

Standard False Cards

This would be an obvious case: South, who is in Six some-things, leads the Queen of trumps from dummy:

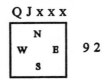

Q J x x x

N
W   E   9 2
S

The chances are that declarer is looking for the King, and it is quite likely that West has it bare. South will probably finesse anyway. But he may be tempted to play for the drop, if he is loath to surrender the initiative before attacking a side-suit—for a quick discard, perhaps. East should mislead him by false carding with the nine. Should South believe him, he will assume that the King is guarded and he will be much more likely to finesse. For if West has the deuce, his King won't drop, and if East has the K 9, the finesse will work.

The position might be:

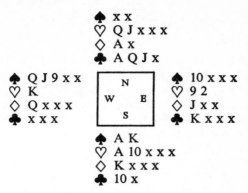

♠ x x
♡ Q J x x x
◇ A x
♣ A Q J x

♠ Q J 9 x x
♡ K
◇ Q x x x
♣ x x x

♠ 10 x x x
♡ 9 2
◇ J x x
♣ K x x x

♠ A K
♡ A 10 x x x
◇ K x x x
♣ 10 x

South wins the opening Spade lead with the Ace, crosses to dummy and plays the Queen of Hearts. He needs one of two finesses for his slam—trumps or Clubs. And he may well be tempted to go up with the Ace of Hearts—just in case the King drops—and to rely on the Club finesse or on an End Play after elimination. East's false card may put him off by creating the impression that the King *can't* drop.

As for West, the question of deceiving him simply does not arise. All he can do is to follow suit. So why worry about him?

Here is another instance:

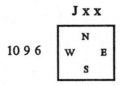

J x x

10 9 6

South leads a small one from dummy and plays the Queen on East's deuce. The suit is trumps and the contract is Four Spades. West must false-card. To tell the truth with the

281

six would be disloyal to East. It looks as if the suit is divided
as follows:

```
                 J 5 4
                ┌───────┐
                │   N   │
      10 9 6    │ W   E │    K 2
                │   S   │
                └───────┘
               A Q 8 7 3
```

Unless West plays the nine, declarer's only hope will be to lay
down the Ace, hoping to drop the King. And that, of course,
is the very thing that will happen. But if South can be made
to think that East has the six, he will have another chance—
to find this distribution.

```
                 J 5 4
                ┌───────┐
                │   N   │
       10 9     │ W   E │    K 6 2
                │   S   │
                └───────┘
               A Q 8 7 3
```

Now he enters dummy again and leads the Knave, hoping to
drop West's ten.

Again, no amount of false-carding can fool East. But
declarer can be easily misled. Even if he is of a suspicious
nature, he will have to guess, which means that—some of the
time—he will guess wrong. The other way, he is bound to
take the right view.

An audacious version of this fraud is to *open* the nine from
10 9 x. It is very pleasing when it succeeds, but West may
have to wait a long time for the right psychological moment.
All the auspices and omens must be right. This is how it works:

```
                 J x x
                ┌───────┐
                │   N   │
       10 9 x   │ W   E │    Q x (or K x)
                │   S   │
                └───────┘
               A K 8 x x
                   or
               A Q 8 x x
```

282

South can take five tricks by dropping East's Queen—or his King—after a first-round finesse. The lead of the nine suggests that East has the ten and gives South ideas. The nine is covered by the Knave and East's Queen—or King—falls to the Ace. Declarer enters dummy and finesses against East, who is " marked " with the ten. West pounces.

Partner, as well as declarer, may be fooled by this play. But why not? There are times when partner asks for nothing better than to be deceived. A common situation is the lead of the Knave from Q J. As with the nine, from 10 9, the stratagem is rarely worthwhile except in the trump suit, when East is innocent and North–South have the high cards.

West leads the Knave to emphasise that he is without the Queen. If South is taken in, he may go to a lot of trouble to finesse against East.

Lying is also advisable in this situation :

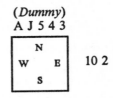

(Dummy)
A J 5 4 3

               10 2

This is a side suit, and declarer leads the King—or a small one from dummy up to his King. East goes up with the ten like a man. It looks as if South started with K x or K x x and has every intention of finessing against West's Queen. The ten may sow doubt in his mind. What if East has the Q 10 alone? Declarer won't fall for it every time. But if a false-card deceives him occasionally, it will show a profit. And even when it fails, there will be some compensation. Knowing that a defender false-cards, declarer will be unable to derive the full benefit from true cards which reveal too much. When East is really dealt the Q 10, South will, perhaps, finesse, refusing to trust the ten. If East never false-cards, South is much more likely to drop that Queen. Once more, observe that the ten can't fool West. He will be only too grateful to have a little protection for his defenceless Queen.

Duplicity is sometimes rewarded in cases like this:

A J 9

Q 10 x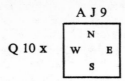

South leads a small one up to dummy, and he can hardly go wrong. West should give him a chance by playing the Queen—" splitting " his imaginary K Q combination. If South believes him, he will play up to the table again and go up with the Knave.

The point to bear in mind is that West has little to lose. If he plays low, South will surely put on the nine. The Queen may deceive. So it is a " free lie ", as it were. Something for next-to-nothing. Of course, if South has the King, duplicity won't help. But neither will the truth. So the lie is still free.

Deceiving Partner

This, too, is an honest lie, which partner will readily forgive.

♠ K x
♡ x x x x
♢ K Q x
♣ A 10 x x

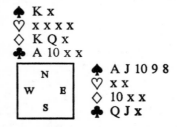

♠ A J 10 9 8
♡ x x
♢ 10 x x
♣ Q J x

North raises South's non-vulnerable No-trump (12–14 points) to Three, and West opens a small Club. Dummy plays low and East goes up with the Queen. By implication, this denies the Knave. But East does not want to boast about it, anyway. Should the Queen hold, East can always make a clean breast of it by returning the Knave. If South has the King, he will look on dummy's A 10 as two certain tricks, and it would be a pity to disillusion him. Of course, West will be taken in as well, but it does not matter, for the suit holds no prospects for the defence. East wants a Spade switch, and he is all the more likely to get it if West is kept in the dark about the Knave of Clubs.

Sometimes, it is of the very essence of the stratagem that partner should be deceived. But be careful to pick the right occasions.

The next piece of fraud is taken from real life.

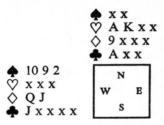

♠ x x
♡ A K x x
◇ 9 x x x
♣ A x x

♠ 10 9 2
♡ x x x
◇ Q J
♣ J x x x x

At game to East–West, the dealer, East, bid Four Spades, and South overcalled with Five Diamonds. West led the ten of Spades. The sight of dummy, bulging with trumps and Aces, was calculated to send a chill down the sturdiest spine.

East won the first trick with the Knave of Spades and laid down the Ace. South followed. That was the first feeble ray of sunshine and inspired a resourceful West to a neat subterfuge. He dropped—not the deuce—but the *nine*. Of course, East thought that South had the deuce and continued Spades, hoping that his partner would ruff higher than dummy. The nine deceived East completely. But it deceived declarer, as well, and two wrongs made a right.

West gambled—and it was a good gamble. He took this view: that for his over-call, at the five level, South would have all the seven missing Diamonds. And that he would have no side losers. The eleventh trick could be the King of Clubs or the Queen of Hearts.

If this diagnosis were correct, the only way to disturb declarer would be to frighten him with the threat of an over-ruff. To promote his Queen of Diamonds, West announced a fictitious shortage. South believed him and ruffed with the

King, hoping to drop the two outstanding trumps on the Ace. The four hands were:

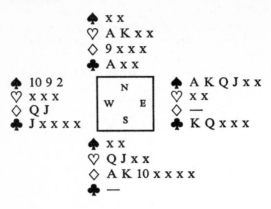

Ars Gratia Artis

At times, lying serves no concrete purpose, but it is right and proper to lie just for the sake of lying.

Dummy has A J 10 x x, and East sits over it with K Q bare. Declarer takes a finesse, and East has the choice of winning the trick with the King or Queen. Which should it be? The answer is that East should play the honour nearest his thumb. It does not matter which it is, so long as his thumb is not always on the same spot. He must vary his tactics. Otherwise, declarer will know whether to finesse again or to play for the drop. An East who false-cards automatically may be digging his own grave. Every time he wins with the Queen, South will know that the King must be with West. And the East who never false-cards will fare no better. The moment he produces the King, he tells the world that the Queen is somewhere else.

But with K Q x over A J 10, false-carding is generally rather pointless. As a rule, declarer is predestined to finesse twice, and encouragement is superfluous. To fool partner without confusing declarer is sabotage—not deception.

286

Deceptive Hold-up

The next example calls for strong nerves.

The bidding was:

South	North
One Heart	Two Diamonds
Two No-Trumps	Three No-Trumps

West leads the deuce of Spades, and dummy goes down with:

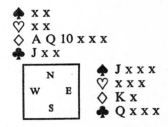

♠ x x
♡ x x
◇ A Q 10 x x x
♣ J x x

♠ J x x x
♡ x x x
◇ K x
♣ Q x x x

Declarer captures East's Knave with the King and runs the Knave of Diamonds. East plays low with an air of innocence. Of course, his King is now unguarded. But South does not know it and has no particular reason to suspect it. What the eye does not see the Ace cannot take.

An alert East will reason this way: " If I take the King, we may collect three more Spade tricks, which is not enough. But if I duck, South is bound to try the Diamond finesse again. And it may well be that he has a doubleton Diamond himself. Then he will be cut off from the table and we can turn really nasty. If dummy yields him one trick only, he is unlikely to find the other eight himself. Of course, South may have three Diamonds, in which case he will doubtless make his contract. But it costs nothing to hope. And the hope will turn to a near-certainty if West follows in ascending order, indicating three Diamonds. His first card is usually revealing.

The same cunning, but even more willpower, will be needed by East when the position is as follows:

Dummy has A K J x x and no entry. Declarer runs the ten, and East holds Q x x. If it is clear that declarer needs four tricks in the suit, East should hold off. All the chances are that South will repeat the finesse, and if he has a doubleton, he will find himself cut off from the table.

It is not always possible to tell how many tricks declarer needs from his dummy, but often enough East will make a good guess. The bidding, as a rule, provides a valuable clue.

Suppose that South opens One Club and rebids Two No-Trumps over his partner's Diamond. North raises to Three and goes down with :

♠ 10 x x   ♡ J x x   ◇ A K J 9 x   ♣ x x

Now it is unlikely that South can produce six tricks on his own. Perhaps the distribution in the other suits is right for him, but he knows nothing about it, and if his ten of Diamonds holds, he will probably finesse again. That is the time for East to play low on the first round. Of course, if the defence have already set up enough tricks to break the contract, the question does not arise. But if East wants to hold up an honour he should not be deterred automatically by the absence of an additional x. A little effrontery can take its place.

Deceptive Discards

The same precept applies to those situations in which a defender is put to a lot of discards and finds that, sooner or later, he will have to bare a King. Seeing the danger ahead he should perform the denuding process nonchalantly and with rhythmic insouciance. Above all, he should do it early on. No use waiting until the last agonising moment and then writhing in pain. That gives the whole show away. Bare the King in advance and throw less vital cards afterwards.

In the above examples deception has ranged from scientific false-carding to sheer impudence. Here is a case of bamboozling, pure and simple.

The bidding was:

South	North
One Spade	Four Spades

West led the King of Hearts and beheld dummy with:

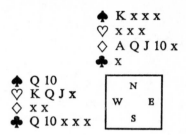

```
        ♠ K x x x
        ♡ x x x
        ◇ A Q J 10 x
        ♣ x

♠ Q 10          ┌─────────┐
♡ K Q J x       │   N     │
◇ x x           │ W     E │
♣ Q 10 x x x    │   S     │
                └─────────┘
```

The King held and West continued with the Queen, noting East's high–low signal. South won with the Ace and laid down the Ace of trumps. West dropped the Queen—not for any clear-cut purpose, but to introduce an element of confusion into an otherwise deplorably tidy situation. Of course, declarer intended to draw a couple of rounds of trumps, and then to settle down to the Diamonds. West felt that, even if his partner turned up with the King, prospects would still be dismal. East had no Heart, and West had no entry. As for that Queen of Spades, she was not much use anyway, for declarer was clearly on the point of leading another trump, and it made no difference whether the Queen dropped on the Ace or on the King.

Confusion was its own reward. South switched to Diamonds, hoping to clarify the position before facing a possible 4–1 break in trumps. East held back the first time. Then, when South repeated the finesse, he took the King and played another Diamond, giving West a ruff. Declarer had to lose two more tricks.

289

The hands were:

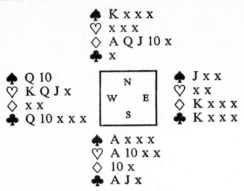

```
                    ♠ K x x x
                    ♡ x x x
                    ◇ A Q J 10 x
                    ♣ x
♠ Q 10                              ♠ J x x
♡ K Q J x          N               ♡ x x
◇ x x          W       E           ◇ K x x x
♣ Q 10 x x x        S              ♣ K x x x
                    ♠ A x x x
                    ♡ A 10 x x
                    ◇ 10 x
                    ♣ A J x
```

It is not suggested that South played the hand with particular brilliance. For all that, he would have made the contract if West had not rattled him.

Choosing the Right Victim

Declarers have had a poor time in the preceding pages, but it does not follow that they are a gullible tribe who believe everything East–West say. To lie artistically, first learn to pick your victim. Often a brilliant false card will be wasted on the rabbit, who will not notice it. Or worse still, he will ponder deeply and draw the wrong deduction. Conversely, a crude piece of fraud will deceive the novice, but will give the show away to a good player. This sort of situation arises again and again.

```
                 K J
                  N
A 7 x x      W        E      Q 10 8 x x
                  S

                 x x
```

South is trying to locate the Ace and Queen. East peters with the eight to fool him.

Against the tyro this may be quite effective. But an experienced declarer will be helped by so cheap a lie. He will reason: If East had the Ace, he would not tell me about it. So I bet he has the Queen and the Ace is with West.

Résumé

(1) Since almost every card carries a message, it may be more important to withhold information from declarer than to convey it to partner.

(2) The very fact that a defender is known to false card is an advantage. Declarer is made suspicious of the true cards and cannot derive full benefit from plays which reveal the distribution.

(3) It is permissible to lie to partner, so long as the deception cannot lure him into the wrong course of action. Sometimes his hand is dead anyway or his line of play is so obvious that no signal can affect it.

(4) When a defender can win a trick with the King or Queen —the Queen or Knave—the correct procedure is to be inconsistent. Sometimes do the one, sometimes the other, so as to prevent declarer from spotting your habits and drawing inferences.

(5) When dummy has a long suit, without the King or Queen, and no side entry, East may be justified in holding up the missing honour—even if he has to bare it. Declarer is unlikely to guess the situation. If he has a doubleton, and repeats the finesse, he may be cut off from the table.

(6) In all the above situations, defenders should play smoothly and at normal speed. A long pause is the antithesis of deception. It gives the show away.

(7) Suit the deception to the declarer. A blatant false card often helps a good player, but is the only way to deceive a bad one.

Exercises

(1) K J 3

Q 10 2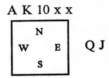

South, declarer, leads up to dummy and wins the trick with the Knave. He then plays the King. What card should West play?

(2) The contract is Three No-Trumps.

A K 10 x x

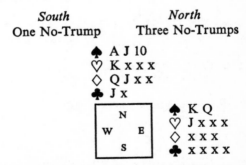 Q J

South leads the King from dummy. What should East play?

(3) The bidding was:

South	*North*
One No-Trump	Three No-Trumps

♠ A J 10
♡ K x x x
◇ Q J x x
♣ J x

      ♠ K Q
      ♡ J x x x
      ◇ x x x
      ♣ x x x x

West leads a small Spade, and declarer plays dummy's ten. What should East play?

(4) South, who bid Clubs and Hearts, ends up in Three No-Trumps.

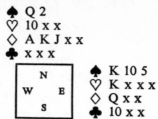

♠ Q 2
♡ 10 x x
◇ A K J x x
♣ x x x

```
      N
   W     E
      S
```

♠ K 10 5
♡ K x x x
◇ Q x x
♣ 10 x x

West leads the seven of Spades. East covers dummy's Queen with the King, and South plays the Ace. The ten of Diamonds is led from the closed hand and ducked in dummy. What should East do?

(5) The bidding was:

South	North
One Spade	Three Diamonds
Three Spades	Four Spades

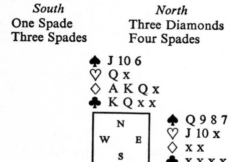

♠ J 10 6
♡ Q x
◇ A K Q x
♣ K Q x x

```
      N
   W     E
      S
```

♠ Q 9 8 7
♡ J 10 x
◇ x x
♣ x x x x

West opens the King of Hearts.
What card should East play?

(6) The contract is Three No-Trumps.

A J 8 7 5

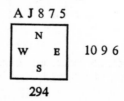

10 9 6

South leads up to dummy and plays the Knave on West's deuce. What card should East play?

(7) The contract is Three No-Trumps by South.

A Q 4 3 2

K 10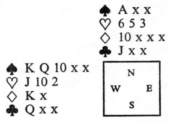

South leads the six towards dummy. What card should West play?

(8) The contract is Three Hearts by South.

♠ A x x
♡ 6 5 3
◇ 10 x x x
♣ J x x

♠ K Q 10 x x
♡ J 10 2
◇ K x
♣ Q x x

Declarer wins the opening Spade lead with dummy's Ace and plays a Heart.
East produces the four and South the King.
What should West play?

DUMMY PLAY

CHAPTER XIX

Squeezes

A squeeze is either difficult or painful. It depends on where you sit. Declarer may have difficulty in bringing it off. His victim has no problem. He just suffers, knowing that his next discard—whatever it is—cannot fail to be wrong. It is this element of inevitability which characterises the successful squeeze. The defender can choose *which* trick he throws. To that extent he exercises free will. The rest is predestination.

Why does a defender find himself in so awkward a predicament? The answer is that he is MENACED in two places at once, and cannot protect himself in both.

Positional Squeeze

This is how it looks from the receiving end.

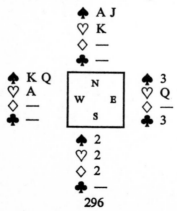

Declarer leads the deuce of Diamonds—the SQUEEZE CARD—and West is doomed. Whether he is an expert or a novice makes no difference. An inexorable fate compels him to present South with a trick. Because he has to play *before* dummy, he is forced to unguard the Spades or the Hearts. This is the POSITIONAL squeeze. It functions because the victim must play first—before the hand with the MENACE CARDS. Note the term—MENACE. You will come across it again and again. North's Knave of Spades and King of Hearts are *potential* winners. By threatening to materialise, they MENACE the defence.

In the POSITIONAL SQUEEZE the menaces are *always* over the victim. If East held West's cards there would be no squeeze. For TIME is the crucial element, and it is West who must play first.

Divided Menaces

But the Greenwich Observatory itself can do nothing here:

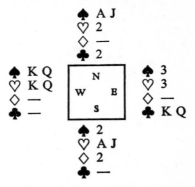

Again South leads his deuce of Diamonds, and to add insult to injury, he can throw dummy's Club *before* West has so much as a chance to writhe or wriggle. This time, the victim's position is of no interest. East and West can change places. No one will care. The defender will be squeezed wherever he sits.

What is the difference between the two hands? Why is it

that TIME and POSITION no longer matter as in the last example?

The explanation lies with the MENACES. The first time, *both* were in dummy—over West. Now the MENACES are divided. North's Knave of Spades and South's Knave of Hearts threaten, simultaneously, whichever defender happens to guard both suits.

Numerical Superiority

What really happens is that the victim is outnumbered. West has to guard the Spades and Hearts all by himself. But declarer can use dummy's cards, as well as his own. The trouble from West's point of view is that his partner is of no help. And the DIVIDED MENACES catch him in a pincer movement. Hence the squeeze.

Note the plural—menaces. There must always be two against the same defender, for the essence of the stratagem is to force his surrender to one or other. And one of the menaces must have not less than two cards—a combination of winner plus potential winner. An Ace with an x behind it can be a two-card menace, compelling one of the defenders to retain two cards, lest the x should turn into a winner. One menace of two or more cards, headed by a winner, is the prerequisite of every squeeze.

The Link

To complete a description of the squeeze mechanism one more piece must be fitted into place—the LINK between the two hands. An entry is not enough. The LINK must be with the two-card menace. Otherwise the victim escapes.

The Squeeze Apparatus

To recapitulate, here are the three essential parts of the squeeze apparatus.

First, two menaces against the same defender. One of the two must be extended—not less than two cards. Next, there must be a LINK between declarer's hand and dummy, and this link must be with the two-card menace.

298

Last comes the SQUEEZE card, which sets the mechanism in motion. The victim cannot follow to it, and the essence of the play is that he should be unable to discard without unguarding one of the suits in which he is menaced.

We have seen already what actually happens when the blow falls. In the POSITIONAL squeeze the defender is helpless, because the menaces are over him and he must play first. In all the other squeeze situations the menaces are divided and the victim is outnumbered.

Double Squeeze

And how about this:

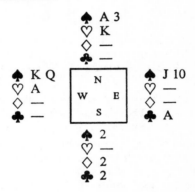

Declarer leads the deuce of Diamonds, and West hangs on grimly to the Ace of Hearts. One of his Spade honours goes, leaving East to look after the Spade suit.

South throws dummy's King of Hearts—which has done its work—and it is East's turn to squirm. He can neither part with a Spade nor with his Ace of Clubs.

What was it? A DOUBLE SQUEEZE—the synthesis of both the types discussed above. West was in trouble, because he had to discard before dummy. East could not cope with superior numbers. The positional aspect was against the first defender. Divided menaces were too much for the second.

If only the pack contained fewer cards, squeeze play would be far easier. It is the superfluous cards which get in the way

299

and make it complicated. In the quintessential diagram the position is clear. With fifty-two cards about, the menaces, the link and the squeeze card itself are blurred in a mist.

The Execution

Let us deal all four hands and bid Seven Spades. We begin with a grand slam—not just to be spectacular, but for a very important reason, which will emerge later. Don't ask how we got there. No doubt, partner bid badly. Never mind.

♠ A K Q J x x   ♠ x x x
♡ A x x   ♡ K Q x x
◇ A J   ◇ x x x x
♣ A K   ♣ x x

North opens the King of Diamonds and we begin to count. Twelve top tricks are there for all to see, and one more if the Hearts break. And if they don't? There is still a chance. Can you see it?

No, it is not the hope that someone will carelessly throw a Heart from four. That is bad defence. A true squeeze succeeds against any defence. Try it.

First, the menaces. Can you threaten the same defender in two suits? How about Hearts and Diamonds? North's lead marks him with the K Q of Diamonds. What if he has four Hearts—or five for that matter? Won't he have to guard both suits?

West's menaces are divided—the Diamond Knave in his own hand and the long Heart in dummy. So it would not really matter if South, not North, guarded the red suits.

♠ x   ♠ —
♡ A x x   ♡ K Q x x
◇ J   ◇ x
♣ —   ♣ —

North—or South, if he started with four Hearts and the K Q of Diamonds—will be reduced to:

♠ —   ♡ J 10 9 x   ◇ Q   ♣ —

and he will have to discard something on the last trump. The victim is squeezed, because he cannot guard both red suits.

In real life, and given that distribution in Hearts and Diamonds, this particular grand slam would doubtless be made by most players. It requires no special technique, because the squeeze is *automatic*. So long as West plays off *all* his winners—apart from the Hearts—there can be no hope for the defender with four Hearts and the K Q of Diamonds. There is nothing he can do.

Preparation

But most squeezes, of course, are not automatic. They must be PREPARED. Before a squeeze materialises, the stage must be set and the scenery moved into position.

And the first thing to remember is that a squeeze yields one trick, only one trick and nothing more than one trick. There is an exception—the PROGRESSIVE squeeze, which really means two *successive* squeezes on the same hand. This occurs too rarely to justify a digression. Meanwhile, the crux of the matter is that when the squeeze card is played, declarer must be able to count every card in his hand as a winner—except *one*.

That is why our first example of a full deal was a grand slam. The COUNT was right from the start. With twelve ready-made winners, no preparation was required.

To bring the point home, try a little alchemy. Take away West's King of Clubs and make the contract Six Spades instead of Seven. Imagine that the same defender holds the Hearts and the K Q of Diamonds. This time, however, North opens a Club. Suppose that West wins. Here we go.

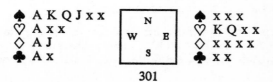

♠ A K Q J x x   ♠ x x x
♡ A x x   ♡ K Q x x
◇ A J   ◇ x x x x
♣ A x   ♣ x x

The last six cards will be:

♠ x
♡ A x x
◇ J
♣ x

♠ —
♡ K Q x x
◇ x
♣ x

As before, West leads the squeeze card, his last trump. But nothing happens. North (or South) discards a Club and declarer is tied to eleven tricks. Why? Because the count was not right. There was an IDLE card about, which the intended victim of the squeeze could throw away with impunity.

The Count

And yet West should have made his small slam. All he had to do was to *give up* the first trick by holding up the Ace of Clubs. That would have *RECTIFIED THE COUNT*.

Look again at that last diagram. Remove the Club x. It is no longer there. Now, once more, the defender with the red suits is squeezed. All his cards are BUSY. He cannot follow to that Spade without unguarding the Hearts or letting go his King of Diamonds.

The first essential step in the preparation of a squeeze is to make sure that the *idle* cards have been eliminated. They represent space, and the whole idea of a squeeze is to compress space—to leave the victim no room to breathe.

This is so important that it will bear repetition. A squeeze yields ONE trick. Therefore, to bring it about, declarer must have ONE loser and no more. If he happens to have two, he must first concede a trick to the defence. Then, and then only, will the squeeze mechanism function.

If South hopes to make Four Spades on a squeeze, he must first give up three losers. With nine winners and ten cards left, he looks to the squeeze for the extra trick. If he concedes two losers only, the IDLE card will provide the defence with room to breathe—and a card to jettison.

When declarer has eight winners in a Three No-Trump contract, a squeeze may yield the ninth trick. But only *after* four losers have gone. Not before.

Rectification

Turn the searchlight on this diagram.

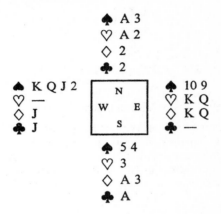

```
                    ♠ A 3
                    ♡ A 2
                    ◇ 2
                    ♣ 2
    ♠ K Q J 2      ┌───────────┐      ♠ 10 9
    ♡ —           │     N     │      ♡ K Q
    ◇ J           │  W     E  │      ◇ K Q
    ♣ J           │     S     │      ♣ —
                  └───────────┘
                    ♠ 5 4
                    ♡ 3
                    ◇ A 3
                    ♣ A
```

South needs one more trick besides his four Aces. Can he do it by squeezing East? He has two perfectly good menaces in Hearts and Diamonds. Entries are plentiful. And the Ace of Clubs is an impeccable squeeze card.

For all that, the squeeze will not function without preparation. Declarer has *two* cards that are not winners—one too many.

What, then, should he do? He must lose a trick quickly to leave himself with five cards and four winners. Only Spades provide a suitable loser, for all the red cards are needed to threaten East. Since South cannot afford to surrender control, he *ducks* a Spade in both hands. West's return can

303

make no difference.   Suppose that he plays a Diamond.   The position will be:

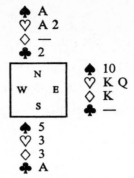

```
              ♠ A
              ♡ A 2
              ◇ —
              ♣ 2
        ┌───────────┐      ♠ 10
        │     N     │      ♡ K Q
        │ W       E │      ◇ K
        │     S     │      ♣ —
        └───────────┘
              ♠ 5
              ♡ 3
              ◇ 3
              ♣ A
```

South lays down the Ace of Spades and the Club squeezes East.

Vienna Coup

Rectifying the count—leaving yourself with only one more card than you have winners—is the crux of the preparation. More often than not, it will suffice.   Sometimes, however, the menaces are not quite in place and another adjustment is needed.   Like this:

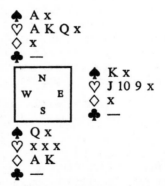

```
              ♠ A x
              ♡ A K Q x
              ◇ x
              ♣ —
        ┌───────────┐      ♠ K x
        │     N     │      ♡ J 10 9 x
        │ W       E │      ◇ x
        │     S     │      ♣ —
        └───────────┘
              ♠ Q x
              ♡ x x x
              ◇ A K
              ♣ —
```

Theoretically, South's second Diamond will squeeze East.   In practice he will bare his King of Spades, and declarer will be

304

unable to take advantage of it. For dummy must discard first, and East won't throw his small Spade until that x has gone from dummy. Then South will be unable to get back to cash his Queen.

To make the Spade menace effective, the Ace is cashed *first*. That leaves the way open for the Queen. On the second Diamond—the squeeze card—declarer throws dummy's Spade x and the position is:

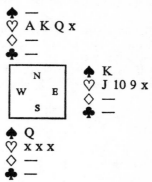

East is squeezed.

This play is known as the Vienna Coup. It consists in cashing a winner *opposite* a menace card, when the winner is in the way. Technically, the Vienna Coup is an unblocking play. It helps when the menaces need a little unscrambling.

A Choice of Two Squeezes

To illustrate in more detail the mechanism of PREPARATION let us deal all the cards.

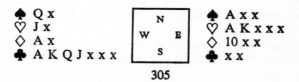

305

Six Clubs is a nice contract, but, at duplicate, West lands in Six No-Trumps.

North opens the King of Diamonds. Seeing eleven tricks in his thirteen cards, declarer ducks. That makes the count right for a squeeze, if there is one—every card a winner, *less one*.

The Queen of Diamonds follows. West wins and notes that dummy's ten is a menace against North. For surely he would not have played the Queen if he did not hold the Knave as well.

What is the next step? If North made a bid at some stage or doubled the final contract, declarer will assume that he must have the King of Spades. And if the assumption is right, the last Club will subject North to a positional squeeze in Spades and Diamonds. The final diagram will show:

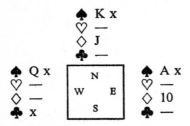

Having to discard before dummy, North is helpless. In this case, rectifying the count at the first trick ensures the contract. No further preparation is necessary.

But what if West decides that South is more likely than North to hold the Spade King? That is the time for the Vienna Coup. Otherwise, after the Spade xs have been thrown from dummy, the Ace will obstruct the Queen.

Observe what this play does to the Heart suit. A third menace has appeared, for one of the defenders must look after the Hearts, and the same man won't be able to look after the Queen of Spades or the ten of Diamonds as well. He will be too busy.

West lays down the Ace of Hearts—just in case. Unless the Queen drops, he plays off the Ace of Spades—the Vienna Coup

—and settles down to the Clubs. When the last one touches the table, the position is :

The ten of Diamonds is thrown from dummy as soon as North has followed with something other than his Knave. If South started with the King of Spades, he, too, is squeezed.

The contract was made on a DOUBLE squeeze. And the motif, as always in a double squeeze, was the third suit. North had to look after dummy's ten of Diamonds. South was compelled to hang on to his King of Spades. Neither defender had room for a guard in Hearts.

Note the difference in technique. If declarer assumes—because of an intervening bid or double—that North has the King of Spades, he plays off the tops in Hearts. For a positional squeeze, two suits only matter—in this case, Spades and Diamonds.

Not so for a double squeeze. Hearts—the third suit—is brought into play. The Heart link is carefully preserved, and the Ace of Spades is played off.

If North and South remain apathetic throughout the auction, the expert West is more likely to adopt the second approach than the first. Only 12 points are outstanding. And if North is credited with six of them—the K Q J of Diamonds—it is reasonable to expect the King of Spades to be with South. After all, why should North have 9 points or more out of the missing 12?

Planning

The time has come to put the question : When should declarer turn his thoughts to a squeeze?

In the foregoing pages we have made numerous contracts—some of them far from easy—without resorting to the squeeze technique. It was not necessary. How, then, should we recognise the right occasion? And what makes one hand better suited for squeeze play than another?

First, there are certain broad indications. Declarer needs *one* more trick, and he can't find it. There is no finesse position, and suit establishment holds out no prospects.

Starting on his quest, declarer looks for a defender who may be guarding two suits. Sometimes, only one of the defenders will fill the bill. All the menaces are in one hand, and the situation lends itself only to a POSITIONAL squeeze. More often, the menaces are divided—one in the closed hand, and the other in dummy. Then East is as good a victim as West.

Finally, as in the last example, a third suit can be brought into play. Declarer knows or suspects that each defender, in turn, must guard a particular suit. Is there a menace in a third suit? If so, a double squeeze may be indicated.

Spotting the Chances for a Squeeze

A long suit often suggests a squeeze. But that is more a case of local colour than of hard fact, and the experienced player looks for opportunities, whatever the distribution. What are the chances on this very ordinary hand?

	N	
♠ K x x x	W E	♠ A x x
♡ A x		♡ K 10 x
◊ 10 9 x x	S	◊ A Q J x
♣ A x x		♣ x x x

North opens a Club against Three No-Trumps. Declarer holds up twice, and the suit breaks 4–3. But the Diamond finesse loses and the last Club is with South. West must take the rest of the tricks. How? Admittedly prospects are not particularly bright, for it is too much to hope that the Q J of Hearts are bare. There is a better chance than that. The odds are that the Spades will break 4–2. Does that suggest anything?

If the same defender has four Spades—or more, of course— and the Q J of Hearts, he will be squeezed out of existence. When declarer leads the last Diamond, the position will be:

	N	
♠ K x x	W E	♠ A x
♡ A x		♡ K 10 x
◊ x	S	◊ J
♣ —		♣ —

308

And the victim will hold:

♠ 10 x x   ♡ Q J x

His partner—if he started with a doubleton Spade—won't be in the argument. This contract does not call for the squeeze technique as such. If the cards lie right, the squeeze is automatic. But declarer must know the technique to spot the situation, and the hand is only given as an exercise in RECOGNITION.

Continue to be squeeze-minded on the next deal:

♠ x x x		♠ x x x
♡ A K x x	N	♡ Q J x
◇ x x x	W E	◇ A K x x
♣ J x x	S	♣ A K x

West is once more in Three No-Trumps. North collects the first four tricks with Spades and switches to a Heart. On the last Spade, declarer throws a Diamond from both hands. West can see eight tricks. Where should he look for the ninth? The Queen of Clubs may drop. But what if it does not? Then a squeeze is the only hope. One of the defenders may hold four (or more) Diamonds and the Queen of Clubs, and if he does, his pips will rattle on the last Heart.

The last three cards will be:

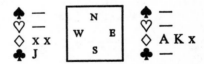

♠ —		♠ —
♡ —	N	♡ —
◇ x x	W E	◇ A K x
♣ J	S	♣ —

At this stage, neither defender can retain three Diamonds *and* the Queen of Clubs. So it is just a case of hoping that the same defender has the Club Queen and the long Diamonds.

The Importance of Hoping

The wheel has turned full circle. In the opening pages of this book declarer *hoped* that a missing honour was in the right place. So he finessed. Now, as we near the end—and in what is reputed to be the most difficult play in Bridge, the squeeze—declarer still puts his faith in hope, the hope that the same defender guards two suits. That means that two menaces must point in the same direction. And it is the search for *menaces* which characterises the planning of a squeeze.

Creating a Menace

To avoid any trouble with the COUNT, the contract is Seven Hearts. North leads a Diamond.

```
♠ A x              N            ♠ K x x x
♡ A K Q J x x   W     E         ♡ x x x
◇ A                             ◇ x x
♣ A x x x          S            ♣ K Q x x
```

What are the prospects? The barometer points to " Fine ". Still, a bad Club break can wreck the contract. Can anything be done to overcome a 4–1—or 5–0—Club division? How about a squeeze? The victim will have to be the defender with the long Clubs—if that suit does not break. So that is one menace. Spades will have to provide the other. Declarer's hope is that whoever holds the Clubs was dealt long Spades as well.

After drawing trumps declarer plays three rounds of Spades, ruffing the third. That assures that only one defender can guard the suit. The five-card end position will be :

```
♠ —               N            ♠ x
♡ x            W     E         ♡ —
◇ —                            ◇ —
♣ A x x x         S            ♣ K Q x x
```

Dummy throws a Club on the last Heart. North—or South, provided our hope is borne out—will have :

$$\spadesuit \text{ J} \quad \clubsuit \text{ J 10 9 x}$$

And thanks to the Spade ruff, his partner will have no more Spades left.

310

This play is known as ISOLATING THE MENACE. The purpose is to prevent *both* defenders from guarding the same suit. In this particular example, ISOLATING the Spade menace is a safety play. It creates an additional chance—in case the Clubs break badly.

But beware! You cannot afford to play off the Clubs, just to see if they break, and to curse your luck if they don't. The Club suit provides the essential LINK with the Spade menace. And in squeeze play the LINK always takes precedence over curiosity.

The next example, based on the same principle, will seem particularly difficult to players who are not familiar with squeezes.

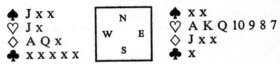

```
♠ J x x              ♠ x x
♡ J x         N      ♡ A K Q 10 9 8 7
◇ A Q x    W     E   ◇ J x x
♣ x x x x x    S     ♣ x
```

East opens Four Hearts, and all pass.   Declarer ruffs the third Spade and takes stock.

Three top losers stare him in the face. So the Diamond finesse must be taken for granted. But even then there are only nine winners. Unless the King of Diamonds drops, a Diamond —the fourth loser—will have to be given up at the end.

A little addition shows that there are not enough entries to ruff the Club suit out and to get at it afterwards.

What are the prospects of a squeeze? The Diamonds provide one menace—assuming, of course, that South has the King. A second menace can only be found in Clubs, which means that the Club menace must be ISOLATED. If South alone is forced to look after the Clubs—as well as the King of Diamonds—he will be in trouble. Test it.

At the third trick play a Club. The best defence is a trump. This you take on the table and ruff a Club. Then a successful Diamond finesse, and another Club ruff. No matter how the suit breaks, only one of the defenders can now look after it. You hope that it is South. With two menaces—Clubs and

Diamonds—poised nicely over him, he will be a prey to the positional squeeze. This will be his last spasm.

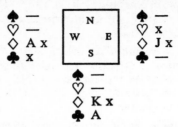

What can he do on the ultimate Heart, except leave the room?

The key to the hand lies in pointing the second menace against South. If North has the long Clubs, it cannot be done. But if South has them, the Club menace can be isolated.

There are many complex squeezes, each one rejoicing in a name of its own. They make suitable material for double-dummy problems and Christmas teasers in the Sunday Press. But none of them occur often enough to justify detailed analysis. The student who masters the technique set out above will be able, eventually, to work out by himself the more intricate types of squeeze. It is the other kind that matter—the kind that arise regularly in day-to-day Bridge. And it is our purpose to impart the winning technique for the hands you will be actually dealt—not for the ones you will occasionally read about. Look after the humdrum, and let the exotic look after itself.

Résumé

(1) A simple squeeze takes effect when a defender cannot discard without unguarding one of two suits, thereby presenting declarer with a trick.

(2) A double squeeze takes effect when *both* defenders—first one, then the other—are placed in that position.

(3) Every squeeze demands two MENACES (or more). The first can be a one-card menace, but the second must have at least two cards, headed by a winner. The two hands must have a link, and this must be with the *two-card* menace.

(4) In a POSITIONAL squeeze both menaces are in the same hand—over the victim. The squeeze takes effect because the victim has to discard *before* the hand with the two menaces.

(5) In every other type of squeeze the menaces must be *divided*—one in declarer's hand, the other in dummy. The squeeze takes effect because the victim is OUT-NUMBERED. He cannot keep in his one hand as many ACTIVE cards as declarer and dummy between them.

(6) To make a squeeze effective, it is necessary to reduce the victim's hand to the point at which *all* his cards are ACTIVE. There must be no IDLE cards.

(7) In preparing a squeeze the above is of paramount importance. The first step is to concede the inevitable losers, relying on the squeeze for ONE extra trick only. If the defenders do not cash all their winners, declarer must FORCE them to do so before giving effect to a squeeze. This is known as RECTIFYING THE COUNT.

(8) Sometimes a further step in preparing a squeeze is needed : a menace position must be " re-arranged ". This play, known as the Vienna Coup, arises when a menace is blocked by higher cards opposite (e.g., Q x opposite A x or J x x opposite A K x). The high cards are played first, " releasing " the menace card opposite to do its work.

(9) In planning a squeeze declarer looks for two menaces against the same defender. Sometimes one menace is

313

readily available, but the other is doubtful; perhaps the suit is being held by both defenders. To ISOLATE the menace, declarer endeavours—by ruffing or ducking—to exhaust the partner of the intended victim of this particular suit. Then the menace points at one defender only. Declarer hopes that it is at the defender who is already threatened in another suit.

(10) As in the case of a simple finesse, the hope that the cards are well placed often guides declarer in planning a squeeze. He knows or guesses that one of the defenders guards a certain suit. The next step is based on the hope that he guards a second suit as well. It is vulnerability on *two fronts* which lays the victim open to a squeeze.

Exercises

(1) ♠ x x x 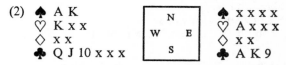 ♠ x x x
♡ A K x ♡ J x x x
◇ Q x x ◇ A K x
♣ A K Q x ♣ x x x

North opens a Spade against Three No-Trumps by West, and the defence take the first four tricks. On the fourth Spade West throws a Diamond from his own hand and a Heart from dummy.

(a) If the Clubs break 4–2, and the Queen of Hearts is twice guarded, will declarer still have a chance to make his contract?

(b) If there is still hope, on what will the contract depend?

(c) What should be the last four cards in the East–West hands?

(2) ♠ A K 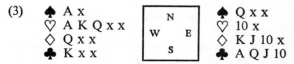 ♠ x x x x
♡ K x x ♡ A x x x
◇ x x ◇ x x
♣ Q J 10 x x x ♣ A K 9

North leads the two top Diamonds against Five Clubs, and then switches to a trump.

(a) What should West do after drawing trumps, which break 2–2?

(b) What should be the last three cards in the East–West hands?

(3) ♠ A x 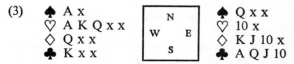 ♠ Q x x
♡ A K Q x x ♡ 10 x
◇ Q x x ◇ K J 10 x
♣ K x x ♣ A Q J 10

The nine of Clubs is led against Six No-Trumps by West.

(a) How should declarer plan the play to allow for a bad Heart break?

(b) What should be the last three cards in the East–West hands?

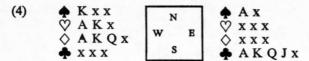

(4)
- ♠ K x x
- ♡ A K x
- ◇ A K Q x
- ♣ x x x

- ♠ A x
- ♡ x x x
- ◇ x x x
- ♣ A K Q J x

North opens the ten of Clubs against Six No-Trumps by West. South shows out.

(a) Can declarer make certain of the contract?

(b) What East–West cards should make up the second trick?

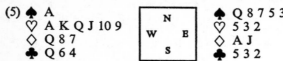

(5)
- ♠ A
- ♡ A K Q J 10 9
- ◇ Q 8 7
- ♣ Q 6 4

- ♠ Q 8 7 5 3
- ♡ 5 3 2
- ◇ A J
- ♣ 5 3 2

After North had opened the bidding with Three Diamonds, West becomes declarer at Four Hearts. North leads the Knave of Clubs. South wins with the King, lays down the Ace and plays a small Club, which North ruffs. A Diamond return is won by dummy's Knave. Declarer leads a trump and North shows out.

(a) What is declarer's only chance?

(b) What should be the last three cards in the East–West hands?

(6)
- ♠ J x x
- ♡ x
- ◇ A Q J x x
- ♣ A Q x x

- ♠ A Q x x
- ♡ Q x x x
- ◇ K x
- ♣ K J x

North, who had intervened with One Heart during the bidding, opens the King of Hearts against Six Diamonds. At the second trick he switches to a trump.

(a) Assuming that the Spade finesse wins, can declarer put his hand on the table?

(b) In explaining his line of play, what will he tell opponents about his last three cards?

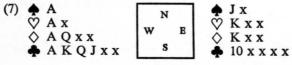

(7)
- ♠ A
- ♡ A x
- ◇ A Q x x
- ♣ A K Q J x x

- ♠ J x
- ♡ K x x
- ◇ K x x
- ♣ 10 x x x x

Seven Clubs is, of course, icy cold, but playing in duplicate pairs with matchpoint scoring, East–West reach a contract of Seven No-Trumps.

North opens the King of Spades. Later, he shows up with a singleton Heart.

(a) Can the contract be made?

(b) What should be the last four cards in declarer's hand and in dummy?

DEFENCE

CHAPTER XX

Defending with Bad Cards

Bad cards have a charm of their own—though it is not widely appreciated. It takes a good player to defend well with a collection of tram-tickets, but the reward is commensurate with the skill. When East–West have next to nothing, North–South bid their slams. And that is the time to stop them, if possible.

Now get ready for the cascade of rock-crushers that is about to descend upon you. And remember: every Goliath may meet a David.

Sometimes, declarer's hand overflows with Aces and Kings and all the good things of the pack. The distribution is not especially unkind. Yet there is a hoodoo of some sort, and things won't go right. To cast an evil spell on declarer requires expert defence. And that begins with the opening lead, which is especially important against slams.

Leading Against a Slam

The most striking success for an opening is to present partner with a ruff or to contrive a ruff for oneself. It needs no Gremlin on South's shoulder for West to open a singleton. The next best thing for East–West is to *set up* a trick. Against a small slam the defence can generally reckon on one trick somewhere, and the idea is to develop another—all ready to cash when the first one comes along.

Let us start with the obvious. Expert and novice alike will make the same lead against Six No-Trumps from:

♠ K Q x ♡ A x x ◇ x x x ♣ x x x x

West opens the King of Spades, because he expects to come in with the Ace of Hearts, and he looks to the Spade Queen for the setting trick. He would make the same lead, and for the same reason, against a suit contract.

Change the hand slightly, substituting an x for the King of Spades:

♠ Q x x   ♡ A x x   ◇ x x x   ♣ x x x x

Now the novice won't think of touching Spades. The expert might. It will depend on the bidding.

If North–South reached the slam by some such means as: Two No-Trumps—Six No-Trumps, then the Spades must be left strictly alone. Presumably, declarer and dummy have balanced hands. Therefore, the Spades may be expected to provide them with more than two tricks, and that means that South will look for the Queen. Don't tell him where she is. Left to himself he may look in the wrong place. The bidding shrieks for a passive lead.

An Aggressive Lead

But perhaps the auction followed some such lines as:

North	South
	One Heart
Three Diamonds	Three Hearts
Four Diamonds	Four No-Trumps (Blackwood)
Five Hearts (Blackwood)	Six No-Trumps

Clearly, North–South have two long suits and can make plenty of tricks, given *time*. West can intervene once, and once only—when he takes his Ace of Hearts. At that precise moment he must have a ready-made trick. And with that in mind, he leads a small Spade from:

♠ Q x x   ♡ A x x   ◇ x x x   ♣ x x x x

It is an aggressive lead based on the hope that the King is with East.

Of course, this may cost a trick. But it is imperative to take the initiative, for this time the bidding suggests that declarer's problem will be—not to make twelve tricks, but to avoid losing two. The risk of giving him a winner, which he does not need, is outweighed by the prospect of creating for him a loser, which he cannot afford.

319

In fact, there is no harm in presenting declarer with a winner —so long as it is not his *twelfth*. Sometimes the bidding shows that declarer can be reasonably certain of eleven tricks, but may have work to do in developing one more. That is the time for a *passive* lead—one that will give nothing away. Often enough—and more often in suit contracts than in No-Trumps—the bidding suggests good, long suits with plenty of winners. That is when West must look for a weak spot. An *aggressive* lead is then the order of the day.

All this has a bearing on one of the favourite vices of the uninitiated—the vice of leading out Aces. With a certain trump trick, West may be justified in laying down an Ace quickly. There is always the possibility that declarer has a singleton in the suit and can get a quick discard. But that is an exception. As a regular habit, opening an Ace against a slam is thoroughly unprofitable. It may clear a suit for declarer, and it loses a tempo. With the Ace gone, it will be too late to *develop* a trick. For without an entry, there will be no opportunity to cash it.

The Lightner Double

A new element enters the picture when partner doubles. In a slam contract this is a special bid and calls for special treatment. Part score and game contracts are doubled for penalties. Not so slams. Unless it is a sacrifice, there can be no expectation of a sizeable penalty and the double is inspired by a different motive. It is *lead directing* and calls for an UNUSUAL opening—an opening that would not be made normally.

That rules out any suit bid by defenders, and also the unbid suit(s). Such leads would be normal, and the double calls for the *abnormal*. This is known as the *Lightner double*, after Theodore Lightner, one of Culbertson's famous partners, and today the convention is in universal use.

This would be a case in point.

North	*South*
One Diamond	Two Hearts
Three Hearts	Four Diamonds
Five Hearts	Six Hearts

East doubles.   West holds:

♠ Q x x   ♡ x   ◇ x x x x   ♣ Q J 10 x x

The Queen of Clubs is the natural lead, so West looks else-where.   The search is soon over, for surely East is screaming for a Diamond.   Almost certainly he is void of the suit.   The bidding shows that East is short in Diamonds, though that, of course, would be no reason for leading one.   The double settles the matter, as far as West is concerned.   It is a com-mand, and it follows that East must not double a slam unless he is fully prepared for an unusual lead.   The Lightner double is too valuable a weapon to be brandished frivolously.   And that puts a responsibility on both sides of the East–West axis.

Look at it from the East angle:

North	South
	One Heart
Two Clubs	Three No-Trumps
Five Hearts	Six Hearts

East has:

♠ J x x x x x   ♡ A x   ◇ x x x x x   ♣ —

Unless West receives specific instructions, he has no reason to lead a Club.   But the Lightner double cannot be misunder-stood, for only a Club lead would be "unnatural".

Sometimes the light is not so blinding.   Perhaps three suits have been bid and West is in doubt.   For such cases no ready-made rule can be laid down.   A player's holding, taken in conjunction with the bidding, will usually supply all the clues.   Often, though by no means always, the Lightner double proclaims a void.   But it may be a situation of this sort.

North	South
One Spade	Three Clubs
Three Spades	Four Diamonds
Four Spades	Four No-Trumps (Blackwood)
Five Hearts (Blackwood)	Six No-Trumps

East holds:

♠ K x x   ♡ x x x x x   ◇ A x x   ♣ J x

and sets his mind to work. Declarer has not less than nine cards in the minors and maybe more. His Spades must verge on the imperceptible—probably a singleton. No doubt, South chose to play the slam in No-Trumps because he did not want to commit himself to a trump suit—in case the one he picked broke badly.

To upset the apple-cart, East must make sure of a Spade lead. A double conveys the request to West, and a Spade opening sets up East's King, while he still retains the Ace of Diamonds.

That is the purpose of the Lightner double—to summon a slam-destroying lead, which West would be unlikely to produce on his own.

Technique in Discarding

The opening is often the decisive factor, which is why more slams against South are given away by West than by East. Thereafter, the initiative passes to declarer. East–West lead lives of enforced rectitude with little to do but follow suit. When six or seven cards have gone and the defenders begin to run out of South's suits, every discard seems to present a problem. That is the critical phase.

Fortunately, no two hands are alike, and each one must be treated on its merits. For all that, the art of discarding correctly is governed by certain principles.

The first and foremost is to count declarer's hand. The second is to deduce his intentions from his play. Card reading and interpretation will often tell the defenders which suits they can unguard—because South must be short in them himself, or because he has no losers in them anyway.

Against slams, and other high contracts, East–West must be especially wary of the squeeze. This may take one of three forms:

The *true* squeeze against which there can be no defence.

The *potential* squeeze, which can sometimes be broken up by good play.

And finally, the *imaginary* squeeze, which exists only in the minds of the defenders.

This last type is by far the most common, for it takes in all those situations which range from honest delusion to vague apprehension. Sometimes a defender just does not know what to throw, and the resulting confusion is as helpful to declarer as the most lethal squeeze.

Psychologically, South starts with an initial advantage in every slam contract. Because he holds the great preponderance of cards, East–West are inclined to wallow in gloom and melancholy. Defeatism undermines their will to win. In point of fact, their optimism should rise with every card declarer plays. That he cannot spread his hand after the first few tricks is in itself an encouraging omen. When a slam is watertight, South can usually make an announcement at an early stage. If he does not, there must be some hope for the defence.

So much for morale. Now for technique. Try to discard correctly from East's hand.

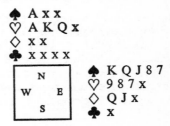

♠ A x x
♡ A K Q x
◇ x x
♣ x x x x

♠ K Q J 8 7
♡ 9 8 7 x
◇ Q J x
♣ x

Bidding:

South	North
One Diamond	One Heart
One No-Trump	Three No-Trumps

West opens the Queen of Clubs, holds the trick and continues with the Knave. Declarer wins with the King, lays down the Ace of Clubs and leads another, which falls to West's ten.

East has to find three discards. The first two present no insuperable problem. He lets go the eight, then the seven of Spades. But what should he throw on the last Club? The answer is: a Diamond. And if he had to find two discards, he should relinquish two Diamonds.

If East throws a Heart, dummy's x becomes a *certain* winner. West cannot stop the suit, for the bidding marks South with not less than a doubleton Heart. So West can have three at most.

If South holds the Knave of Hearts and the A K of Diamonds, the contract is cold. If he is missing any one of those three cards, he can probably be beaten—so long as East does not allow himself to be mesmerised into a faulty discard by South's Diamond bid.

In letting go a Diamond East can take comfort from declarer's line of play. If he had five Diamonds or even something like A K 10 9, he would have surely set about developing the suit instead of playing back West's Clubs. South's hand is probably:

♠ 10 x x   ♡ x x   ◊ A K x x   ♣ A K x x

Breaking up a Potential Squeeze

Against the infallible squeeze the defence is helpless. It is a case of the irresistible force and the mobile object. But sometimes the force is not quite irresistible and the squeeze can be broken up before it gathers momentum. To foil declarer it is first necessary to understand what he is trying to do. The squeeze mechanism has already been explained in the previous chapter. For present purposes, the briefest outline will suffice.

In executing a squeeze, declarer relies on MENACES—potential winners in two (or three) suits. The stratagem materialises when one of the defenders—both in a double squeeze—throws a vital card(s), unguarding a suit. Before this situation can come about, declarer must concede his inevitable losers. Otherwise, the defenders will have *idle cards*—cards not engaged in guarding anything—and these they can throw away with impunity.

So, declarer's first step in preparing a squeeze is to RECTIFY THE COUNT—to concede *all* the tricks he can afford to lose. He stoops to conquer by losing to win.

The defence counters by refusing to win until the last possible moment. The count remains *unrectified*, because East–West prefer to keep their idle cards.

It works like this:

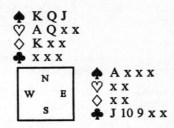

        ♠ K Q J
        ♡ A Q x x
        ◇ K x x
        ♣ x x x

                        ♠ A x x x
                        ♡ x x
                        ◇ x x
                        ♣ J 10 9 x x

South opens One No-Trump, vulnerable, advertising 16–18
points. North bids Four, and South calls the small slam.
West leads the Knave of Hearts, which declarer wins with the
King in his own hand. Next comes a Spade, and if East holds
up his Ace, another Spade. Should East hold up a second
time?

Good defence does not call for clairvoyance. East has no
particular reason to suspect that South is thinking of squeezing
anyone. Perhaps he is not. But still East should hold off.
It is the correct technique, *in case* of a squeeze. And he has
nothing to gain by going up with the Ace. He can only take
one Spade trick, just as South cannot fail to win two.

Now look at all four hands:

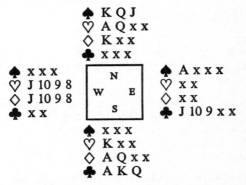

                ♠ K Q J
                ♡ A Q x x
                ◇ K x x
                ♣ x x x

    ♠ x x x   ♠ A x x x
    ♡ J 10 9 8   ♡ x x
    ◇ J 10 9 8   ◇ x x
    ♣ x x   ♣ J 10 9 x x

                ♠ x x x
                ♡ K x x
                ◇ A Q x x
                ♣ A K Q

Observe the disagreeable consequences for the defence if
East uses his Spade Ace prematurely.

One Heart has gone. By the time South has played three

Clubs and *three* Spades, West will be left with six cards. And he needs seven—badly. For he must retain three Hearts and four Diamonds.

Now work out the play if East holds up his Ace twice. West will have a card to spare (a Spade)—an idle card to throw on the third Club—and there will be no squeeze.

East—unless he is an expert—is not expected to foresee the exact position, but he has nothing to lose, and a possible squeeze to avert, by not taking his trick too soon. It is the right stroke, and it pays in the long run.

The Suicide Squeeze

South opens a non-vulnerable No-Trump and North bids Three.

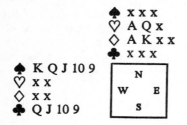

```
            ♠ x x x
            ♡ A Q x
            ◇ A K x x
            ♣ x x x
♠ K Q J 10 9   ┌─────────┐
♡ x x          │    N    │
◇ x x          │  W   E  │
♣ Q J 10 9     │    S    │
               └─────────┘
```

West leads the King of Spades, then the Queen. South wins and plays back another Spade. East throws a nondescript Club.

Of course, West is overjoyed. He did not expect to get in till the session after next, and his lovely Spades were already wilting in his hand. Suddenly, a magnanimous South puts him on the road to Spades and fortune. It is too good to be true. And that is just what it is—*too* good.

If West pauses to think, he will realise that South must have a purpose. Why this unexpected generosity? Presumably, because declarer cannot develop nine tricks himself and looks for assistance. And the only form that assistance can take is a squeeze against East. South can't do it himself, because he has no squeeze card. West has, and South blandly asks him to work on his behalf. The stratagem is known as a SUICIDE SQUEEZE—a squeeze perpetrated by a defender against his own partner.

Again West is not expected to be psychic. But he can see that East must have a lot of red cards. Dummy has four Diamonds. If, as is not unlikely, South has four Hearts, East may be panting for breath sooner or later. Therefore, West resists the temptation to turn on the heat with his Spades and switches to a Club.

Is that dangerous? Can it cost the contract? Surely not, for if South had some way of developing nine tricks, he would not have been so polite to West. Beware of the Greek gift.

And now we can look at the four hands.

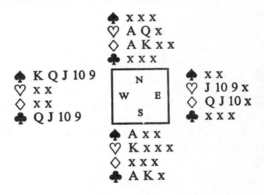

```
                    ♠ x x x
                    ♡ A Q x
                    ◇ A K x x
                    ♣ x x x
♠ K Q J 10 9      ┌──────────┐      ♠ x x
♡ x x             │    N     │      ♡ J 10 9 x
◇ x x             │ W     E  │      ◇ Q J 10 x
♣ Q J 10 9        │    S     │      ♣ x x x
                  └──────────┘
                    ♠ A x x
                    ♡ K x x x
                    ◇ x x x
                    ♣ A K x
```

Removing the Link

Rectifying the count is one of the essentials for a squeeze. Another, quite as important, is a LINK—or LINKS—between the two hands. For a MENACE is of no use to declarer if he can't get at it at the critical moment.

To break up a potential squeeze, the defence should look for opportunities to disrupt communications—to *remove* the LINKS.

To illustrate the mechanism, let us first take a complete deal.

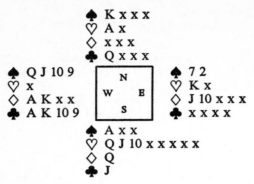

♠ K x x x
♡ A x
◇ x x x
♣ Q x x x

♠ Q J 10 9   ♠ 7 2
♡ x   ♡ K x
◇ A K x x   ◇ J 10 x x x
♣ A K 10 9   ♣ x x x x

♠ A x x
♡ Q J 10 x x x x x
◇ Q
♣ J

South, the declarer, opens Four Hearts, and West, yielding to temptation, doubles.

The King of Clubs is the opening lead and the King of Diamonds comes next. Then West shifts to the Queen of Spades, which South wins in his own hand. Nothing to note, so far, except, perhaps, East's play of the seven of Spades. South now takes the trump finesse, which loses to East's King. What should he do? Knowing that partner started with the A Ks in both minors, the average East will lead a Club. What is more, that is just what the average West will want him to do—to clear up the situation, in case South was foxing with that Knave.

A little concentrated thought shows that neither a Club nor a Diamond will help the defence. If South has a loser in either he will have to come clean with it—providing that East returns a Spade. Any other lead will expose West to a squeeze, and East can get there without seeing all four hands. It is enough for him to know that he cannot stop the Spades and that his partner has the Ace of Clubs *under* dummy's Queen. When South leads relentlessly the last of his trumps, West will wriggle and writhe, but he will have to unguard the Spades or let go the Club Ace. And declarer will wait patiently to see which he does, *before* touching his dummy.

328

The actual position will be:

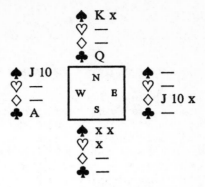

Now observe what happens if East returns his deuce of Spades. The King goes up and the essential LINK with dummy is severed. South cannot use the black cards on the table as menaces against West. He will have no way of getting at them—at the critical moment.

To break up a potential squeeze, East attacks the LINK. It is relatively easy for the player, who is conversant with the squeeze mechanism—and almost impossible for the player who is not.

A Real Teaser

The next example will tax every reader to the limit. The preceding hand paves the way. For all that, it is a real teaser, and all who succeed will have just cause to be proud of themselves.

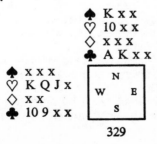

Bidding:

South	North
One Spade	Two Clubs
Three Diamonds	Four Spades
Six Spades	

West leads the King of Hearts, East plays the deuce and South the three.

Now go into a huddle. Let the brain sparks fly in all directions, but admit, candidly, that sitting West, in real life, you would lead another Heart. So would all good players and most of the very good ones, too. A master will lead a Club.

Examine the inferences, beginning with the bidding.

South has shown a rock crusher with not less than five Spades and four Diamonds. He must have five Spades, for North has shown no more than three, and that was enough for South to go slamming.

Now the inferences from play.

Who has the Ace of Hearts? South, without a doubt. East would have overtaken or petered violently, if he had it. He played the deuce instead.

Why, then, did South duck that first Heart? What possible object could it serve? The answer must be that he was conceding the inevitable loser at the first opportunity. He was RECTIFYING THE COUNT in preparation for a squeeze. No other explanation will fit his play.

Having reached that stage, West must go back to the bidding and visualise South's hand, brimming over with Spades and Diamonds.

What sort of squeeze can he have in mind? The Spades must be solid, for a trump loser would put him down straightaway. Therefore, the squeeze will hinge on declarer's Diamonds, and dummy's Clubs and Hearts. East will have to keep Diamonds. West will have to retain a Heart. Who will be left to look after the Clubs?

Eleven cards in South's hand can be identified—five Spades, four Diamonds and two Hearts. If there is a third Heart, there must be a singleton Club.

This is where an expert will project his mind into the future and picture the end position. If South was dealt two Clubs,

330

West can do nothing. But what if it was a singleton? Quite right. A Club switch at the second trick will destroy the LINK with dummy and so avert the squeeze. The deal could be:

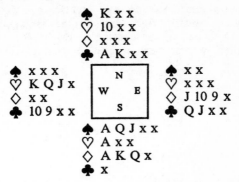

Should West persist with Hearts, the end position will be:

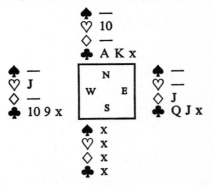

South's last Spade will be the killer, for neither defender will be able to keep three Clubs.

Even a good player in the West position may fail to foresee every detail. But the expert will be helped by his experience and knowledge of technique. He will suspect from the play that South is preparing a squeeze. From the bidding he will deduce that South may well have a singleton Club. So he will switch to a Club in the hope that it will break up a potential squeeze. And he will be fortified by the thought that a second Heart can't help anyway.

West does not know that a Club will beat the slam. He only knows that a Heart won't. And next to backing winners, the best thing is not to back losers. But don't be disappointed if you failed to find the right play on that last hand. It was not easy. And one of the charms of Bridge is that there is always room for improvement, just as there is no danger of perfection.

Résumé

(1) A passive lead against a slam is indicated when the North–South bidding proclaims *balanced* hands. But . . .

(2) When the bidding suggests that declarer and dummy have long suits, and plenty of winners, West should try to *develop* a trick on the lead. On such occasions it is permissible to open from holdings headed by a King or a Queen.

(3) The Lightner slam double is a convention calling for an *unusual* lead. It generally shows a void or a major tenace —an A Q over a suspected King—in a suit bid by dummy.

(4) A squeeze can only become effective *after* declarer has conceded all his losers. When declarer appears anxious to give up a trick(s) in the early stages, it is an indication that he may be planning a squeeze.

(5) The defenders can sometimes avert a squeeze by refusing to win a trick(s) prematurely. This prevents declarer from RECTIFYING THE COUNT.

(6) To execute a squeeze, declarer must retain a LINK with his menace in dummy. The defence may be able to break up the squeeze by attacking the LINK.

DEFENCE—CHAPTER XX

Exercises

(1) Bidding:

South (dealer)	*North*
Two Hearts	Four Diamonds
Four Hearts	Four No-Trumps
Five Hearts (Blackwood)	Six Hearts

What should West lead from:

♠ K x x   ♡ x x   ◊ x x x   ♣ J 10 x x x

(2) The bidding is the same as in (1), but this time East doubles the final contract.
What should West lead?

(3) Bidding:

South (dealer)	*North*
Two No-Trumps	Six No-Trumps

What should West lead from:

♠ K J x   ♡ Q x x   ◊ 10 x x   ♣ J x x x

(4) Bidding:

South (dealer)	*North*
One Spade	Three Hearts
Three Spades	Four Spades
Six Spades	

East doubles.   What card should West lead from:

♠ x x   ♡ J x x x x   ◊ A x x   ♣ J 10 9

(5) Bidding:

South (dealer)	*North*
One Club	Two Diamonds
Two Spades	Three Clubs
Three Spades	Five Spades
Six Spades	

East doubles. What should West lead from:

♠ x x   ♥ K Q J 10   ♦ 10 x   ♣ x x x x x

(6) Bidding:

South	North
Two Clubs	Three Clubs
Three Hearts	Four Clubs
Four Hearts	Six Clubs
Six No-Trumps	

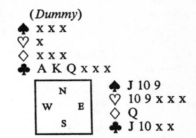

(*Dummy*)
♠ x x x
♥ x
♦ x x x
♣ A K Q x x x

♠ J 10 9
♥ 10 9 x x x
♦ Q
♣ J 10 x x

West leads a small Spade. Declarer wins with the Ace and leads a small Diamond. East is forced to overtake his partner's nine. What card should he play?

(7) Bidding:

North (dealer)	East	South	West
Three Diamonds	No Bid	No Bid	Four Hearts
No Bid	No Bid	No Bid	

(*Dummy*)
♠ A J x x
♥ x
♦ x x x x x
♣ x x x

♠ K Q 9 x
♥ x x x x
♦ x
♣ K Q J x

335

North leads the King of Diamonds and switches to the eight of Spades. Declarer ducks in dummy, and South wins with the Queen. At trick three, South plays the King of Clubs. West wins with the Ace and reels off seven top Hearts. Dummy's last three cards are A J of Spades and a Club x.

Which three cards should South keep?

(8) Bidding:

South	North
Two Clubs	Two Diamonds
Two Spades	Three Diamonds
Three Spades	Three No-Trumps
Four Clubs	Four Spades
Four No-Trumps (Blackwood)	Five Diamonds
Six Spades	

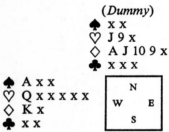

(*Dummy*)
♠ x x
♡ J 9 x
◇ A J 10 9 x
♣ x x x

♠ A x x
♡ Q x x x x x
◇ K x
♣ x x

West leads his fourth highest Heart, and declarer takes East's eight with the Ace. Hoping for an informative discard, West holds up his Ace of trumps till the third round. East follows twice, then throws the three of Diamonds. What should West now play?

DUMMY PLAY

CHAPTER XXI

TRUMP-REDUCING PLAYS—PART I

You can perish of a surfeit of trumps, as well as of lampreys.
Consider South's predicament.

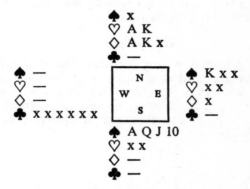

Spades are trumps. The last trick was taken in dummy and
South must make the rest. West does not count. His last six
cards are small Clubs, so that he can't even revoke.

Declarer leads a trump and finesses. West's Club discloses
the position, and South goes into a huddle. What now? He
can enter dummy and lead out three red winners. Alas, he
will have to ruff the third one and lead trumps from his own
hand. Why? Because he has one trump too many. If he
had one fewer, all would be well. Put it to the test.

After the first, tell-tale finesse, South enters dummy with
a Heart, leads the Ace of Diamonds and *ruffs*. Another Heart

takes him back to dummy and the position is:

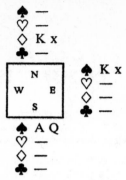

```
        ♠ —
        ♡ —
        ◇ K x
        ♣ —
  ┌─────────────┐        ♠ K x
  │      N      │        ♡ —
  │  W       E  │        ◇ —
  │      S      │        ♣ —
  └─────────────┘
        ♠ A Q
        ♡ —
        ◇ —
        ♣ —
```

Now all is well. South has reduced his trumps to East's level, and the lead is in dummy.

Grand Coup

Let us have a full deal for a demonstration of the GRAND COUP, a grandiloquent term for this type of trump-reducing play. The idea—as in the above diagram—is to "finesse" against a missing trump honour, without the necessary trump in dummy. In the process declarer ruffs winners—but that is purely incidental.

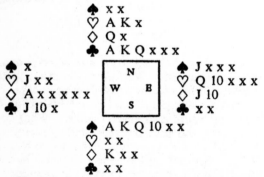

```
              ♠ x x
              ♡ A K x
              ◇ Q x
              ♣ A K Q x x x
   ♠ x        ┌─────────┐    ♠ J x x x
   ♡ J x x    │    N    │    ♡ Q 10 x x x
   ◇ A x x x x x │ W   E │    ◇ J 10
   ♣ J 10 x   │    S    │    ♣ x x
              └─────────┘
              ♠ A K Q 10 x x
              ♡ x x
              ◇ K x x
              ♣ x x
```

West leads the Ace and another Diamond against Six Spades. South takes two rounds of trumps and puckers his brow when

West shows out. Then he slowly unpuckers, for he has learned the trump-reducing technique and knows that he must get rid of two surplus trumps. His objective is to leave himself with the same number of trumps as East, and then to play from dummy. That will be as good as finessing.

Any trouble? Not in this case, but generally speaking, declarer's main preoccupation is with entries. He must be able to get into dummy often enough to shorten his trumps—and once again after that.

Let us put theory into practice. Two Diamonds and two Spades have gone. South leads two rounds of Clubs and ruffs a Club. That is one superfluous trump out of the way. Now a Heart to the table and another Club ruff. This is what is left.

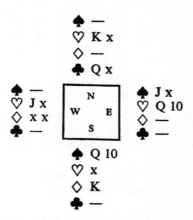

South leads a Heart—for the final, decisive entry—and plays another Club from dummy. Unless East ruffs, declarer throws his King of Diamonds. The next lead from the table catches East's Knave.

Transfer the Ace of Hearts to the South hand and the Grand Coup misfires. Dummy will be short of one entry. Declarer has to shorten his trumps *twice*. Therefore, he needs *three* entries to dummy and the Clubs provide one only—for that is the suit that yields the ruffs.

A Trump Coup

On the next deal South will again have all the fun of making Six Spades. It won't be a Grand Coup, because declarer will not be called upon to ruff winners. But Trump Reduction remains the motif.

West leads the Knave of Clubs.

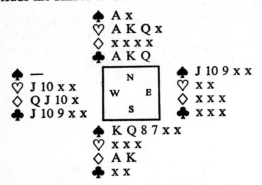

```
              ♠ A x
              ♡ A K Q x
              ◇ x x x x
              ♣ A K Q
  ♠ —                      ♠ J 10 9 x x
  ♡ J 10 x x      N        ♡ x x
  ◇ Q J 10 x   W     E     ◇ x x x
  ♣ J 10 9 x x     S       ♣ x x x
              ♠ K Q 8 7 x x
              ♡ x x x
              ◇ A K
              ♣ x x
```

At first view of dummy, South probably regrets that he is not in Seven. Then, at the second trick, he leads out the Ace of trumps—and seeing West show out—regrets that he is in Six.

Put yourself in declarer's place and decide what you would do. With all four hands before you, are you sorry that you bid a slam?

Of course not! As long as you don't drown in your own trumps, the story will have a happy ending.

A trump from dummy will produce the Knave, ten or nine from East. Otherwise, you draw trumps in the kindergarten fashion, conceding one trick to East.

The Ace and King of Diamonds follow. Then a Heart—or Club—to dummy, and a Diamond *ruff*. That is the key to the hand, for you had one trump too many—one more than East.

Now all is plain sailing. Another Heart (or Club) to dummy, and if East does not ruff, you have made it. The

Queen of Clubs comes next. You throw a Heart, lead a Heart from dummy, and this is the position.

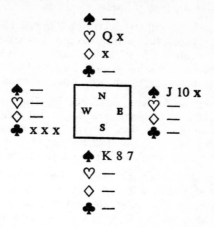

```
                    ♠ —
                    ♡ Q x
                    ◇ x
                    ♣ —
    ♠ —          ┌─────────┐      ♠ J 10 x
    ♡ —          │    N    │      ♡ —
    ◇ —          │ W     E │      ◇ —
    ♣ x x x      │    S    │      ♣ —
                 └─────────┘
                    ♠ K 8 7
                    ♡ —
                    ◇ —
                    ♣ —
```

If East ruffs with the ten or Knave, South can please himself. If he feels like it, he can let East hold the trick, leaving him to play into the K 8 tenace. But observe that as long as South has reduced his trumps to East's level, he can afford, at this stage, to lead from his hand. The eight or seven will end play East, who will have to play away from his J x.

The Advantage of Betting on Certainties

Grand Coups are few and far between, but trump-reducing plays are an everyday affair. We have had our fair ration of slams in the last few pages, so let us turn modestly to a part-score. Three Hearts is the contract. North leads Clubs, declarer ruffing on the third round.

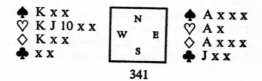

```
    ♠ K x x       ┌─────────┐      ♠ A x x x
    ♡ K J 10 x x  │    N    │      ♡ A x
    ◇ K x x       │ W     E │      ◇ A x x x
    ♣ x x         │    S    │      ♣ J x x
                  └─────────┘
```

West can see four tricks in his two A Ks, and another five maybe if the Queen of Hearts is with South.

Assume that the trump finesse succeeds. What next?

Many a declarer will lay down the King of Hearts, only to utter a painful groan if North shows out. Needless to say, the odds are 2–1 against a 3–3 Heart break. But it would hardly affect the issue if the odds were 2–1 on. West should avoid betting altogether—except on certainties, of course.

He plays off any outstanding Ace or King and exits with whatever small card happens to be nearest his index finger. As long as he retains the K J of Hearts, he must make both. If South was dealt Q x x x, he will be compelled to ruff—*under* declarer—when two cards only remain to be played.

Of course, this is a variation on the Grand Coup theme. It is not grand, and it is hardly a coup. But it has the merit of occurring at frequent intervals, and that makes it important. Coups are made largely for the onlookers—who don't even pay table money. Declarers need not bother with them overmuch—until they cut out and join the onlookers.

TRUMP-REDUCING PLAYS—PART II

Throughout these pages, Thrust and Parry has been the constant refrain. To every lunge by declarer in one chapter, the defence has found a riposte in the next. That is as it should be, for it is an even struggle, and though the tactics differ, neither side has an advantage in weapons. Each can say to the other in the words of the song : " Anything you can do I can do better." It is all a matter of technique.

In Trump-reducing Plays the technique for both sides is almost identical. That is why our study of the subject falls into two parts, rather than into separate chapters. For declarer, as for the defence, the objective is the same—to get rid of surplus trumps, because they stand in the way, compelling the wrong hand to be on play at the wrong time. To switch the lead across the table there is need of some small, humble card, which a trumpless partner can overtake.

Compare the mechanics of the Grand Coup with defender's play on this deal:

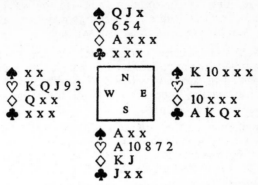

♠ Q J x
♡ 6 5 4
♢ A x x x
♣ x x x

♠ x x
♡ K Q J 9 3
♢ Q x x
♣ x x x

N
W E
S

♠ K 10 x x x
♡ —
♢ 10 x x x
♣ A K Q x

♠ A x x
♡ A 10 8 7 2
♢ K J
♣ J x x

East bids One Spade. South calls Two Hearts and West Doubles.

The King of trumps looks the best opening. Declarer wins, plays the King of Diamonds, crosses to dummy with the Ace, and runs the Queen of Spades. Next he ruffs a Diamond in his own hand, lays down the Ace of Spades and exits with a small one.

That leaves six cards. Which six should West be clutching to his bosom? If he retains too many trumps, it will cost his side a trick. The position will be:

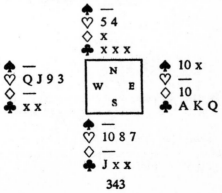

♠ —
♡ 5 4
♢ x
♣ x x x

♠ —
♡ Q J 9 3
♢ —
♣ x x

N
W E
S

♠ 10 x
♡ —
♢ 10
♣ A K Q

♠ —
♡ 10 8 7
♢ —
♣ J x x

343

East, winning the seventh trick with the King of Spades, can cash two Clubs. If he plays the third (or the ten of Diamonds) West will be forced to ruff—for he will have only trumps left, and that will mean playing away from his tenace, allowing South to make a trick with the ten.

To avoid the indignity, West must ruff the third Spade. His trumps will then be reduced to the same length as declarer's. And at the vital moment, when *both* South and West have nothing but trumps, the lead will come from East—*through* declarer.

That is very much the technique of the Grand Coup. This time, it is true, the glory of ruffing winners rests with the defence. But the tactics are identical—trumps are shortened, then the lead is passed across the table in preparation for the kill.

The next example is more difficult.

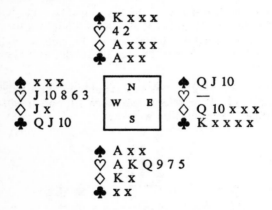

```
                 ♠ K x x x
                 ♡ 4 2
                 ◇ A x x x
                 ♣ A x x
  ♠ x x x       ┌─────────┐      ♠ Q J 10
  ♡ J 10 8 6 3  │    N    │      ♡ —
  ◇ J x         │ W     E │      ◇ Q 10 x x x
  ♣ Q J 10      │    S    │      ♣ K x x x x
                └─────────┘
                 ♠ A x x
                 ♡ A K Q 9 7 5
                 ◇ K x
                 ♣ x x
```

West leads the Queen of Clubs against Four Hearts. Declarer wins in dummy, leads a trump and absorbs the shock of East's void. Eleven tricks begin to look like nine. But there is still hope—for both sides. The issue will hinge on technique, though victory will rest with the defence, if West is as good a player as South.

344

At the third trick declarer leads a Club. West wins and leads another. South ruffs, cashes the two top Spades, the two top Diamonds and ruffs a third one with the King of Hearts. Eight tricks are in the bag, and this is the position:

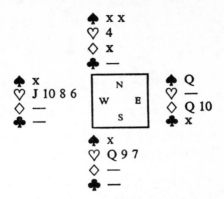

It is West's turn to play. If he jettisons a Spade, it will be all up. And trump-asphyxiation will be the verdict at the inquest. For declarer will exit with his small Spade, and West will be compelled to ruff—and to play into South's trumps.

To counter the end-play West should under-ruff at the ninth trick. This will allow East to come on play with the Queen of Spades, and at the decisive moment the lead will come through declarer—not up to him.

Observe the close parallel with the technique outlined in Chapter XVI—the defence against End Plays. The victim-designate must hug an EXIT CARD—or perish.

Occasions for under-ruffing or trumping partner's winners are comparatively rare. More frequent, if less spectacular, are opportunities for attacking declarer's entries and upsetting his timing.

The following hand, which occurred during an ordinary, unfriendly rubber, carries a lesson in reverse. It is a trump coup by the defence—on declarer's behalf.

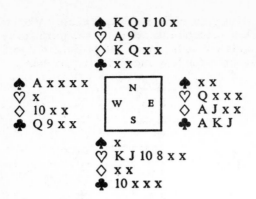

                    ♠ K Q J 10 x
                    ♡ A 9
                    ◇ K Q x x
                    ♣ x x

♠ A x x x x   N   ♠ x x
♡ x   W   E   ♡ Q x x x
◇ 10 x x   S   ◇ A J x x
♣ Q 9 x x   ♣ A K J

                    ♠ x
                    ♡ K J 10 8 x x
                    ◇ x x
                    ♣ 10 x x x

At game to East–West, South opened a dashing Three
Hearts. North restrained himself, and East's double closed
the auction.

A small Diamond brought forth dummy's King and East's
Ace. The King and Ace of Clubs followed, West dutifully
completing a peter with the nine and deuce. Then a Spade to
the Ace, and . . .

This is the time to pause. But do not look for good play.
The interest of the hand lies in bad play—the bad play to give
declarer his contract.

Having lost four tricks, South must somehow catch the
Queen of Hearts. That requires a trump coup and calls for
three entries to dummy—to shorten trumps twice, establishing
parity with East, and again to get back to the table for the final
curtain. Alas, South has two entries only, the Diamond and
the Ace of trumps. To ruff a Club with the nine of Hearts
would, of course, upset the tumbril and ruin the whole
execution.

In theory the coup must fail. In real life it succeeded,
because West—innocent of trump-reducing problems—returned a Spade, presenting declarer with the third decisive
entry, which he could not hope to create for himself.

South still had to be careful. After discarding two Clubs
and ridding himself of two embarrassing trumps, the position
was:

346

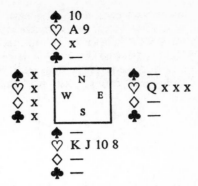

```
              ♠ 10
              ♡ A 9
              ◇ x
              ♣ —
   ♠ x                      ♠ —
   ♡ x      ┌──────┐        ♡ Q x x x
   ◇ x      │  N   │        ◇ —
   ♣ x      │W    E│        ♣ —
            │  S   │
            └──────┘
              ♠ —
              ♡ K J 10 8
              ◇ —
              ♣ —
```

Here the stage is set, but even now negligence can ruin the performance. South must lead the Knave (or ten) of trumps. This is no deception against West, but an unblocking play, for the nine of Hearts—which East, of course, will not cover— must hold the next trick. The essence of the trump coup is its timing. At the crucial moment the lead must come *through* the victim.

Needless to say, there would have been no crucial moment— and no victim—if the defenders had not fallen asleep. Everything about the hand shrieked for a third Club to remove dummy's nine of Hearts. East, especially, should have known that his Queen, despite her escort, could be ravaged by a trump coup.

The hand is instructive as a warning. When declarer has too many trumps, defenders should pursue the reverse of a forcing game; they should prevent declarer from "forcing" himself. And that means attacking the entries to the hand from which the forcing can be done.

Epilogue

The last deal provides an object lesson in the anatomy of luck, and that makes it a fitting epilogue to this book.

Against perfect defence, there are no lucky declarers. South's good fortune lay not so much in the lapses of East and West, as in his ability to exploit them. To paraphrase Hamlet: " Cards are not good or bad but playing makes them

347

so." Many a contract cannot be won until the defence to it is lost—and vice versa. For winners are not born, they are made; whereas a loser is born every minute.

Holding good cards is not lucky. It is only difficult. To acquire the technique needs a little imagination, a grasp of logic and the ability to draw inferences. And therein lies the Art of being Lucky.

Résumé

(1) In certain situations, either side can have *too many* trumps. This arises when the only loser(s) is in the trump suit itself, and the superfluity of trumps forces a player to take the lead at the wrong time—when he cannot avoid leading into (or away from) a trump tenace.

(2) To overcome this obstacle, a player reduces his trumps, so as to retain a card in a side suit with which to EXIT or switch the lead across the table.

(3) In a Grand Coup declarer's object is to catch a trump honour on his right, when no trump is left in dummy for a straightforward finesse. To do this:

   (a) Declarer shortens his trumps to the same level as that of the defender on his right.
   (b) Eliminates the side suits.
   (c) Contrives to put dummy on play at the critical moment —when the hand under him, having only trumps left, must ruff any card led from the table.

(4) All trump-reducing plays depend on entries to dummy.

(5) Therefore, the best defence is to disrupt declarer's communications.

(6) Like declarer, a defender may find that having too many trumps can be a liability. Coming on play with a ruff at the wrong time, he may be forced to lead into declarer's trump tenace—or away from his own.

(7) Anticipating such a situation, a defender may have to ruff his partner's trick or to under-ruff declarer, so as to retain a card in a side-suit for partner to overtake.

Exercises

(1)

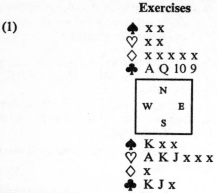

♠ x x
♡ x x
◇ x x x x x
♣ A Q 10 9

♠ K x x
♡ A K J x x x
◇ x
♣ K J x

Bidding:

East (dealer)	*South*	*West*	*North*
Three Spades	Four Hearts	Double	No Bid
No Bid	No Bid		

West leads the Ace of Spades, then the King of Diamonds, followed by the Queen, which East overtakes with the Ace. Declarer ruffs and lays down the Ace of Trumps to which all follow.

How should South continue?

(2)

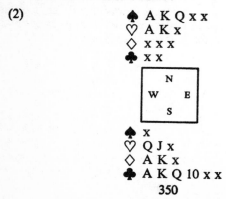

♠ A K Q x x
♡ A K x
◇ x x x
♣ x x

♠ x
♡ Q J x
◇ A K x
♣ A K Q 10 x x

West leads a small Diamond against Seven Clubs. East plays the ten. South wins and lays down two top trumps. On the second round West throws a small Diamond.

How should declarer play the hand?

(3)

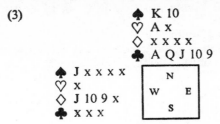

♠ K 10
♡ A x
♢ x x x x
♣ A Q J 10 9

♠ J x x x x
♡ x
♢ J 10 9 x
♣ x x x

The Contract is Seven Hearts by South.

West opens the Knave of Diamonds, on which East plays the deuce and South the Queen. Declarer leads a trump to the Ace and another to his Queen. West throws a Spade. The King of Clubs from the closed hand is overtaken with the Ace. A second Club is ruffed by declarer, who leads a small Spade. Sitting West, what view have you formed of declarer's line of play, and what chances do you foresee for the defence?

(4)

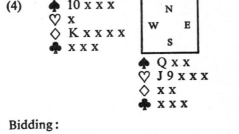

♠ 10 x x x
♡ x
♢ K x x x x
♣ x x x

♠ Q x x
♡ J 9 x x x
♢ x x
♣ x x x

Bidding:

North (dealer)	*East*	*South*	*West*
One Spade	Four Hearts	No Bid	No Bid
No Bid			

South opens a small Spade. North wins with the King and leads the Ace, which East ruffs. Declarer lays down the Ace and King of trumps, North discarding a small Spade on the second round. A Diamond to dummy's King—on which

North throws the Queen—and another Spade is ruffed in the closed hand. The next trick is East's Ace of Diamonds, to which North plays the ten. Then the Ace and King of Clubs, North playing the Queen, followed by the nine.

With four cards left (South has ♡ J 9 x ♣ x) declarer leads a small Diamond.

(*a*) What card should South play?

(*b*) After North's Spade continuation to the second trick, can declarer make his contract against any defence?

DUMMY PLAY—EXERCISES

Answers to Questions Based on Chapter I

(1) Ace first, then a small one towards the Q J x x. If the Queen holds, re-enter your hand and lead again towards dummy. The point of the hand is not to finesse. This cannot gain—since you are missing the ten—and it can easily cost a trick if the suit breaks 4–2.

(2) A small card *away* from the Ace. If the Queen holds, the Ace will provide an entry to play once more towards the dummy.

(3) A small card towards the Queen. Then finesse against the Knave.

(4) Play for split honours. Lead the ten and run it. If it loses to the Knave, finesse against the King next time.

(5) Ace first, then a small one. If no honour appears, it is a guess. But—if there is no indication—the ten is the best bet. The opponent under the Q 10 x x may have started with K J x x.

(6) Run the ten, hoping that the Knave is under the Queen. If the trick is taken by the Ace or King, re-enter your hand and finesse again.

(7) This calls for a ruffing finesse. Draw trumps, ending in dummy, and lead the King of Hearts. Unless it is covered, discard a Diamond.

(8) The *Knave* of Diamonds. It is essential to be able to play from dummy again if the finesse against the King succeeds.

(9) A small Diamond. This time, since the ten is missing, the only hope is to find K x—or the bare King—under the A Q. Note that the play of the Knave will lose against the bare King under the Ace, for then the other defender will have 10 x x.

DEFENCE—EXERCISES

Answers to Questions Based on Chapter II

(1) Yes. You may make a trick if declarer finesses against the ten next time. If you don't cover, you cannot hope to make a trick at all.

(2) No. Cover the second time, if declarer leads the Knave. You cannot gain by playing the King the first time.

(3) Yes. You may promote partner's holding. If you don't cover, you will probably have to play the King on the *deuce* next time.

(4) No. There is only one case where you could gain by covering: if declarer's holding is K J x. This play must be dismissed as being too remote.

(5) Yes. Covering will confine declarer to two tricks. Not covering will enable him to make three.

(6) Not the first time. By playing low you will retain a tenace over the ten. Wherever the Ace and King may be, you cannot *gain* by covering the first time.

(7) Yes. This time, you must hope that declarer will finesse against the nine on the next round. This may well happen if declarer has the King and partner the Ace.

(8) Small. If declarer intends to take the double finesse there is nothing you can do about it. But he does not know the position and may play the King. Don't help him to locate the cards. Last but not least, there is obviously nothing to PROMOTE.

(9) No. On the bidding it is evident that partner cannot have more than one Heart. There is, therefore, nothing to promote.

(10) The seven of Hearts. Any other lead may cost a trick. Adopt a passive defence.

DUMMY PLAY—EXERCISES

Answers to Questions Based on Chapter III

(1) (*a*) In dummy.

(*b*) The small Heart.

You cannot afford to touch trumps before clearing the stage for Heart ruffs in dummy.

(2) A small Heart. The Heart is a probable loser anyway. But you cannot afford to ruff high, in case the Spades break 4–1. Still less can you afford to ruff small and to be over-ruffed.

(3) One trump (taken in declarer's hand), the Ace of Diamonds and the Ace of Clubs. The hand must be played on a cross ruff. That is why dummy's deuce of trumps must be used at the first opportunity, leaving three trumps that cannot be over-ruffed. The Ace of Clubs must be cashed quickly to avoid the danger of a ruff in the end game. By then defenders may have had the opportunity to discard their Clubs.

(4) A trump. The catch is that there is no catch. Declarer can count eleven winners, so long as a Club is not ruffed. There is no need to ruff a Heart in dummy and every reason to draw trumps before allowing the defence to come in.

(5) (*a*) The King of Hearts; the Club and Diamond Aces; and *seven* trumps.

(*b*) The King *and Ace* of Hearts; the Club and Diamond Aces; and six trumps.

Unless a trump is opened, declarer cannot afford to lay down the Ace of Hearts. He can count ten tricks without it. But if the Ace is ruffed and a trump is returned, the contract will be broken. On a trump lead, the Heart Ace must be played, because without it, the cross-ruff will only yield nine tricks.

(6) (*a*) Ace and King of trumps.

(*b*) The three top Clubs.

If the Clubs break 4–2—or worse—the eighth trick will have to be a Club ruff. To prevent a Club over-ruff by a defender's *losing* trump, declarer draws two round of trumps, leaving the defence with the *best* trump. That is always a loser, and declarer does not mind if it is used to over-ruff a Club.

355

(7) (*a*) A Spade.

(*b*) The four Aces, the King of Diamonds and three trumps.

The lead indicates that the Spade suit is divided 4–4–4–1, and dummy has enough entries to give declarer three ruffs, which is all he needs for his contract.

Without the partial dummy reversal, the contract may fail against a bad trump break, for declarer needs four winners out of his six trumps.

DEFENCE—EXERCISES

Answers to Questions Based on Chapter IV

(1) *Not* over-ruff. The King will take a trick anyway, but if partner turns up with the ten, the K 9 7 combination will take *two* tricks—so long as West does not over-ruff.

(2) *Not* over-ruff. The position is fundamentally the same as in the previous example. Though the King is under the Ace, it cannot fail to make a trick now that the Knave is out of the way.

(3) Over-ruff. East's Ace of Clubs is obviously a singleton. West should give him a ruff. East will return a fourth Heart, allowing West to over-ruff again with the ten. If declarer ruffs high, the ten will take a trick later. The reason for over-ruffing is that West wants to *be on play* to lead a Club.

(4) No. The next trump lead must come from East, who is marked with the Ace of Spades.

(5) (*a*) One of the top trumps, intending to lead two more rounds. Declarer will clearly find ruffing value in dummy and the defence should limit it to as few tricks as possible. There is a temptation to open the King of Clubs, but it must be resisted. Dummy may have a void, and if so, the initiative will immediately pass to declarer.

(*b*) A small trump. The reasoning is the same as above. The bidding shrieks of ruffing value in dummy, and it must be attacked at once.

(6) (*a*) Small Spade. The thoughtless lead would be the singleton Diamond. West does not require a ruff. He

expects to collect two trump tricks, and probably the Ace of Clubs. To break the contract he needs one more trick, and Spades seem to offer the best chance.

If partner can get in at all, the contract will almost certainly go down—an additional reason for not looking for a ruff which can only materialise if partner has an entry.

(b) Queen of trumps. All the reasons in (a) apply here, but West can safely look at the table before committing himself. Time is on his side.

DUMMY PLAY—EXERCISES

Answers to Questions Based on Chapter V

(1) A small Spade from *both* hands. To dispose of the Club losers you must set up a long Spade. One ruff will not do it, unless the Spades break 3–3. By ducking once, you can establish that Spade x against a 4–2 break.

(2) (a) The Ace, the King, then a small Diamond. You can afford to lose to the Queen, if she is with North. He can do no harm. But you must try to keep out South, because a Heart *through* the K J could wreck the contract. Playing off the top Diamonds succeeds, also, when South holds a doubleton Queen.

(b) This time, play off the Ace—in case East has a singleton Queen—and finesse on the next round. In Four Spades, you cannot afford to lose a Diamond and must give yourself the best chance to catch the Queen.

(3) A small trump from both hands. You will win the next trick, lay down the Ace of trumps and cross-ruff the hand. So long as the trumps break 3–2, the contract is unbeatable. Ducking a Spade ensures that you will remain in control, *after* you have drawn two rounds of trumps. Only the best trump will then be out and an over-ruff will not hurt.

(4) (a) A trump. If he discards a Heart, he may find a 3–1 Diamond break, in which case he may lose four tricks—two Clubs, the Ace of Diamonds and a ruff.

357

(*b*) A Diamond.   Now a ruff will not matter, because the defender who is short of Diamonds will not be able to put his partner in to give him a *second* ruff.   If declarer draws trumps prematurely, and finds a 4–2 break, he will lose control.   The defence will come in with the Ace of Diamonds and continue with Clubs.

(5) (*a*) A Club to the Ace.

    (*b*) A small Club, ruffing high.

    (*c*) A Diamond to the Ace.

    (*d*) Another small Club, ruffing high.

Declarer must retain a *small* trump in his hand.   Then he can draw trumps ending in dummy.   The contract is made so long as both black suits break 3–2.

(6) (*a*) Yes.   He cannot afford to discard a loser, because the defence is likely to collect another trick—it would be their fourth—in trumps.

    (*b*) A small trump towards dummy's ten.   This takes care of the probable 4–2 trump break.   Another Heart will not matter, because declarer can ruff it in dummy.

DEFENCE—EXERCISES

Answers to Questions Based on Chapter VI

(1) The Queen of Spades.   With four trumps it is rarely wise to play for a ruff.   Besides, the Diamond lead may help declarer to set up dummy's suit.   The Spade is both safe and constructive.

(2) A small Spade.   The bidding shows that South has a two suiter with five Spades, maybe six.   North, who opened a No-Trump, must have at least a doubleton Spade.   It follows that East has one Spade or none.   Having two entries, including the Ace of trumps, West may be able to give his partner two Spade ruffs.

(3) The Ace.   Declarer has almost certainly Q x x in Spades in view of his bid of Two No-Trumps.   Partner is, therefore, marked with a singleton and can ruff a Spade return.

(4) The Ace.

(*a*) This time partner cannot possibly have a singleton, as that would leave five Spades for South. But East needs an immediate entry, because—

(*b*) he wants to give West a Diamond ruff. South's Two No-Trumps rebid promises a balanced hand, and that means no singleton. Therefore, South has two Diamonds and West none. When he comes in with the Ace of trumps, East will give his partner a second Diamond ruff and—

(*c*) the contract will be beaten.

(5) The thirteenth Diamond. It is clear that declarer can have no losing Spades, and since the Club King is under the A Q J, he has no losing Clubs either. The only hope is the " uppercut ". If East can ruff the last Diamond with an honour, West's ten will win a trick eventually.

(6) The Queen of Clubs. Unless South was dealt ten tricks in his own hand, he is almost bound to have A x in Diamonds. Without a fit, he would not bid Four Spades, since North has promised nothing beyond a string of Diamonds. If South has two Diamonds, East must have a void. That suggests a switch to a Diamond at the second trick. The temptation must be resisted, because East is unlikely to have three trumps, and one Diamond ruff will not beat the contract. West switches to a Club, and when he comes in with the Ace of Spades, returns a Diamond. East ruffs and plays back a Club for West to ruff. If, by some chance, East has three trumps after all, declarer will go two down.

(7) The Queen of Spades. West is obviously setting the stage for an " uppercut ". If he has as much as K 10 of Spades, this defence ensures two trump tricks and beats the contract. Declarer is marked with six Spades, but they may be A J 9 x x x. Compare this hand with (5) above.

DUMMY PLAY—EXERCISES

Answers to Questions Based on Chapter VII

(1) (a) Dummy.

(b) A Diamond, finessing against the King. If the King of Diamonds is with East, you are safe. But if West has it, the lead will be lost twice. Should West hold both the King of Diamonds and the Club Ace, the contract is doomed. But if East has the Ace of Clubs, he may not have a *third* Heart to return, when he gains the lead.

(2) Small. The Heart finesse must be taken into East's hand. If he has three Spades, West cannot have enough to worry you. If East has a doubleton and returns a Spade at trick two, he will not have another to put West in should he later gain the lead with the Queen of Hearts.

(3) (a) Yes.

(b) A small Club or Diamond to dummy, followed by the Knave of Hearts. Unless covered, run it. The contract cannot be beaten, so long as declarer does not allow East to gain the lead. But it would be careless to play the Ace of Hearts first. If East holds Q x x x, declarer must finesse twice; otherwise he will make three Heart tricks only, and that is not enough. If the Heart Knave wins, declarer runs the ten.

(4) A *small* Spade. Dummy's Spade honours guarantee an entry to the Hearts, so long as the Q J are retained *intact*. Declarer wins the first trick with the Ace and drives out the Ace of Hearts.

(5) (a) Hold up once.

(b) A Club.

The Diamond finesse can be delayed, because it will be taken into East's hand. But West, the DANGEROUS opponent, may have the Club Ace, and it must be removed first. The hold-up on the first round makes certain that, unless the Hearts break 4–4, East will not have one to play back, if he gains the lead with the King of Diamonds.

(6) The King of Diamonds. If East has Q 10 x of Diamonds, you can do nothing about it. But if West has that

holding, East will show out on the first round, and the Queen can be finessed. The question of keeping out the DANGEROUS opponent does not arise.

DEFENCE—EXERCISES

Answers to Questions Based on Chapter VIII

(1) (*a*) The Knave of Spades. There is a danger of playing into declarer's A Q, but this lead from an interior sequence still offers the best chance to set up enough tricks to break the contract.

(*b*) The Queen of Diamonds. This is safe while the Spades are too short to justify the risk, which was worth taking in (*a*).

(*c*) The four of Spades. It is the natural opening, and with reasonable luck may lead to three tricks in defence. If the Spade suit contained four cards only, the Diamond lead would be preferable.

(*d*) The Knave of Spades. It offers about the same prospects as the Knave of Hearts, but is less risky. Even if declarer has K Q x of Spades, the lead will not cost a trick. The same is true if there is a doubleton Spade honour in dummy. But in Hearts—unless partner has an honour—the lead is more likely to present declarer with a trick.

(*e*) The Queen of Diamonds. This is safe, and the suit may develop two tricks. Let declarer play the Spades himself. Alternatively, wait for partner to play them.

(*f*) The King of Spades—the orthodox opening from this combination. Partner may have an opportunity later to play through declarer into West's tenace.

(2) The Ace of Hearts. A small Heart would block the suit.

(3) (*a*) The Ace.

(*b*) K J 10 x x. West is missing the nine and eight and he cannot be leading from J 10 x x. The fourth highest would be the right lead from such a holding—not the top. By going up with the Ace, East can play through declarer's Queen.

(4) (*a*) The eight.

(*b*) The Ace. The bidding marks South with J x x x. East must, therefore, overtake the Queen and clear the suit. If he does not, he will have only one trick (the Ace of Spades) to cash when he comes in with his Ace of Clubs. The point to bear in mind is that West cannot have a third Spade.

(5) The nine. Peter to encourage West. You like Spades and you don't want a switch.

(6) The deuce. East wants a switch to Hearts, and hopes that West will gain the lead, before his probable Diamond entry is driven out.

(7) (*a*) The seven.

(*b*) The ten. By applying the Eleven Rule, East can tell that declarer has only one card higher than the four. With the Ace, declarer would have probably played an honour from dummy. It is safer, however, for East not to play the King, in case South has the Ace after all. Playing the King cannot gain, but can lose a trick.

DUMMY PLAY—EXERCISES

Answers to Questions Based on Chapter IX

(1) (*a*) No.

(*b*) In his own hand, three top Hearts and two top Clubs. In dummy, one Spade and the three top Diamonds.

The point of the hand is to create an entry to dummy's Diamonds by throwing the King of Spades on the Ace at the first trick.

(2) (*a*) Yes.

(*b*) After the Ace of Clubs, declarer lays down the Ace and King of Spades, then the two top Diamonds, followed by the *nine*. The object is to create an entry to dummy with the six of Diamonds. Two entries are required—to drive out the Queen of Spades, and then to reach the two good Spades. The Club provides one entry. The six of Diamonds will be the other.

(3) (*a*) The Ace.

(*b*) North would not have led a small card from a suit

headed by: K Q J; K Q 10; Q J 10 or K J 10. Therefore, South must have two honours. If North has five Hearts—which alone can worry declarer—South holds two *bare* honours, and the play of the Ace from dummy to the first trick will BLOCK the suit.

(4) (*a*) The King. Declarer cannot afford a HOLD-UP, for he may lose three Clubs, as well as the Ace of Diamonds.

(*b*) A small Spade.

(*c*) The finesse against the Knave of Spades. Declarer needs two entries to dummy—to drive out the Ace of Diamonds, and then to get at the suit after it has been established. His only hope of reaching the table twice is to find North with the Knave of Spades.

(5) The King first. If North shows out, declarer can still catch South's J 10. If North follows with the Knave or ten, the Ace is laid down to clarify the position. There is no certain way of making all four Diamonds, because North may have a singleton x, which will reveal nothing. But declarer must realise from the bidding that North is likely to be short in Diamonds and may have a void or singleton.

(6) The Ace first. This time South is likely to be short in Diamonds, but declarer can still make four tricks in the suit if South has a singleton Knave or ten. Nothing can be done against J 10 x x (x) in North's hand.

DEFENCE—EXERCISES

Answers to Questions Based on Chapter X

(1) (*a*) The Three of Spades. You may be able to set up four Spade tricks, and conceivably, to reel off the whole suit. If you open anything else, partner will never credit you with so good a suit.

(*v*) The Knave of Diamonds. This time, the Spades are too threadbare, and the entry position is not promising.

(*c*) The Queen of Spades. It is a good suit, and will

probably yield three tricks, if partner has as much as x x x. The Ace of Diamonds should be retained as an entry.

(d) The four of Diamonds. This will help partner to set up his suit. Even if he is no better than Queen high, declarer's A J x will take one trick only. But *don't* open the King. Leave yourself with a tenace position over declarer.

(2) The ten of Spades. East has no certain entry and can make four Spade tricks only if partner can get in. He must, therefore, preserve communications.

(3) The Ace. Partner has signalled (the eight *before* the seven) that he holds a doubleton Diamond. Therefore, declarer has three, and his play suggests that he is trying to steal his ninth trick in Hearts quickly.

(4) The Knave. East has a certain entry, whichever suit declarer tries to set up. On the bidding, West cannot have more than 2 or 3 points, probably the Queen of Spades. If East plays his Ace, declarer will *hold up* his King. If, however, East plays the Knave, South is almost bound to take the trick, and communications between East and West will remain open.

(5) The seven of Hearts. On the lead, declarer must have the A J 10, so that East will have to concede two tricks anyway. Since he has one entry only, he must leave West a second Heart to return, if he gets in first. If East plays the Queen, declarer will hold off, and another Heart will leave partner with none.

(6) (a) The Ace of Spades.

(b) The Queen of Diamonds. On the lead, declarer is bound to make two Spade tricks, whatever you do. So play the Ace, followed by the Queen of Diamonds. This will drive out declarer's King, and West, if he gets in, will play through dummy's Knave of Diamonds to break the contract.

(7) The King of Spades. The entry to dummy's Clubs must be removed at all costs. There is no other line of defence, because declarer is marked with the Ace of Hearts and must have reasonably good Diamonds on the bidding.

DUMMY PLAY—EXERCISES

Answers to Questions Based on Chapter XI

(1) Yes, because the Clubs *must* yield these tricks.

West's bidding shows ten red cards. He has rebid Diamonds, so he should have five. And he bid Hearts first, so he should not have fewer Hearts than Diamonds. Since he has followed to two rounds of Spades, we know of twelve cards in his hand. That leaves room for one Club only. If West's Queen does not drop on the Ace, the finesse is a certainty.

(2) (*a*) Yes.

    (*b*) A Club.

The play to the first trick shows that West had six Clubs. Since he had three red cards only, he is marked with four Spades. If he discards one, all South's Spades will be good. If West discards four Clubs, he will leave himself with one Club and four Spades. South will then set up dummy's Club with the loss of one trick only.

(3) (*a*) Yes.

    (*b*) Six Spades, the *Ace of Hearts*, two Diamonds and a Club.

The point of the hand is *not* to play the Ace of Hearts on any of the first three tricks, but to use it later—after ruffing the third Heart and drawing trumps—for a discard. This play cannot lose, and ensures the contract against a probable Heart void with East.

(4) (*a*) Yes.

    (*b*) Dummy.

    (*c*) Double finesse.

West is most unlikely to have a Club. His Four Heart opening, missing the A J 10, suggests a seven-card suit. And he has shown up with three Diamonds and three Spades. Since declarer needs two entries on the table, he must be careful, in drawing trumps, to be in dummy with the third trump trick.

(5) Declarer enters his hand with a Club and leads a Diamond, ducking in dummy. The purpose of the play is to take *three* rounds of Diamonds, before tackling the Club.

This will give a complete count of West's hand. He has shown eight cards in the majors. If he follows to Diamonds twice only, he must have three Clubs. If he follows three times, the Clubs must break 4–2, in which case declarer finesses against the Knave on the third round.

(6) The Ace of Spades is with South, and the Queen with North. North has shown up already with 15 points—10 in Clubs and 5 in Hearts. Holding the Ace of Spades as well, he would surely have made another bid, despite South's pass. Probably he would have doubled One Diamond. But if South has the Ace of Spades, he cannot have the Queen, too. For then he would have responded to his partner's opening Club bid.

(7) The King of Spades. The key to the play is to realise that North *must* have that Knave of Spades, as well as the Ace. Even with both the honours, his hand adds up to a bare 16 points, a minimum vulnerable No-Trump, and there is no reason to assume that he made a shaded opening. The King of Spades compels North to lead away from his Knave of Spades or to concede a ruff and discard.

DEFENCE—EXERCISES

Answers to Questions Based on Chapter XII

(1) A small Spade. East is marked on the bidding with not less than ten red cards. If his Spade holding is A x, he will discard the small Spade on the King of Clubs. But he may have two losing Spades, and in that case the contract can be beaten by taking two Spade tricks quickly. The setting trick will be a trump.

(2) A small Club. The only hope is that declarer holds K x in Clubs, in which case he is bound to play the King. Should declarer hold K x x, he will not cover the Queen the first time, and the suit will be blocked. The lead of the Queen will succeed only if partner holds A 9 x, and if that is the position, declarer has K x, and a small Club will do just as

366

well. Note that the Queen lead will lose if declarer holds
K 9, for then dummy's ten will stop the suit.

(3) A *small* Club. Declarer has no more losers in the other
three suits, so the contract can only be beaten if the defence
take three Clubs. This is only possible if North has the
Knave and declarer makes the wrong guess.

(4) The Knave of Clubs. Declarer has shown up already
with 13 points—the A K of Spades, the Queen of Diamonds
and the K J of Hearts (if North had the King of Hearts, he
would have played it to the first trick). Therefore he cannot
have the Ace of Clubs, which would give him a 17 count. He
may well have the ten, and that is why South must not play a
small Club. Should declarer cover the Knave with dummy's
Queen, North will win the trick with his Ace and return a Club,
trapping the ten. If dummy plays low to the Knave, North
will naturally duck.

(5) A small Heart. The only chance to beat the contract
lies in collecting three Heart tricks. This is possible if North
holds the King. To play the Ace first will cost a trick if
declarer's Hearts are Q x x. The bidding suggests that East
has ten cards in Spades and Diamonds, and since he is void in
Clubs, he is pretty well marked with three Hearts. If the
Heart tricks are not cashed, some of dummy's Hearts may be
discarded on declarer's Diamonds.

(6) The King of Hearts. Declarer's bidding shows eight
cards at least in Diamonds and Spades. Partner's lead of the
deuce indicates four Clubs, which leaves four for declarer.
That means that he has one Heart—conceivably none. If,
as is more likely, declarer has a singleton, it may be the Queen.
That is why South must lead his King, not a small Heart.

DUMMY PLAY—EXERCISES

Answers to Questions Based on Chapter XIII

(1) The Ace first. Then a small one towards the King.
If North follows low, finesse the nine. Should North show
out, go up with the King and play towards the Knave. Observe

that if the nine loses to South's ten, the suit must break 3–2 and declarer has no more problems.

(2) To guard against Q J x x with South, declarer should lay down the King and then finesse the ten. So long as South follows to the second round of trumps declarer need not worry. Nothing can be done if North holds four trumps.

(3) The Queen of Diamonds. The contract is an easy make so long as the trumps do not break 4–0. If North has four trumps there is no hope, but if South has them, declarer can still get home—providing he retains the K J 8 in his hand. This will enable him to lead through South's ten and nine twice, losing one trump trick only.

(4) Run the nine. If South wins, the suit will break 3–1 or 2–2, and there will be no more trump losers. The only danger is that North started with Q J 10 2, and if that was the case, the nine will win the first trick. If North covers the nine and South shows out, the finesse is taken again.

(5) (a) Yes.

(b) A low Club is led from dummy, and unless the ten or Queen appear, declarer plays the eight. This is a safety play to shut out South, who may have started with Q 10 x or Q 10 x x in Clubs. The contract is safe as long as South does not get in to play through the Spades.

(6) The Knave of Diamonds. With ten of a suit between the two hands, the finesse is obligatory. Playing the Knave gives declarer the chance to finesse a second time, against the ten, if North shows out. South may have K 10 x. If declarer leads a small trump from dummy, intending to play the Queen from his hand, South will play low and still make a trick if he started with K 10 x.

(7) (a) Yes.

(b) A small Heart. Then a small Club from dummy and the eight from his hand. North may win with the Knave, but he can do no harm, and declarer will be certain of nine tricks—one Spade, two Hearts, one Diamond and five Clubs.

This safety play ensures against J x x x of Clubs with South, who must not be allowed to lead through declarer's J x of Spades.

(8) (a) Yes.

(b) The deuce. The only danger is that North started

with all four Diamonds. If that was the case, declarer will make six Diamond tricks by finessing against North's Queen next time. If declarer plays the Knave on the first round, North may retain Q 10 9 and the Diamonds will yield three tricks only—not enough to make the contract.

(9) A small Spade.

Declarer can afford to lose two trump tricks, but not three. The danger is that his King will fall to the *bare* Ace. If the Spades break 3–2, he will not mind losing the first trick to the seven.

DEFENCE—EXERCISES

Answers to Questions Based on Chapter XIV

(1) (*a*) The Knave of Spades. East is obviously strong in Hearts and expects a Heart lead. West, however, can only lead the suit once, and will probably have a chance to do it later.

(*b*) The Knave of Clubs. The position is similar to (*a*), and having two Hearts, this time, a Heart lead is reasonable. West's Diamond honours are so well placed, however, that declarer is unlikely to run off many tricks before letting him in. There is, therefore, no hurry. Meanwhile, the Knave of Clubs is safe, and if East has the right cards this may turn out to be more profitable than a Heart.

(*c*) Queen of Hearts. On this hand East's double can hardly be based on Hearts, but with so compact a holding it is a safe lead and allows West to avoid guessing which of the black suits to choose.

(*d*) Knave of Hearts. If East is as good as K 9 8 x in Hearts—and he may be better—the lead through North can be very helpful. It is unlikely to do much harm, whatever the situation.

(2) The Queen of Spades. West's trump signal—high–low —shows that he can ruff Spades, and that he has a third trump to do it with. The King of Diamonds may then provide the setting trick.

(3) The deuce. This is a suit-preference signal, asking for a Club. East, of course, has every reason to fear that a second Spade will be ruffed. If East wanted a Heart, he would drop the Spade King. And if he wanted Spades to be continued, he would encourage partner with the nine. The deuce, coming from a player who should have six other cards to choose from, is a demonstratively low card, and therefore a McKenney suit signal.

(4) The three of Spades. This will tell West that he can put his partner in with a Club for another ruff. The Knave of Spades would ask for a Diamond.

(5) The King. East is anxious for a Heart switch, and he knows that West is unlikely to come in again later. Unless a Heart is played at once, South may be able to discard a loser in that suit on the Clubs. The Spade King must be a suit-preference signal, for East has bid Spades and could encourage a continuation without going to such extremes. It is an unnecessarily high card, and therefore a McKenney.

(6) A small Diamond. If South has the King of Diamonds, the contract is unbeatable, for he can afford to give up a Diamond to West's Knave. Therefore, West must assume that the Diamond King is with East. This, incidentally, is what declarer's play suggests. East's high–low in Clubs—the six, followed by the five—shows that he has four. It indicates that South will take three Club tricks only. He probably has the King of Spades, and may have K x x x. If that is the case, a Spade discard by West will present declarer with his ninth trick.

DUMMY PLAY—EXERCISES

Answers to Questions Based on Chapter XV

(1) (a) Yes.

(b) West draws trumps, ruffs two Clubs in his hand and a Heart in dummy. Then he leads a Spade from the table, covering the card played by South. If North wins with the Knave, he must lead into declarer's Spade tenace or concede a ruff and discard.

(2) (a)

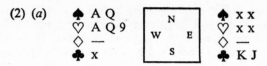

(b) Dummy.
(c) Hearts.
(d) Nine of Hearts.

Diamonds having been eliminated, North will be compelled to : (i) give declarer a ruff and discard ; or (ii) play into one of his tenaces. If North leads a Heart, declarer discards a Spade from dummy.

(3) (a)

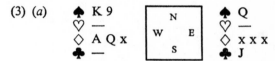

(b) The Knave of Clubs and a small Diamond.

North is marked on the lead with the Queen of Clubs. Declarer discards a loser on a loser, throwing in North to play into his A Q of Diamonds or to give him ruff and discard. Hearts must be eliminated to make the End Play effective.

(4) (a)

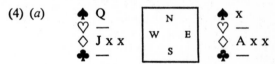

(b) Dummy (East).
(c) A small Diamond.

It is crystal clear that South was dealt seven Diamonds to the K Q. His bid indicates a seven-card suit, and North's Heart lead points to a void in Diamonds. South wins the tenth trick with the Queen, but is now forced to play away from the King or to give declarer a ruff and discard.

(5) (a)

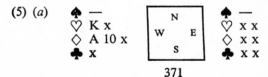

(*b*) A small Diamond from both hands.

Declarer End Plays North, forcing him to lead up to the King of Hearts or into the A 10 of Diamonds. If South shows out on the second Club, which is very unlikely, declarer throws North in with a Club, not a Diamond. North is no better off. He will cash his last Club, on which West will throw away a small Diamond, but his next lead will give declarer his ninth trick.

If South has four Clubs, which is much more likely, he can only get in if he has the Ace of Hearts. West will then discard the ten of Diamonds on the last Club, but his contract will be safe with: four Spades, a Heart, two Diamonds and two Clubs.

(6) (*a*)

♠ x x x		♠ Q 10 9
♡ J	N	♡ x
◇ K 9 x	W E	◇ A J x
♣ —	S	♣ —

(*b*) A Spade from West.

(*c*) Declarer's first hope is to find a favourable Spade position, but he is prepared, if need be, to lose three Spade tricks. The main point of the END PLAY is to force North–South to make the first move in Diamonds. If South leads a Diamond, there is no problem. If North takes the initiative, declarer lets the lead run up to his K 9 x. That is why the Spades must be eliminated first.

The strip play gives West several chances and costs nothing, for if the Queen of Diamonds is under the A J, he cannot fail anyway.

The contract will be beaten only if: the Knave of Spades is wrong; North is on play after the third Spade trick; and South has the Q 10 of Diamonds.

DEFENCE—EXERCISES

Answers to Questions Based on Chapter XVI

(1) Drop the Queen of trumps on the Ace.

West is in imminent danger. After the Ace of trumps, South will probably lead a small one to the King, and seeing West's Queen, he may let him hold the trick. If South started with the A Q of Clubs, which is likely enough, West will be forced to lead into the tenace.

To avoid the END PLAY, West must get rid of the Queen of Spades. East may turn up with J x x, and in that case the defence will eventually come to a trick in Clubs.

Note that dropping the Queen is most unlikely to cost a trick, whatever the distribution. If South has six Spades, he has no trump loser anyway, and if he started with A x x x x, he will lose one trump whatever card West plays.

(2) Small. Declarer has shown up with six Spades and four Diamonds. If his remaining three cards consist of one Club and two Hearts, East must not allow himself to be END PLAYED. If South has K x in Clubs, he has twelve tricks anyway. The only hope is that West has the King of Clubs and that South will be forced to take the Heart finesse.

(3) The Ace. West has an exit card—his fourth Club. East has only red cards left. A Heart will give declarer a ruff and discard, while a Diamond will eliminate a possible guess. South is pretty well marked with the King and two other Diamonds. If one of them is the ten, he may play East for the Queen. Since East has no safe EXIT, he must not be allowed to hold the trick.

(4) The ten. Declarer has stripped the hand, obviously preparing the ground for an END PLAY. Unless West covers the eight of Spades, South will certainly run it, and East—whatever his holding—will be forced to lead into the A Q or to play a Club, giving declarer a ruff and discard. South may have the nine of Spades and still make his contract. West does not know. But he does know that the Slam is unbeatable if he does not cover.

(5) ♠ A Q 9 8   ♡ x   ◇ —   ♣ 2

373

The important thing is to get rid of the Queen of Clubs—the throw-in Card. West is obviously looking for his ninth trick in Clubs, and South's only hope is that before the thirteenth Club is set up, North will come in to lead Spades. If declarer has the Knave of Clubs—unlikely on the play—the contract is unbeatable, but on the fall of the cards North probably holds J 10 8, and if that is the case, South must get out of the way.

(6) ♠ K 10 9 x x   ♣ x

The Queen of Clubs must be discarded at the first opportunity. It is a menace—to West. Declarer will probably play on the Club suit, and West will be thrown in with nothing but Spades to lead. West's only hope is to find partner with J x x of Clubs. The bidding makes it pretty certain that South has the Queen of Spades.

DUMMY PLAY—EXERCISES

Answers to Questions Based on Chapter XVII

(1) He should lead the *nine*. If the ten is led, North is more likely to cover with the Queen, promoting his own or South's fourth Spade. Of course, if dummy had a certain entry, it would make no difference which card was led.

(2) The Knave of Spades. South may have the Ace, and West should try to convey the impression that he is finessing against the Queen. He could have K 10 or K 10 x. If South is deceived, he may duck and declarer will make his singleton King.

(3) The King. North knows that South cannot have the King, since he did not play it. But he might have the Queen. Declarer should keep him guessing.

(4) The Knave from his own hand. If North has the Queen, he may cover and save West the guess. If he plays low, West can overtake and finesse against South.

Note. West should not attempt this play without the eight. The suit is likely to break 4–2. With nothing to guide him, it would then be better to lead the King and another, finessing against South. But having the eight, West can afford to tempt North into an indiscretion. It costs nothing.

(5) The five. Obviously, West wants the suit continued. He tries, therefore, to confuse North, who may place his partner with the deuce or three—or both—and interpret the four as a come-on signal.

(6) The deuce. South's three may be a singleton. West must not peter on his behalf. Needless to say, declarer will welcome any switch by North.

(7) The ten of Spades. Declarer obviously does not want to ruff a Spade at all, but North does not know that, and may decide to lead a trump, helping declarer to find the Queen.

(8) Declarer should cover the eight of Diamonds with dummy's nine and *duck* South's ten. Not suspecting declarer of leaving himself with the bare Ace, South is far more likely to switch to a Spade than to lead another Diamond. If declarer parts with his Diamond Ace on the first trick, he abandons all hope. North is bound to have an entry, and a second Diamond through dummy will wreck the contract.

DEFENCE—EXERCISES

Answers to Questions Based on Chapter XVIII

(1) The Queen. South *knows* that West has the Queen, because dummy's Knave won the previous trick. His holding may be A 9 x x, and he may play East for the ten. If you have the choice, play the card you are *known* to hold.

(2) It does not matter in the least. But vary your tactics to prevent declarer from spotting your habits and drawing inferences.

(3) The Queen. Declarer is most unlikely to play on Spades himself, and the King might prejudice the defence by deceiving West. A false card in this position would fool partner unnecessarily.

(4) Win with the Queen. By applying the eleven rule East can see that South has no further stop in Spades. Therefore, the defence can cash enough Spade tricks to defeat the contract.

(5) The Knave of Hearts. If East can mislead declarer into

thinking that he has two Hearts only, South will probably ruff the third Heart with the ten (or Knave). This will allow East to make two trump tricks. East has nothing to lose by his fraudulent signal, because it is apparent that, unless he can take two tricks in trumps, the contract is unbeatable.

(6) The nine. South's holding is probably Q x x, and unless the nine or ten falls, he will inevitably play the Ace, dropping West's King, for that will be his only chance. South must be given the opportunity to go wrong. If he can be made to believe that East started with 10 9 alone, he will lead the Queen from his hand, setting up a trick for East.

If South's holding is not Q x x, East's play is unlikely to make any difference.

(7) The King. This may gain a trick if South holds J 9 x. Playing West for a singleton, he may finesse against East's supposed ten. The King play can hardly lose, for if East holds J x x he will make a trick, whatever West does.

(8) The ten. If declarer's trumps are A K x x x—or better —it won't matter what West plays. But it is possible that South's Hearts are K Q 9 x x. If neither the Knave nor the ten drop on the first round, he will have one chance only—to lead a small one, hoping to drop the Ace. Without a second entry in dummy, he has no alternative. West's false card puts South off the scent. If he believes it, he will play the Queen, expecting to crash West's second honour and East's Ace.

DUMMY PLAY—EXERCISES

Answers to Questions Based on Chapter XIX

(1) (*a*) Yes.

(*b*) On finding the same defender with the Queen of Hearts and four (or more) Clubs.

(*c*) West will have the A K Q x of Clubs. The table will have the Knave of Hearts and three Clubs, and the lead will be in dummy.

This hand is an example of the Vienna Coup. Declarer plays off the Ace and King of Hearts so as to UNBLOCK the suit. Then he leads the Queen of Diamonds, crosses over to dummy's Ace and discards his small Heart on the King of Diamonds, which is the SQUEEZE CARD. With four cards left, the same defender cannot retain four Clubs *and* the Queen of Hearts.

(2) (*a*) Declarer should isolate the Spade menace. His only hope is to find the same defender with four (or more) Hearts, and also four (or more) Spades. Therefore, he lays down his two top Spades, enters dummy with a trump and ruffs a Spade. Only one defender can now retain a Spade. If the same defender started with four Hearts, he is squeezed in the three-card end position, which is:

> (*b*) *West:* ♡ K x x
> *East:* ♠ x ♡ A x

(3) (*a*) If either defender holds the King of Spades, and also long Hearts, he can be squeezed. That is the basis of declarer's plan of campaign.

> (*b*) *West:* ♡ K Q x
> *East:* ♠ Q x ♡ 10

After driving out the Ace of Diamonds, declarer lays down the Ace of Hearts—in case the Knave is bare. Then he plays the Ace of Spades—the Vienna Coup. Now divided menaces come into operation, with the Spade threat in dummy and the Hearts in the closed hand. Dummy's last Club (or Diamond) is the squeeze card, and the ten of Hearts is the link.

(4) (*a*) Yes.

(*b*) A small Heart from both hands.

Since there are eleven winners, it is necessary to RECTIFY the count for a squeeze. Hence the small Heart, which removes an IDLE card—available for a cheap discard—from defenders.

Declarer then starts on Diamonds. If South has four, West plays off his two Hearts. North is squeezed in the black suits and lets go a Spade to guard the Clubs. Now the Clubs are cashed, and South is subjected to a positional squeeze in Spades and Diamonds. In the four-card end position he must discard on the Knave of Clubs *before* West, who retains K x x of Spades and one Diamond.

If North has four (or more) Diamonds, West squeezes him by playing off his Hearts and Spades.

(5) (*a*) A squeeze against North in Spades and Diamonds.

    (*b*) *West:* ♠ A   ♢ Q x

          East: ♠ Q x   ♢ A

North is marked with the King of Diamonds—since the finesse succeeded. If he also started with the King of Spades, declarer's last Heart will force him to bare one of his Kings. This type of play is called the " Criss Cross Squeeze ".

(6) (*a*) Yes.

    (*b*) When declarer plays his last trump, his two other cards will be the Knave and a small Spade. Dummy will retain the Ace and a small Spade, and the Queen of Hearts. Unless North throws his Ace of Hearts, he will be forced to bare his King of Spades. The Heart will then be thrown from the table and West's Knave of Spades will take the last trick.

(7) (*a*) Yes.

    (*b*) *West:* ♢ A Q x x

          East: ♠ J ♡ x ♢ K x

A double squeeze now takes effect. North cannot keep four Diamonds, since he must retain the Queen of Spades—which he is known to hold on his opening lead. South must retain a Heart—since North has none—and cannot keep four Diamonds either.

DEFENCE—EXERCISES

Answers to Questions Based on Chapter XX

(1) A small Spade. The bidding calls for an aggressive lead. It is clear that dummy has solid Diamonds, which will yield enough discards. East may have the Queen of Spades and perhaps a trump trick.

(2) A Diamond. The Lightner double calls for an " unusual " lead, and neither a trump nor an unbid suit would be unusual. The implication is that East is void of Diamonds.

(3) A small Diamond. The only passive lead, and that is what the bidding demands. Declarer will be anxious to locate the missing honours in the other suits, and West must not help him.

(4) The Knave of Hearts. As in (2) the Lightner double calls for an " unusual " lead, which must be Hearts. The Knave is a McKenney or suit-preference signal, inviting East to return a Diamond—the higher-ranking suit.

(5) A Club. The Lightner double makes it clear that East has no Clubs.

(6) The Knave of Clubs. South's play suggests that he is rectifying the count for a squeeze. The bidding, and East's holding in Clubs and Hearts, reinforce the warning. East's only hope is that South has a singleton Club, for then the squeeze can be broken up by removing the *link* with dummy. South's hand may be :

♠ A K Q   ♡ A K Q J x   ◇ A 10 x x   ♣ x

and if a Club is not returned, East will be squeezed. The Club switch can help declarer only if he has no Clubs at all, and that is well-nigh impossible on the bidding.

(7) ♠ K 9   ♣ x. To avoid being thrown in, South must get rid of all his Club honours, hoping that his partner has the ten of Clubs. Declarer intends, no doubt, to try a throw-in instead of a Spade finesse, which he expects to be wrong. Note that if West has the ten of Clubs, South has no defence.

(8) A small Diamond. Declarer has shown up with six Spades, and his bidding suggests four Clubs. It is possible that his Ace of Hearts was bare, but it is more likely that the King is behind it. That leaves a singleton Diamond. If his hand is as good as :

♠ K Q J 10 x x   ♡ A K   ◇ x   ♣ A K Q x

a double squeeze will develop in the three-card end game. The last trump will force West to let go a Diamond. Declarer will throw dummy's Knave of Hearts, and East will have the dismal choice of baring his Diamond (probably the Queen), or discarding a winning Club.

By attacking the Diamond link with dummy West breaks up the squeeze.

If declarer has two Diamonds (and the Heart Ace was singleton) the play costs nothing.

Note, that since South applied the Blackwood convention, he is unlikely to have a void in Diamonds.

DUMMY PLAY AND DEFENCE—EXERCISES

Answers to Questions Based on Chapter XXI

(1) Since East has shown up with the Ace of Diamonds, declarer must assume that West had four Hearts (Q 10 x x). Otherwise he would not have enough to double. To shorten his trumps, South crosses into dummy twice with Clubs and ruffs two Diamonds. So long as West has four Diamonds, all is well. For then he is pretty well marked with a 4–4–4–1 distribution. He follows to all four Clubs and is forced to ruff the next card (a Spade or Diamond) and to lead into South's trump tenace.

(2) This is a typical Grand Coup. Declarer enters dummy with a Spade, discards a small Diamond on a second Spade, ruffs a third one, cashes the King of Diamonds and gets back to dummy with a Heart for another Spade ruff. Dummy is entered with another Heart, and so long as East follows, all is over. On dummy's Queen of Spades, South throws a Heart. His last two cards are Q 10 of trumps, and the lead is from the table—through East's J x.

(3) Clearly, declarer has embarked on a Grand Coup. Otherwise his Club ruff makes no sense.

He must have six trumps, for with five he could not afford to shorten himself at all.

With six trumps (presumably K Q 10 x x x) he requires three entries for the Grand Coup. The Ace of Clubs was one and the King of Spades is another. The third vital entry must be the ten of Spades—assuming that the finesse against the Knave succeeds. If South started with A Q x x, West can do nothing about it. But if, as is more likely, declarer's Spades are A Q x, West can break the contract by going up with his Knave of Spades. This will remove dummy's third decisive entry.

(4) (a) A small trump. If South discards a Club, he will be forced to come on play at the next trick and to lead away from his J 9 into declarer's Q 10 of trumps. Ruffing the Diamond enables South to put North on play with a Club at the decisive moment.

(*b*) Declarer can make his contract by playing as he did up to the ninth trick, but then exiting with a Club instead of a Diamond.   South must follow, and cannot, therefore, shorten his trumps.

Note that at the ninth trick South can read every card. Since declarer has three Diamonds (no more, for North's discards show Q J 10), he must have three Clubs.   This, of course, is confirmed by North's Club discards—Queen, followed by the nine.